BEACH BOYS ARCHIVES
VOLUME 7

FOREWORD

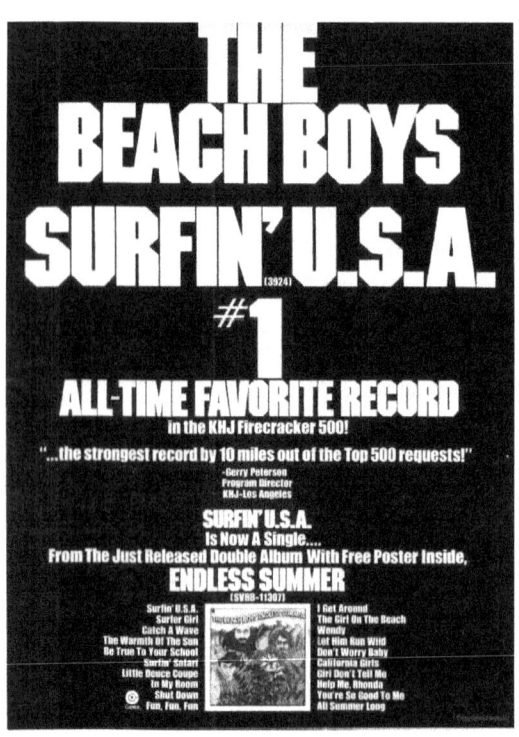

A LITTLE BIT OF EVERYTHING. This time around, we found a treasure trove of things that, quite honestly, we never saw or even knew about while compiling the first four Archives volumes. Some of these came from private collections and others from internet searches, where the materials were buried in newspaper archives or other obscure places.

So the good news is that there is still more stuff to be uncovered. The challenge is in grouping the material together. It comes in drips and drabs and runs the gamut of topic. So we basically didn't try too hard to group things and made this a true scrapbook. Solo act items were reserved for Achives Volume 6, which was fine. This volume serves as a catch-all for the interesting stuff.

We should also make a note about quality. If we were lucky enough to locate all of the original materials, they would have been in super-high resolution scans. Unfortunately, some source material is mediocre copy machine repros; others are lower resolution scans. Where we can, we make adjustments to contrast and brightness to improve the image reproduction. The goal is to present you with good, readable copies of materials.

And remember that we need to find copyright-friendly or copyright-free items. If there are favorite items that you know about, but haven't been presented, it could very well be because we can't use them. You;d be surprised how many publications won't even respond to multiple requests for permission to reprint their pieces. Still, hopefully you find the items that we have included to be of interest and worthwhile.

All reprinted materials believed to be in the public domain, copyright abandoned as the publishing companies have folded or we have received permission to reprint the materials within. If you believe we are in error, please contact us with proof of ownership and copyright status so that the pieces can be removed from subsequent printings.

April 9, 1983

JAMES WATT CONTROVERSY

Watt edict on 'rock' raises row

Compiled from wire services

WASHINGTON — In the face of an uproar from rock fans across the country — including some on the White House staff — Interior Secretary James Watt has rescinded a ban on rock music on the Capitol Mall.

But Watt said the rescission is too late to allow the Beach Boys and other rock groups to appear at a Fourth of July celebration on the Mall.

Watt emerged from a White House meeting carrying a plaster of paris foot with a hole in it — a trophy of his symbolically shooting himself in the foot. He said President Reagan gave it to him during a meeting in the Oval Office in which Reagan ordered him to rescind the ban.

Nancy complained

Lifting of the ban occurred after first Lady Nancy Reagan and some White House staffers complained to the president about the ban and Watt became the butt of jokes on the floor of Congress.

The Interior secretary said he couldn't change the program for the annual Fourth of July celebration, in which Wayne Newton will star instead of the Beach Boys or other rock groups. But Watt promised the Beach Boys will be back at some future time.

"We'll look forward to having them here in Washington to entertain again, as soon as we can get that worked out," he said. He added that the Mall was the only area big enough to hold the crowd the Beach Boys would attract.

Watt's change of heart came after Nancy Reagan and deputy White House chief of staff Michael K. Deaver rushed to the defense of the Beach Boys.

"I like the Beach Boys," Mrs. Reagan said.

Watt said the first lady told him "that the Beach Boys were fans of hers, and her children had grown up with them, and they're fine, outstanding people, and there should be no intention to indicate that they cause problems, which I agree with." Watt said earlier that he was banning rock groups from the Mall because they attracted the "wrong sort" of people — people who brought drugs and perpetrated crimes on the Mall.

Earlier, Deaver said, "There are a lot of us who think they (the Beach Boys) are a national institution. Anybody that thinks that the Beach Boys are hard rock must think Mantovani plays jazz." Watt had referred to the bands on the Mall as "hard rock" groups.

As for Reagan's opinion of the Beach Boys, Deaver said, "I wouldn't be a bit surprised if he is a fan."

Lit up switchboards

Watt's ban decision lit up switchboards at local radio stations, the Park Police and even the White House. Most of the calls were protests.

Tom Gaugher, a disc jockey for WMAL, said, "We've gotten more calls than any news event since the hostages in Iran."

On Capitol Hill, one member of Congress who is a Beach Boys fan responded to Watt's ban by pleading, "Help me, Ronald" and another suggesting that Watt take a permanent "Surfin' Safari."

In a series of one-minute speeches, several members complained about Watt's decision with puns that played upon the names of Beach Boys tunes or lines from their popular songs.

"Help me, Ronald, don't let him run wild," said Rep. George Miller, D-Calif., in a slight twist to the tune. "Help Me, Rhonda."

Rep. Thomas Downey, D-N.Y., said he was sure Watt had never heard the Beach Boys and, to cure that, he was sending the secretary "my own copy, slightly scratched from overuse, of

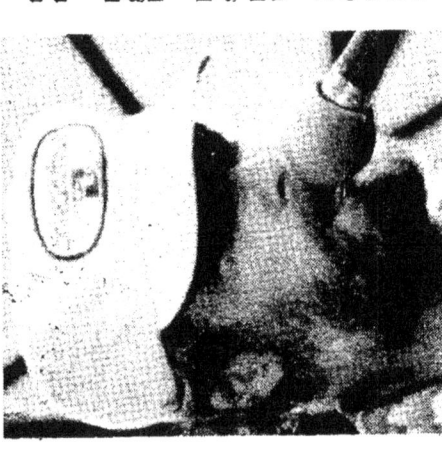

Mike Love

'Good Vibrations — the Best of the Beach Boys.'"

"The idea of listening to 'Danke Schoen' (a Wayne Newton hit) instead of 'Sail on Sailor' and 'Good Vibrations' . . . is deeply troubling," added Downey. "If he (Watt) doesn't recant, I hope he goes on a permanent Surfin' Safari."

Rep. Bill Richardson, D-N.M., said the decision to opt for Wayne Newton instead of the Beach Boys "may be the first and last time that Secretary Watt has promoted someone (Newton) of American Indian descent — I like that."

But Richardson quickly added in a statement that Watt was "turning a deaf ear to millions of Americans."

"So what else is new?" he asked. "He turns a deaf ear to protecting our environment, to the problems our native Americans face, to the Congress. Maybe we should all chip in and buy Secretary Watt a hearing aid."

In announcing his ban on rock music, Watt said he had arranged for "patriotic, family-based entertainment" on the Mall — U.S. Army Blues Band in addition to Newton.

Watt, as Interior secretary, controls the National Park Service, which runs the celebrations on the Mall.

In Los Angeles, the Beach Boys' publicist, Sandy Friedman, said the group found Watt's assessment "unbelievable."

"Over their 20-year career, the group has participated in many events geared specifically to the very families — parents and children — Watt claims they turn away," the statement said.

In Moncton, New Brunswick, Mike Love, the Beach Boys' lead singer, commented: "It's kind of rough when the secretary of the Interior . . . is now telling us (Americans) what kind of music we can have."

The Beach Boys performed at the annual fireworks display in 1980 and 1981, and the Grass Roots performed last year. Hundreds of thousands of people attended the celebrations.

Deaver said: "My wife and children went to that concert (by the Beach Boys) and loved it."

Bush likes them

In 1980, the Beach Boys performed a benefit concert for Vice President George Bush when he was running for the presidency. "Those guys are friends of his," said one White House aide.

Other White House aides recalled that the group performed at one of the many inaugural concerts for Reagan.

After one of their concerts, the Beach Boys got a guided tour of the Reagan White House.

Shirley Green, Bush's press aide said the vice president had a "personal friendship with the Beach Boys. He likes Mike Love very much. He likes the group; he likes their music. He expresses again the appreciation he had felt for their personal friendship and support, and for the fact they have entertained on the Fourth of July for free."

NEWS/OPINION

BY TOM CAMPBELL
ON THE SCENE

As the mercury soars, the roads to local watering holes are jammed with sweating pilgrims, their cars of vans packed with bodies, blankets, coolers and transistor radios.

The sounds emanating from the radios — the sounds of summer '76 — recall, for the most part, other summers, all of them long gone.

June, July and August of most of the 1960s belonged to the Beatles, who frequently released their new albums during the hot months.

This summer, the defunct group has an oldie on singles surveys ("Got to Get You Into My Life") and four dusty albums on LP charts. An anthology album, "Rock 'n Roll Music," soared to the Top Ten and was certified a platinum disc for sales of over one million copies within ten days of its release June 11.

But the biggest news this summer predates the Beatles. Strangely enough, the stuff the surfer sound was made of is back again. Todd Rundgren revamped the Beach Boys' "Good Vibrations" and has a hit with it.

The Beach Boys themselves, no longer the fresh-faced youths they were in '62, have a hit, "Rock & Roll Music." In re-release in various areas around the country, there's an 11-year-old film featuring the music of the Beach Boys, California girls, sun, sand and surf. Originally titled "Girls on the Beach," it's now called "Summer of '64."

The Sands of Time cut a single, "Tribute to the Beach Boys '76." Jan & Dean's "Sidewalk Surfin,'" a hit in '64 when skateboards were all the rage, was reissued in time for the current reincarnation of the craze.

Meanwhile, Papa Doo Run Run, a package show featuring Dean Torrence (half of the Jan & Dean duo of bygone years), the Safaris, Sandy Nelson and Billy Zoon Rockabilly Band have been doing a multi-tour in Southern California.

Of course, there's some new material tailor-made fo the season. Roy Clark has a country hit, "Think Summer;" MFSB has an LP, "Summertime;" Gordon Lightfoot's current collection is "Summertime Dream." And there's the Impressions' "Sunshine" and Sylvia's more specific "L. A. Sunshine."

Summertime means summer rains for some parts of the country, so Chicago's "Another Rainy Day in New York" and Fools Gold's "Rain Oh Rain" are both appropriate. Starbuck's "Moonlight Feels Right" also fits the seasonal mood.

THE BEACH BOYS SURFIN' U.S.A. (3924)

#1 ALL-TIME FAVORITE RECORD

in the KHJ Firecracker 500!

"...the strongest record by 10 miles out of the Top 500 requests!"

-Gerry Peterson
Program Director
KHJ-Los Angeles

SURFIN' U.S.A.
Is Now A Single....
From The Just Released Double Album With Free Poster Inside,

ENDLESS SUMMER
(SVBB-11307)

Surfin' U.S.A.
Surfer Girl
Catch A Wave
The Warmth Of The Sun
Be True To Your School
Surfin' Safari
Little Deuce Coupe
In My Room
Shut Down
Fun, Fun, Fun

I Get Around
The Girl On The Beach
Wendy
Let Him Run Wild
Don't Worry Baby
California Girls
Girl Don't Tell Me
Help Me, Rhonda
You're So Good To Me
All Summer Long

ADS

ADS

PROMOTIONAL ITEMS

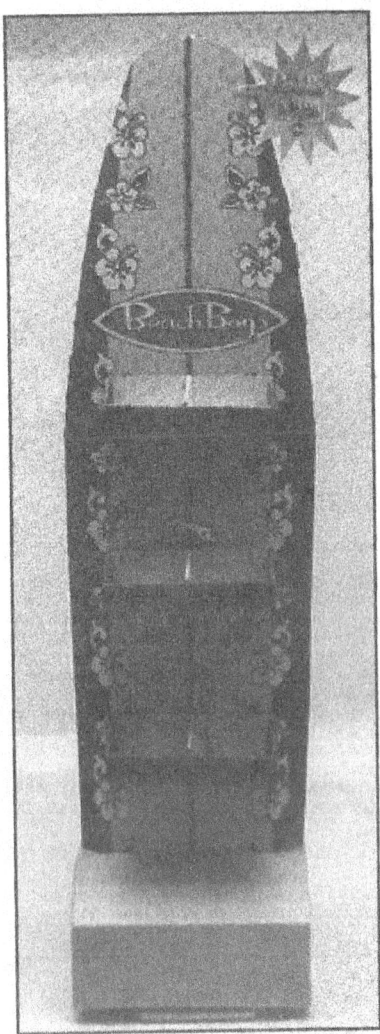

Beach Boys Display
Assembly Instructions

ADS

A NEW RADIO SPECTACULAR FROM WATERMARK

6 Hours of Fun, Sun and Rock and Roll in the Golden State

Now, a new audio adventure saluting the free-wheeling rock and roll life style that made the splash heard 'round the world. THE CALIFORNIA SPECIAL covers the great Southern California hits from 1960 through 1975 ... all the unforgettable surf songs, car songs and girl songs. Along for the ride: the rock celebrities who made the music ... like Brian Wilson, Mike Love, Jan Berry, Dean Torrance, Cher, Michelle Phillips, Rick Nelson, David Cassidy, Neil Young, Seals and Crofts, Lou Adler, Jimmy Webb, Alice Cooper, Cheech and Chong ... interviewed in action, on location, all over the world. And every step of the way, we track the all-time California supergroup, The Beachboys. There's more to the incredible CALIFORNIA SPECIAL story — and it's yours to see and hear ... free ... in the complete presentation package. Send in the coupon and we'll have a gift-wrapped box of good vibrations on your desk in 10 days.

Produced & Directed by Ron Jacobs
Written by Jerry Hopkins
Narrated by John Stewart
Original Music by Rick Kellis
Researched by John Gibson
Executive Producer Tom Rounds

THE CALIFORNIA SPECIAL
Watermark, Inc.
10700 Ventura Blvd.
No. Hollywood, Calif. 91604
(213) 980-9490

THE CALIFORNIA SPECIAL sounds like The programming and sales blockbuster for the summer of '75 ... and beyond. Please send free brochure, demo tape, price and market exclusivity info.

Name _____ Title _____
Call Letters _____ Address _____
City _____ State _____ Zip _____

THE CALIFORNIA SPECIAL: 6 hours of great radio, including 72 commercial or news minutes. Delivered on compatible stereo LP's by WATERMARK, makers of THE ELVIS PRESLEY STORY, AMERICAN TOP 40 and AMERICAN COUNTRY COUNTDOWN.

© 1975 WATERMARK, INC.

WAIVER OF NOTICE AND CONSENT TO HOLDING OF
SPECIAL MEETING OF BOARD OF DIRECTORS

OF

THE BEACH BOYS INTERNATIONAL FAN CLUB

The undersigned, being all of the directors of THE BEACH BOYS INTERNATIONAL FAN CLUB, a California corporation, do hereby waive notice of and give our written consent to the holding of a special meeting of the Board of Directors of said corporation, to be held on the 1st day of January, 1967, at the hour of 4:00 o'clock P.M., at Suite 808, 9000 Sunset Boulevard, Los Angeles, California, for the purpose of conducting such business as may come before the meeting.

We do further consent and agree that any business transacted at said special meeting shall be valid and legal and of the same force and effect as though said meeting were held after notice duly given.

Dated: January 1, 1967.

[signature]
BRIAN WILSON

[signature]
DENNIS WILSON

[signature]
CARL WILSON

[signature]
MICHAEL E. LOVE

MAGAZINE

The Beach Boys

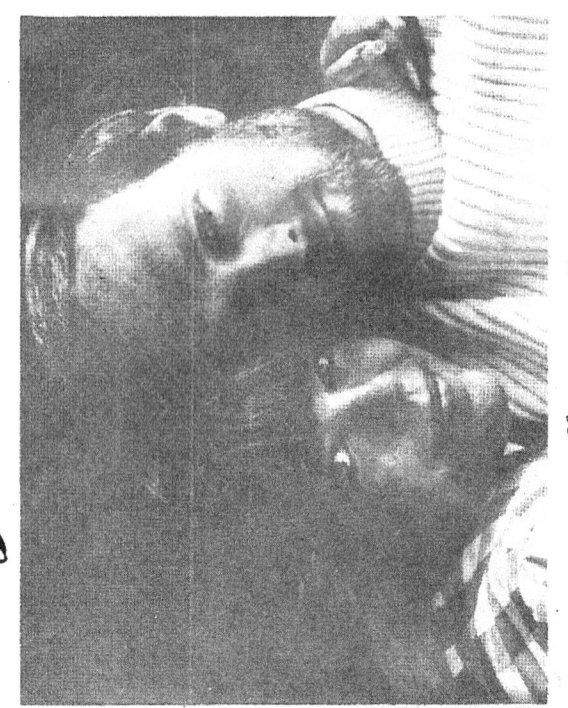

Suzanne & Mike

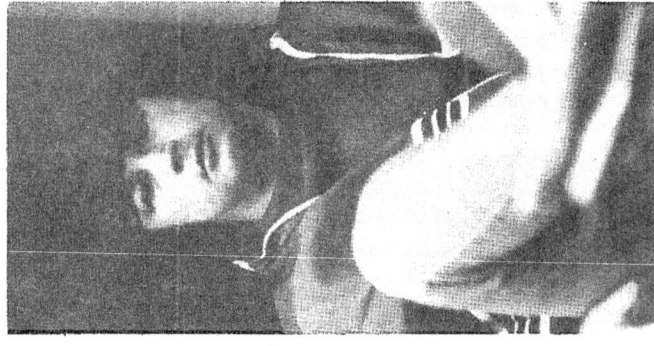

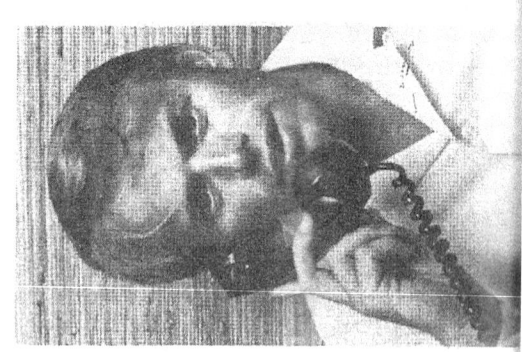
Brian Wilson

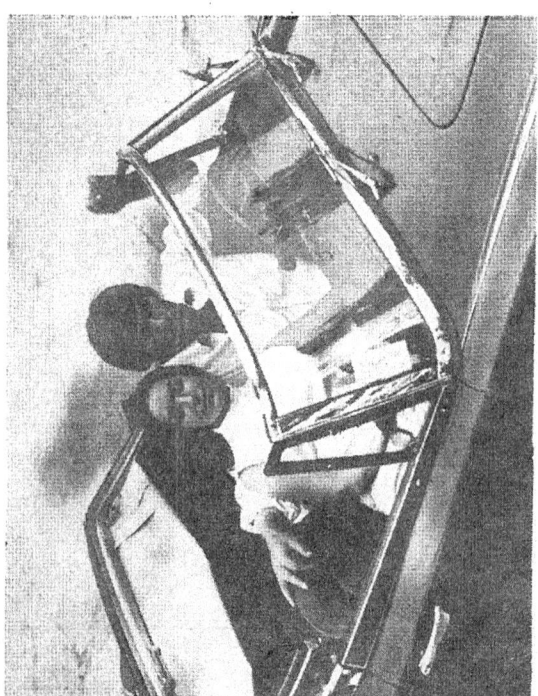

Carol & Dennis

MAGAZINE

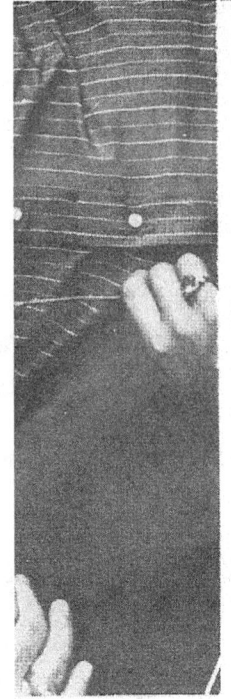
Annie & Carl

Linda & Al

Photos By Cyril Maitland

Al Jardine

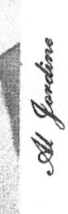

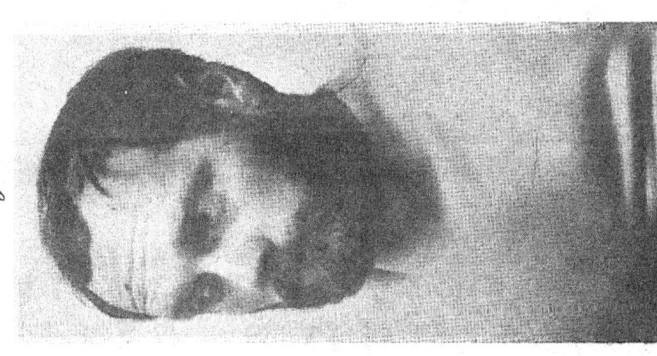
Mike Love

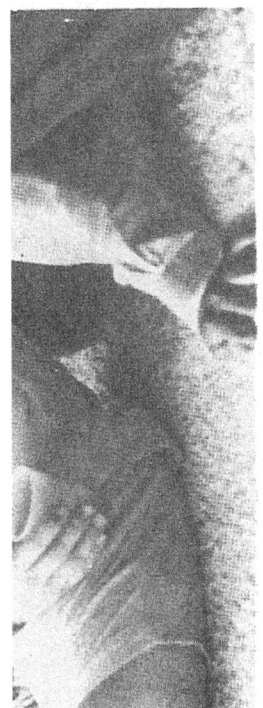
Bruce & Dennis

KFWB PROMOTIONAL MATERIAL AND CONCERT AD

HEY! HEY! L.A.!
A Salute to KFWB

WITHOUT A DOUBT, the grooviest radio station in America today is KFWB, which is located smack-dab in the middle of Los Angeles, California — where everything's *AT*, baby! So let's take a trip to the far west and say hi to those swinging KFWB-cats.

Beach Boy Dennis Wilson relaxes . . . .

. . . . while Carl and Al listen.

That's Mike Love in the beard, dollies — and Ian Whitcomb in the weskit.

INCREDIBLE FESTIVAL JOLIET JAM

with

THE BEACH BOYS
And special guest Stars
BACHMAN TURNER OVERDRIVE

Plus...The New Colony Six, Henry Gross, The new super group Fresh Start, Fast Eddie and **SUPER JOCK LARRY LUJAC**

JOLIET MEMORIAL STADIUM
NOON May 19, 1974

8 Hours of Music — Bring your Frisbees, Balloons and rolls of toilet paper!

Tickets available at all Ticketron Outlets, Tiket Service, Mole's Den in Joliet, Sound Spectrum in Joliet, Polk Bros. in Joliet, Echo's Records in Aurora, Albert Audio & TV in Joliet, Earl's Music in Plainfield, The Shop in Kankakee and Pandora's Box in Lockport. Tickets $5 advance or $6 at the door.

A Zoom Presentation

MAGAZINE

THE BEACH BOYS — A CON

Striped shirts are their trademark.

Between shows lead guitarist Carl chats with other members of the show.

Are they really singing behind all those screams?

Some rock & roll groups don't. "Why should we? The audience just comes to see us and *hear themselves* scream", is their excuse.

Many groups do sing...but they don't put much effort into it. They sing off-key, play on out-of-tune guitars and look bored.

Groups with that attitude don't last very long.

But when you see the Lovin' Spoonful or the Beach Boys onstage you know why they've been able to stay on top while so many others have vanished. These two groups aren't faking or copping out. They really enjoy playing their music and their audiences are treated to this rare enthusiasm.

Backstage, their attitude toward their music is evident too. For example, if you've ever seen Carl Wilson, Zal Yanovsky or John Sebastian tune their guitars before a concert you know they're there to play. Anyone who spends that much time tuning has to be sincere about playing groovy music.

Mike Love sports a neat beard.

Carl is on a diet.

CERT

THE BEACH BOYS

Joe Butler listens to Carl talk on and on about guitars, cars, trains, boats and planes.

The Beach Boys demand lots of security.

Everybody flips out when they see Sebastian's autoharp. Al did too.

When we arrived backstage at a Lovin' Spoonful/Beach Boy concert one night John told us, "My autoharp has gone gimp on me!" It had fallen apart. He could have laid it aside until after the show, but without it the Spoonful couldn't do several of their most popular songs, including "Do You Believe In Magic."

So John got a tiny screwdriver, Steven held the loose keys in place and within 15 minutes the autoharp was working again.

Beach Boy fans need not worry about being unable to hear their favorite group - The Beach Boys carry the largest amplifiers of any group we've seen. Even if you're sitting in the last row of a football stadium, they have the power to reach you.

Little things like that are what separates the overnight failures in pop music from the genuine stars. □

MAGAZINE

THE BEACH BOYS / BRIAN Wilson

In a moment we will let Brian Wilson speak, in a Sunset Strip delicatessen, from behind a tomato juice, dwarfed by his enormous hands. He is a big man, more than six feet tall, comfortably over-weight, given to wearing quiet jackets and trousers and the fanciest shirts in Hollywood. He offers— and comprehends – brief, hardly-uttered humour; but he smiles not much and then only with the corners of his mouth.

He appears – and feels himself to be – considerably older than 23. He is a serious man, with a passion for patient explanation; he is swift to misunderstand; chiefly, one suspects, to force chapter and verse from his companion. He has immense personal charm and knows it. Also, he likes it in others. He sleeps extraordinary hours and will break appointments with absolute calm and only the faintest sense of guilt.

His head seethes with ideas, plots, plans – all interwoven, yet capable of instant separation and he is never a fraction of a step behind his companion in conversation.

Permit him now to speak: "I know I'm a creative man, musically – from early days I believed there were ideas waiting to be dumped out if I had time. Now I know it and it's a good feeling.

"I approach my music-making as an art-form – something pure from the spirit to which I can add dynamics and marketable reality.

"I believe in God – in one God; some higher being who is better than we are. But I'm not formally religious. I simply believe in the power of the spirit and in the manifestation of this in the goodness of people. I seek out the best elements in people."

"People are part of my music. A lot of the songs are the result of emotional experiences, sadness and pain."

"Or joy, exultation in nature and sunshine and so on...like 'California Girls,' a hymn to youth."

"I can write through empathy with others. The surf songs are a simple

Brian's mind is always in another world.

example of that – I have never surfed but I was able to feel it through Dennis, who is a fine athlete."

"I find it possible to spill melodies, beautiful melodies in moments of great despair. This is one of the wonderful things about this art form – it can draw out so much emotion and it can channel it into notes of music in cadence. Good, emotional music is never embarrassing. But emotional prose sometimes is."

"Music is genuine and healthy and the stimulation I get from moulding it and from adding dynamics is like nothing else on earth."

"I sat up in the house (by 'the house' Wilson meant his $220,000 mansion, exquisitely furnished, in Beverly Hills) for five months, planning every stage of the album. I didn't mind people being around – there are visitors up there most of the time – so long as there weren't too many and provided I could cop out and sit thinking. I have a big Spanish table, circular, and I sit there hour after hour."

"Or I go to the piano and sit playing 'feels.' 'Feels' are specific rhythm patterns, fragments of ideas. Once they're out of my head and into the open air, I can see them and touch them firmly. They're not 'feels' any more."

"I think that on 'Pet Sounds' the track 'Let's Go Away for a While' is the most satisfying piece of music I've ever made. I applied a certain set of dynamics through the arrangement and the mixing and got a full musical extension of what I'd planned during the earliest stages of the theme."

"I think the chord changes are very special. I've used a lot of musicians on the track – twelve violins (I guess fiddles is the 'hip' phrase), piano, four saxes, oboe, vibes, a guitar with a Coke bottle on the strings for a semi-steel-guitar effect. Also, I used two basses and percussion. The total effect is..."Let's go away for a while,' which is something everyone in the world must have said at some time or other. 'Let's go away for a while.' Nice thought. Most of us don't go away, but it's still a nice thought."

Brain behind the BEACH BOYS

In a recording studio, Brian reigns supreme. He quit touring to spend more time arranging.

"The track was supposed to be the backing for a vocal but I decided to leave it alone. It stands up well alone."

"Now, there's another track called 'Wouldn't It Be Nice' which has a very special and subtle background and for a time, I thought it would be the single after 'Sloop.' But that was before 'Good Vibrations.'

"One of the features of this record is that Dennis sings a special way, cupping his hands. I had thought for hours of the best way to achieve the sound and Dennis dug the idea because he knew it would work. So we practiced for hours until it *did*."

"The thing is I write and think in terms of what the Beach Boys can do. Not what they would find it easy to do, but what I know they are capable of doing which isn't always the same thing."

"I have a governor in my mind which keeps my imagination in order because idiot ideas are just a hang-up. But I don't like to be told 'it can't be done' when I know it can. That's the point. It mostly can be done."

"My musical influences go back to the early days when I worshipped the Four Freshmen, those great guys. That groovy sectional sound!"

"The Beach Boys are lucky...we have a high range of voices; Mike can go from bass to the E above middle C; Dennis, Carl and Al progress upwards through C, A and B. I can take the second D in the treble clef."

"The harmonies we were able to produce gave us a uniqueness which is really the only important thing you can put into records — some quality no-one else has got into."

"Jack Good once told us, 'You sing like boys in a Sistine chapel,' which was a pretty good quote. Another beautiful quote was the other day when Al Jardine said: 'I feel as if you're singing through my mouth.' I dug that because it showed a total musical communication between Al and me. This was what I'd always been trying to achieve in creating tunes for the group."

"Al was talking about a song called 'God Only Knows,' which we may release under Carl's name as he sings the solo. In the harmonies at the end, each group member picks up the phrase 'God only knows that I'd be without you' in sequence so that there's a mingling stream of voices, each picking up on each other."

"I gave the song to Carl because I was looking for a tenderness and a sweetness which I knew Carl had in himself as well as in his voice. He brought dignity to the song and the words, through him, became not a lyric, but *words*."

"I'm very aware of the value of speaking through a song. I'm not talking of 'messages' — just about saying what you have to say to music. This is why I get so much kick out of bending electricity and recording techniques to make work for us. They're there to be used — maximum. Top maximum."

"I love peaks in a song — and enhancing them on the control panel. Most of all, I love the human voice for its own sake. But I can treat it, with some detachment, as another musical instrument. This doesn't imply a lack of respect because I respect all instruments from Jew's harp to spinet."

"I know that in some circles we're not regarded as all that 'hip' or 'in.' This is maybe, because, we haven't just arrived from nowhere with something new with a new label."

"But I don't care too much what anyone says, so long as I know I'm staying ahead — right up to the limit of my present capabilities. I don't put out anything I don't respect. And I know for sure that the Beach Boys brought something new into rock 'n' roll."

"I don't normally walk into any traps about our favourite contemporary groups because I think everyone's into his own things, which is good, but I must mention the Beatles."

"I started to understand just where they were at around 'Rubber Soul' time. Not just when the album came out, but a bit, before, when I really started to dig them for their attitudes and their magnetism as well as the music."

"What's so great is that the recording industry is getting so free and intelligent that we can go into new things — string quartets, auto-harps, instruments from another culture, dynamics. Dynamics. They're the key. Dynamics applied with love."

At this point, Brian stopped talking and retreated into reverie about "Pet Sounds." No father with his first newborn baby was ever in a higher state of grace than Brian Wilson with this album.

Yet, it is justified because it is no ordinary album and it will do for him and his Beach Boys what "Rubber Soul" did for the Beatles. It will most demonstratively make the point that here is more pure musical essence than the disbelievers ever dreamed of. □

MAGAZINE

BUILDING THE BEACH BOYS

Mike & Brian

Brian Wilson is a genius, I think. I can't be sure because I don't know what the word means; but the way I see it, you have to use a very special word to capture the rare, mind-blocking, blinding talents of this 23 year old whose grasp of popular music is iron-clad and total.

He alone in the industry – at the pinnacle of the pop pyramid – is full creator of a record from the first tentative constructions of a theme to the final master disc.

Brian is writer – words and music – performer and singer, arranger, engineer, producer with complete control even over packaging and design.

All of which leaves him with a unique responsibility which he does not wear lightly.

So heavy are the self-imposed burdens of complete control that Wilson has retired from personal appearances altogether, and forever, to enable him to meet the mounting challenges from within his inventive musical soul.

If you can imagine the Beatles on stage without Lennon, the Stones less Brian Jones, the Who without Townsend, you have an idea of the sacrifice in visual appeal which Brian Wilson sought from the militant legions of Beach Boy fans in America.

Maybe you can imagine also what it means to step from the midst of the group you have formed and nurtured and to hand over the spotlight to a substitute performer, not in hot blood, not because of any inadequacy, but simply because you have re-assembled your priorities.

This was what Brian Wilson did a little less than a year ago. He had watched the group expand and mature from the gauche, sun-happy group of schoolboys – musical novices, and performers without a performance – to the richest, most famous, most potent household-name, pop-unit in the nation.

But he had watched, also, the joyous, flexible skills of Lennon and McCartney and the explosive freedoms of the newcomers on the United States musical scene in 1965.

The rigorous tour-demands were becoming impossible for Brian Wilson on top of his writing tasks but with massive earning-power at their mobile feet, it would have been stupidity and downright bad business for the group to stay at home.

Yet, while he was battering across the nation, Wilson knew he couldn't spill from his head the tumbling ideas which would give the group a new musical direction.

So...he himself quit the road and into his place stepped an unknown 22 year old, Bruce Johnston, "phantom" Beach Boy.

Bruce, then unpublicized, had recorded with Terry Melcher and in appearance and attitude and, more important in the range of his voice, he blended swiftly with the Boys.

And, to Brian's delight, the substitution worked and fans, he found, accepted his reasons for absence as valid and important.

"This was confirmation of what I'd believed," he said. "That kids were becoming very aware musically. They had started to wonder where songs actually came from.

"And they come from inside human beings."

So they do. From Wilson's disciplined intensity have poured some incredible sounds, themes, melodies and dynamics in the past five months; plus those matchless cascading harmonies with which the Beach Boys first paid their membership fee to the club of Exclusivity.

Thirteen of the songs emerge on the Boys' thirteenth album – "Pet Sounds," Wilson's proudest product thus far and a certainty to provide the group with their eighth gold album for sales exceeding 1,000,000 Dollars per album.

But the fourteenth new song will be one to send the pop world staggering with delighted wonderment.

It is called "Good Vibrations" and it may well be the contemporary song of the year.

Instrumentally, the track is quite brilliant; no symphony was ever scored with more inspirational patience and, because Wilson is as much a soundfiend as a maker of melodies, he has used four separate recording studios (each in a different neighborhood), to build the four-tracked tape into a most masterly record.

He isn't talking too much about the actual ingredients in the song because the pop world abounds with adept thieves, but I've heard the dub so many times that my head reels and my mind cannot adequately comprehend the intricacies of his phrasing, nor the separate, sparkling attack of each instrument.

Wilson's instinctive talents for mixing sounds could most nearly equate to those of the old painters whose special secret was in the blending of their oils. And what is most amazing about all outstanding creative artists is that they are using only those basic materials which are freely available to everyone else.

'Phantom' Bruce Johnston now both tours and records with the group. Though he is not included in the 2,000,000 dollar a year Beach Boy Corporation, he receives a very handsome salary and he is, in any case, heir to a multimillion drugs and canning fortune.

They started, with no great seriousness, by making a record called "Surfin'," while they were still at school at Hawthorne, on the Californian edge of the Pacific.

Brian recalled the song: "Mike (Love) and I wrote it because surfing was becoming a big craze and someone in school suggested a song about the sport. It was no great musical creation, but it did bring something of the essence of surfing and the sea to music."

So it did. It altered the course of contemporary music in the USA, this one slight song recorded in two hours in Hollywood, on a single-track tape system with little Jardine playing a stand-

MAGAZINE

The Beach Boy Empire

By Derek Taylor

ard double-bass twice as big as himself, 14-year old Carl Wilson on acoustic guitar, Brian himself standing up using brushes on drums and Mike Love singing the vocals with a severe cold.

The record sold more than 40,000 copies in the dying weeks of 1961. And it went to No. 3 in Southern California in a chart distorted beyond belief by the Twist and its many variants. (Chubby Checker was No. 1 at the time.)

In the U.S. as a whole, the record reached 75 which is no bad thing for a first disc by schoolboys reflecting the spirit of an ocean which is as remote from most Americans as the Tiber is from the good people of Nelson and Colne.

From this first single, the Beach Boys drew $900 in royalties which wasn't much — and, in fact, not enough; that is another story — but it was sufficient to take them back into the studio for

Brian, Mike and Al pause during a hike through the woods and think of new songs to sing.

another single, "Surfin' Safari." This, coupled with "409", was offered as a master to Dot records and to Liberty, both of whom, with the wisdom born of experience, turned the Beach Boys down. (Oh! the pain of recollection... the anguished presidential nightmares at Dot and Liberty.)

Capitol, however, said "Yes" and with them the Beach Boys signed a seven year contract which has much of four years still to run and which they may well re-sign. (Incidentally, it was probably the success of their Beach Boy gamble which induced Capitol to take the Beatles two years later. Ironically, neither group has ever recorded a note in Capitol studios).

The Boys started to perform locally, and then nationally and by 1963 they were a very prosperous, virile national touring group and massive hitmakers in a period when, otherwise, American pop music was in a dead faint.

From the beginnings, to date, they have passed through single sales exceeding 15,000,000 copies, twelve albums, every town and city in the Union, most European countries, Japan and the Orient, Australia and Canada.

The songs from "Pet Sounds" will probably be violently plundered by other artists, which will dismay neither Brian Wilson, as composer, nor his father Murry who runs their publishing company, engagingly called "Sea of Tunes."

I asked Brian about his father, their

first and last manager. "He's really grooving now," he said. "Grooving great. But it didn't work as manager. We love the family thing — y'know: three brothers, a cousin and a friend is a really beautiful way to have a group — but the extra generation can become a hang-up. Now we have our own managerial system. But my dad's got about a hundred songs to keep the pot boiling."

Brian talks incessantly about anything which relates either to contemporary music, its improvement, its personalities. Not in a fragmented, gossipy way — day to day activities like, who got drunk, who got pregnant, don't exist for him; he has less small-talk than a Trappist Monk — but in an urgent, eager way almost in the hope that by *willing* them to get into new directions, they will follow in subconscious obedience.

He adores his group, not as a contemporary, but rather like a patriarchal games-coach. He knows their faults and he raps hard and fast and directly when he doesn't get what he wants. And the Beach Boys are not always easy to deal with. How could they be? Or why?

Equally, he seeks constantly for some redeeming quality. It may be the sexual magnetism which draws the nation's girlhood to the bronzed, iron-necked Dennis. Or, the unbelievable niceness of Carl. It could be the loyalty and half-stated

Mike looks for pine needles.

{Continued on next page}

MAGAZINE

THE BEACH BOYS

Dennis trys to spell his name.

BUILDING THE BEACH BOY EMPIRE

(Continued from last page)

simmering wit of little Al Jardine. Or again the show-off, overt, non-toxic appeal of Bruce Johnston.

For each of them Brian has hour, upon hour, of analytical conversation to bestow on a listener.

But it is for Mike Love that he preserves his special praise. I believe this is not only because he respects Love as a remarkable entertainer (whose potential reaches far beyond rock 'n' roll, or any form of music...away into boundless uplands) but also because Brian has a faint but deep sense of personal guilt over Mike who is MC and leader on stage, yet, can never be overall leader.

Carl, Denny, Brian and Santa.

Brian thinks about sounds.

Al tells Denny to watch out for the copperheads.

Dennis tells Carl, never, never do that again.

For while Brian Wilson is founder, musical genius and natural born inspirer, he has, I suspect, no love for the title "Leader."

I think he would gladly hand the title to Mike Love who would refuse it. This reasoning may seem complicated, but isn't. It is simply a symptom of the substantial power within the Beach Boys. For it is power which has kept them ahead. Musical strength, potent chemistry on stage, intellectual rapport away from the theatres, physical fitness off duty. All these are part of the implied discipline which binds what would, otherwise, be a very headstrong, loose, bunch.

Wilson's own summary of the binding-power is "positive thinking."

I'm not quarrelling with that.

Are you? ☐

●HERE TODAY

(As recorded by The Beach Boys/Capitol)
BRIAN WILSON
TONY ASHER

It starts with just a little glance now
Right away you're thinking 'bout romance now
You know you ought to take it slower
But you just can't wait to get to know her
A brand new love affair is such a beautiful thing
But if you're not careful, think about the pain it can bring,
It makes you feel so bad
It makes your heart feel sad
It makes your days go wrong
It makes your nights so long
You've got to keep in mind
Love is here today and it's gone tomorrow
It's here and gone so fast.

Right now you think that she's perfection
This time is really an exception
Well, you know I hate to be a downer
But I'm the guy she left before you found her
Well, I'm not saying you won't have a bit of a whirl
But I keep on remembering things like they were
She made me feel so bad
She made my heart feel sad
She made my days go wrong
And made my nights so long
You've got to keep in mind
Love is here today and it's gone tomorrow
It's here and gone so fast.
© Copyright 1966 by Sea of Tunes Publishing Co.

●GOD ONLY KNOWS

(As recorded by The Beach Boys/Capitol)
BRIAN WILSON
TONY ASHER

I may not always love you
But long as there are stars above you
You never need to doubt it
I'll make you so sure about it
God only knows, what I'd be without you
If you should ever leave
Oh life would still go on believe me
The world could show nothing to me
So what good would living do me
God only knows, what I'd be without you.
© Copyright 1966 by Sea Of Tunes Publishing Co.

●I'M WAITING FOR THE DAY

(As recorded by The Beach Boys/Capitol)
BRIAN WILSON
MIKE LOVE

I came along when he broke your heart
That's when you needed someone to help forget about him
I gave you love with a brand new start
That's what you needed the most to set your broken heart free
I know you cried and you felt blue
But when I could I gave strength to you
I'm waiting for the day when you can love again.

I kissed your lips when your face looked sad
It made me think about him and that you still loved him so
But pretty soon I'll make you feel glad that you belong to me, and love began to show
He hurt you then but that's all gone
I guess I'm saying you're the only one
I'm waiting for the day when you can love again.
© Copyright 1966 by Sea of Tunes Publishing Co.

●CAROLINE, NO

(As recorded by Brian Wilson/Capitol)
BRIAN WILSON
TONY ASHER

Where did your long hair go
Where is the girl I used to know
How could you lose that happy glow
Oh, Caroline, no.

Who took that look away
I remember how you used to say
You'd never change
But that's not true
Oh, Caroline you break my heart
I want to go and cry
It's so sad to watch a sweet thing die
Oh, Caroline, no.

Could I ever find in you again
Things that made me love you so much then
Could we ever bring them back once they have gone
Oh, Caroline, no.
© Copyright 1966 by Sea of Tunes Publishing Co.

●YOU STILL BELIEVE IN ME

(As recorded by the Beach Boys/Capitol)
BRIAN WILSON
TONY ASHER

I know perfectly well I'm not where I should be
I've been very aware you've been patient with me
Everytime we break up you bring back your love to me
And after all I've done to you
How can it be you still believe in me?
I tey hard to be more what you want me to be
But I can't help how I act when you're not here with me
I try hard to be strong but sometimes I fall myself
And after all I promised you, so faithfully you still believe in me
I want to cry, ah, ah.
© Copyright 1966 by Sea of Tunes Publishing Co.

MAGAZINE

• I JUST WASN'T MADE FOR THESE TIMES

(As recorded by The Beach Boys/Capitol)
BRIAN WILSON
TONY ASHER

I keep looking for a place to fit in
Where I can speak my mind
I've been trying hard to find the people
  that I won't leave behind
They say I've got brains but they ain't
  doin' me no good
I wish they could.

• WOULDN'T IT BE NICE

(As recorded by The Beach Boys/Capitol)
BRIAN WILSON
TONY ASHER

Wouldn't it be nice if we were really older
Then we wouldn't have to wait so long?
And wouldn't it be nice to live together
In the kind of world where we belong?
You know it's gonna make it that much
  better
When we can say goodnight and stay
  together
Would it be nice if we could wake up
  in the morning when the day is new?
And have to have to spend the day together
Hold each other close the whole night
  through
Oh, what happy times together we'd be
  spending
I wish that every kiss was never ending.

Oh, wouldn't it be nice?
Maybe if we think and wish and hope
  and pray it might come true
Maybe then there wouldn't be a single
  thing we couldn't do
Oh, we could be married
And then we'd be happy
Oh, wouldn't it be nice?
You know it seems the more we walk
  about it
It only makes it worse to live without it
But let's talk about it
Wouldn't it be nice?
© Copyright 1966 by Sea of Tunes Publishing Co.

• DON'T TALK (PUT YOUR HEAD ON MY SHOULDER)

(As recorded by The Beach Boys/Capitol)
BRIAN WILSON
TONY ASHER

I can hear so much in your sighs
And I can see so much in your eyes
There are words we both could say
But don't talk put your head on my
  shoulder
Come close, close your eyes and be
  still
Don't talk, take my hand and let me
  be your heartbeat
Being here with you feels so right
We could live forever tonight
Let's not think about tomorrow
Don't talk, put your head on my shoulder
Come close, close your eyes and be still
Don't talk, take my hand and listen to
  my heartbeat
Listen, listen, listen
Don't talk, put your head on my shoulder
Don't talk, close your eyes and be still
Don't talk, put your head on my shoulder
Don't talk, close your eyes and be still
Don't talk, put your head on my shoulder.
© Copyright 1966 by Sea Of Tunes Publishing Co.

Everytime I get the inspiration to go change
  things around
No one wants to help me look for places
  where new things might be found
Where can I turn when my fair weather
  friends cop out?
What's it all about?

Each time things start to happen again
I think I got something good goin' for
  myself
But what goes wrong?
Sometimes I feel very sad
Sometimes I feel very sad
Sometimes I feel very sad
I guess I just wasn't made for these times.
© Copyright 1966 by Sea Of Tunes Publishing Co.

• SLOOP JOHN B

(As recorded by The Beach Boys/Capitol)
BRIAN WILSON

We come on the Sloop John B
Your grandfather and me
'Round Nassau town we did roam
Drinking all night
Got into a fight
Well I feel so broke-up
I wanna go home.

So hoist up the John B sail
See how the main sail sets
Call for the captain ashore and let me
  go home
Let me go home
I want to go home, yeah, yeah
Well I feel so broke-up
I want to go home.

The firstmate he got drunk
Broke in the captain's trunk
The constable had to come and take him
  away
Sheriff John Stone
Why don't you leave me alone, yeah,
  yeah
Well I feel so broke-up
I want to go home
(Repeat chorus).

I want to go home
Home, let me go home
Why don't you let me go home
Home, hoist up the John B sail
Feel so broke-up
I want to go home
Let me go home.

The poor cook he caught the fits
And threw away all my grits
And then he took and he ate up all of
  my corn
Let me go home
Why don't they let me go home
This is the worst trip I've ever been on,
(Repeat chorus).
© Copyright 1966 by New Executive Music.

• I KNOW THERE'S AN ANSWER

(As recorded by The Beach Boys/Capitol)
BRIAN WILSON
TERRY SACHEN

I know so many people who think they
  can do it alone
They isolate their heads and stay in
  their safety zone
Now what can you tell them?
And what can you say that would
  make them be pensive?
I know there's an answer
I know now that I have to find it
  by myself.

'Neath the moonlight they're peaceful
  but inside they're sewn up tight
They trip through the day and waste
  all their thoughts at night
Now how can I come and tell them
  the way that they live could be
  better?
I know there's an answer
I know now that I have to find it by
  myself.
© Copyright 1966 by Sea of Tunes Publishing Co.

• THAT'S NOT ME

(As recorded by The Beach Boys/Capitol)
BRIAN WILSON
TONY ASHER

I had to prove that I could make it alone,
  now
But that's not me
I wanted to show how independent I'd
  grown, now
But that's not me
I could try to be big in the eyes of the
  world
What matters to me is what I could be
  to just one girl
I'm a little bit scared 'cause I haven't
  been home in a long time
You need my love and I know that I
  left at the wrong time.
My folks when I wrote and told them
  what I was up to
Said, that's not me.

I went through all kinds of changes
Took a look at myself and said
That's not me
I miss my pad and the places I've known
And every night as I lay there alone
I would dream
I once had a dream so I packed up and
  split for the city
I soon found out that my lonely life wasn't
  so pretty
But when I went on then that's for sure
  that we're ready
I once had a dream so I packed up and
  split for the city
I soon found out that my lonely life
  wasn't so pretty.
© Copyright 1966 by Sea of Tunes Publishing Co.

MEET the BEACH BOYS

THE BEACH BOYS

Brian's stiletto-sharp mind cuts through layers of confusion, disorder and double-talk to get at the meat of the matter at hand. Though inclined to be tense, serious and intellectual, he has a sense of humor that ranges from the whimsical to the way-out. His hearty laugh starts on the first floor of his diaphram and bellows out through the roof of the house.

The other four boys generally accept Brian's judgments and decisions but they sound off loud when they don't see eye-to-eye with him. He readily gives in when a better idea is presented; he doesn't consider himself omniscient - a $64 word meaning all-wise, all-powerful, all-knowing and too doggoned smart to be human. Peace in the family and harmony in the group are more precious than rubies.

Starting in high school, he began organizing vocal and instrumental combos to entertain at parties and dances for peanuts and bread. The greatest of all, he eventually found in his own home and neighborhood.

"In college I took a music appreciation course but the teachers were 100 per cent against anything except operas, symphonies, cantata, chamber and classical stuff," Brian recalls. "Well, I wasn't going to sit there and let any guy tell me that pop music is bad. I love both. After a year-and-a-half, I became a college drop-out and I'm not sorry. My hunger for knowledge is very strong but I can learn more through self-study."

DENNIS WILSON

Dennis Wilson, whose wild drums feed the beat to the Beach Boys music, was the original surfer with dyed hair and wet feet who stirred up the surfin' excitement among his brothers and friends, which led to their first disk smasheroo.

A complete out-going extrovert, Dennis is the group's glad-hander, good-timer, and mad-mixer. He devotes much of his spare time to the gentle art of girl-watching. Once he was nearly caught in the tender trap but got away in time.

Dennis loves to meet people of all types and is the easiest to know of all the Beach troupe. After a performance he likes to mix with the audience and talk with everybody. He often brings new-found girlfriends and acquaintances backstage to meet the other lads.

Quotes from his questionnaire: "Most of my dreams are about money, cars and girls...Three of us are brothers and we naturally have some pretty good scraps which blow over soon. There's no chance of the Beach Boys coming unglued. They tell me I've got a quick temper and a far-out temperament... but when I look into the big baby blue eyes of a long-haired girl I can agree with anything she says..."

BRUCE JOHNSTON

Bruce Johnston, the phantom Beach Boy – he is the one who tours in place of Brian Wilson Beach Boy leader who no longer goes on the road preferring, rather, to stay in his home creating the new music of the Beach Boys.

Bruce Johnston is an admirable fill-in and is achieving a close identity with the Boys on personal appearances.

He is, also, a member of a duo – Bruce and Terry. The other half of the duo is Terry Melcher, A&R man for Paul Revere and the Raiders and The Byrds, for whom he produced two Number One records.

Bruce and Terry have made several records together. One, "Hey Little Cobra" is still played all over the country, another "Four Strong Winds" deserved to be played all over the country but wasn't.

A third - "Come Love" - was played hard by KFWB recently and was picked by Lord Tim but failed to make it in America.

"Come Love," however, is now Number Six in Hong Kong and is doing well elsewhere in foreign markets.

Bruce is 22, extremely cheerful and genuinely pleasant to have around. He was born into a prosperous family - his father was vice-president of Rexall Drug Company.

With the Beach Boys he's toured the U.S. many times and he's visited Japan. He will be with the group when they make their first big English tour this year.

{Continued on next page}

MAGAZINE

THE BEACH BOYS

(Continued from last page)

MIKE LOVE

Mike Love is many things to the Beach Boys. As lead vocalist, he sings both bass and tenor, and he emcees the stage shows.

Marvy Mike is the company comedian and a one-man laugh track when he's in the mood for cutting capers with friends, strangers and especially pretty girls. Yet, he has a complicated dual personality and can be both kind and sarcastic, idealistic and cynical, sympathetic and impatient, playful as a puppy, or serious as a tree full of owls.

When he's playing around, Mike is a delightful idiot but when he settles down to studying, writing or learning new material, he becomes tenacious as a bulldog. Dancing used to be a drag because he wasn't the best on any floor, so he decided to be just that. In a few weeks he could dance the Monkey like a monkey wishes it could. Mike's like that -- he wants to go first class or not at all.

Quotes from a questionnaire:
"I love going barefoot in Bermuda shorts....Femininity has many alluring aspects but long hair turns me on the most... When I'm out in public and feel a sneeze coming on, I let em have it....I don't have any trouble keeping my nails clean as they are usually in my mouth....."

CARL WILSON

Carl is the youngest and most gifted instrumentalist of the Beach Boys Five.

Playing lead guitar, his strings pace the other galloping guitars. Brian says Carl has such exquisite musical taste that he'll change any arrangement that Carl doesn't like.

In his early Beach Boys' career, concert tours and recording dates kept him out of class so often that he was a year late in getting his hands on a diploma.

"It doesn't matter too much anyhow," he said. "Most of my learning has come from being with the Beach Boys. The music business is better than a college education."

Carl has the strongest family resemblance to Brian, his older brother whom he worships. He used to be terribly shy and easily embarrassed but he's growing out of that fast. His warm personality attracts friends to him easily. He is generous, kind, affectionate, conscientious, co-operative, quiet and deep. If you like that type, you'll like Carl the most.

ALAN JARDINE

A folk singer turned dental student, Al Jardine is now happiest as a swingin' songster, rockin' rhythm guitarist and the only married member of the Beach Boys.

He's a devoted husband to his childhood sweetheart and they hope to raise a large family of surfin' boys and belles.

"Being married, my life on tour is less hectic than the other boys," Al explains. "The girls are friendly but not flirty. I suppose it's the same with the married Beatle, John Lennon, who is sort of father image to the teen chicks. The most important thing in my personal life is to concentrate on the success of my marriage."

Al is the quiet and pensive member of the group. During their travels, while the others are sleeping or playing around, Al most likely will have his nose buried in a book that will pack his brain with knowledge or understanding. His quiet strength makes him one of the most popular members of the quintet.

MAGAZINE

JUNE/JULY 1976

MODERN RECORDING

SERVING TODAY'S MUSIC/RECORDING-CONSCIOUS SOCIETY

VOL. 1 NO. 5
$1.50

A Session with the Beach Boys

P.A. Primer
History of Recording
Elton's Producer: Gus Dudgeon
Lab Reports • New Products • Record Reviews

MAGAZINE

A SESSION WITH THE BEACH BOYS

GD: Right. Eight-track at Trident. Just the fact that they were in stereo meant that you had to have more microphones. And then when you started employing more microphones you suddenly found you were hearing all kinds of overtones and things within the drums that you'd never even noticed before. And then along came Ringo Starr, who I think must be responsible more than any other drummer in the whole word, to revolutionize not only drumming as an art (rather than the techniques, because he's not a technical drummer, he's an artistic drummer), but he revolutionized it in terms of the sort of fills he played and his whole approach.

And it's just become a habit now. I automatically spend as much time as I need to on a drum kit. Sometimes it's only 15 minutes, and sometimes it's two days. It's been as long as two, three days to get the drum sound right. But the funny thing is, people will always talk about Nigel [Olssen's] drum sound because, I suppose, they probably know my work with him better than anybody else. And they're always saying, "How do you get that drum sound on Nigel?" And my answer, quite honestly, is, "I don't fucking know!" I s'pose if I got down to it and actually told them, they'd say, "Well, that's what I do!" Because I'm sure we all do the same. But, it seems to be the subtleties that make the difference. There seems to be something that I look for that maybe other people don't look for. I don't know.

MR: There seems to be this consistent "shine" on Elton's tracks even from album to album, specifically drums and piano and vocal. This is really part of the same question. Is this something you work towards or is this something that has to do with the particular kind of echo you use, or what?

GD: Let me put it this way. If I was to go and produce the Beach Boys, we'd both get screwed up. Because the Beach Boys—I've talked to Carl Wilson about it—I would come in and I'd say, "How the hell do you do this? Why on earth do you—and, how do you get this?" And he's saying, "I don't know what you're talking about."

And he's saying to me, "Well, forget about—how do *you* get this piano sound?" And I'm going, "Well, I don't know." And he's saying, "Well, what kind of mics, where do you put the mics?" And I'm saying, "Well, I use

Gus surveys an old watermill outside of London on the River Thames which he has recently purchased. His original plans to build a mixing room have expanded to include a complete 24-track quad studio, rehearsal studio and accomodations for guests and artists.

this and I use that," and he's saying, "Well, that's what I use.

So, why is it different? I don't know. It seems to be that my ears, my taste, tell me that something is right or something is wrong. And I listen to somebody else's album and I think, "Well, that's probably the worst bass sound that I've ever heard in my life." But somebody else may listen to it and say, "Well, that's the greatest, that's just so great." A lot of people, for instance, really like the sound that Chris Squire gets with Yes. The bass sound. I think it's terrible. There's no way that I would ever want to get that sound. And if I tried to get it, I wouldn't know how to get it.

I think we did get it once for "Funeral for a Friend." There's just this very short section in "Funeral for a Friend" where Dee Murray specifically asked for that sound, and we did get it, but most of the work on getting the sound came from him, not from me, because I just looked at him and said, "Well, I don't know where to begin." It's the same with the Beach Boys. I'm sure if the Beach Boys tried to use my techniques, they wouldn't get it right. And if they did, they'd mess up what they do anyway. Because the way they do their thing is amazing. I just love the way the Beach Boys produce their records. But I feel that if I did it, I would just screw them up.

MR: There are some specific things that you do though. For example, you have described a rather involved enclosure system for miking piano. Others have tried that, but there is still something about Elton's piano sound that consistently rides above it.

GD: Well, that's a special one. I don't know what it is. All I can say is I think it's a combination of—number one, it's got to start out with the pianist, and the way he plays. It could be something to do with the weight he plays at.

MR: Would you describe the set-up?

GD: I extend the piano. I think you would agree that the best way to get a piano sound is to get the mics as far away from the strings as possible. You get far too many overtones and far too much unnatural presence from a piano when the mic is three inches from the strings. After all, when you're playing the piano you haven't got your ear three inches from the strings. If you did you'd deafen yourself, and you'd hear all kinds of awful things going on. Ringings, overtones, harmonics, all kinds of gear you don't want to hear.

So, what I did, working on the principle that you don't want the mics further back, I built a box which is exactly the same size and shape as a piano, except that it's about four foot high and sits on top of the piano, so the piano has basically been heightened by about four foot. Now that means that, with the piano being about a foot inside, you've got about five or six feet that you can move up or down with the

The instrumental tracks are complete and it is evident that keyboards have replaced the electric guitar as the instrumental cornerstone of the Beach Boys's music. Brian plays most of the keyboards on the album, although the other Wilsons sit in on some of the tracks. Various combinations of piano, Baldwin organ, MOOG and ARP String Ensemble synthesizer give the cuts a rich sound. Brian calls the synthesizer the "greatest addition to the Beach-Boys sound to come along," and he actually prefers the String Ensemble's unnaturally full sound to an real string section for most songs.

This emphasis on keyboards is a far cry from the early Beach Boys hits which almost single-handedly popularized the Fender Stratocaster. That self-contained electric-combo sound was a radical departure at the time from the orchestral pop/rock sound of the early '60's, and some people think that it helped pave the way for the Beatles and Progressive Rock.

This is not to say that the guitar has been phased out of the Beach Boys' music entirely. Carl has become an excellent guitarist, and, in spite of a bad back, he has been coming in regularly to lay down guitar tracks. In a couple of cases he is literally "laying down" the tracks, since the only position he can play in without considerable pain is flat on his back on the studio floor. Other guitarists featured on the album include studio guitarist Ben Benay, and Ed Carter and Billy Hinsche who are members of the Beach Boys backup band on the road.

Meanwhile, back at the "Chapel", Steve Moffitt sets up the Neuman U-67's for the vocals, and Earl Mankey, Brother's other staff engineer, explains, "The U-67's tube sound is usually perfect for the group's vocal blend, but we will occasionally go to a Sony C-12 when we want a solo vocal to stand out."

Meanwhile, the group is in the midst of deciding who will sing lead. Most artists have a fairly specific plan for vocals before the rhythm tracks are finished but, according to Dennis, "We've all been through the mill together, and we know what to expect. Strengths, weaknesses .... So whatever happens, whoever takes the lead will be the Beach Boy who is right for it at the time."

Brian asks Mike Love if he wants to sing lead on "Chapel," but Mike says he can really hear Brian singing it. Brian, who has not sung a lead in nobody-knows-how-many years, casually agrees and leaves the control room for the studio. Once in front of the microphone, he appears to have some reservations and asks that the control room be cleared of everybody but Beach Boys and engineers.

Through the (almost) soundproof studio door, we can barely hear Brian's still familiar falsetto running through the song. By the third time through he is singing pretty confidently, they have a take, and all of us non-essential personnel have trickled back into the control room.

Listening back, Brian's voice sounds a little rusty in a couple of spots, but basically the track feels good. After some discussion of possible background vocal lines and of who is going to take the high part, Al and Mike move to the studio. As it turns out, Mike (who usually sings the lower leads) takes the high harmony, but the basic quality of the Beach Boys's harmony comes through.

Moffitt, who also mixes for the group on the road, says, "The Beach Boys have naturally unique vocals without even touching them. Their blend is usually accented further by having two or three of them sing backgrounds around the same mic, and by doubling the voices—sometimes with other voices, sometimes with instruments. EQ and echo are added, and the vocal tracks are usually limited a little, then mixed up front." There is nothing really extraordinary in the way the Beach Boys's vocals are recorded any more than there is a trick to recording Eric Clapton's guitar or Miles Davis' trumpet. More often than not, good production is more a matter of highlighting something that is already special than of taking something ordinary and trying to make it special.

When Mike, Al and Brian are satisfied with the back-up vocals, Steve makes some cassette copies of the rough mix for the band to listen to outside the studio. It has been a productive and eventful day and everyone's spirits are high.

As he gets ready to leave, Brian is raving about Phil Spector: "The man is just a hero. He gave rock just what it needed at the time and obviously influenced us a lot. We're doing two more Spector songs on the album: 'Just Once in My Life' which he co-wrote with Carole King and Jerry Goffin, and 'He's So Fine' [written by Margo, Margo, Medress and Siegel]. I guess I chose most of the ballads on the album. Carl and Dennis are more into rock 'n' roll and picked 'Rock 'n' Roll Music,' 'Mony Mony' and 'Palisades Park.' Al and Mike are the R & B fans and they suggested 'Blueberry Hill,' 'A Casual Look' and 'On Broadway.'"

It is easy to see that Brian feels good about today's session and the Oldies album, in general. The group is scheduled to have some publicity shots taken the following day and won't be coming in until late afternoon. This gives a perfect opportunity to sit down with Steve and Earl to get the engineer's viewpoint.

Steve has been with the Beach Boys since Carl and Dennis called him in late 1971 to work on *So Tough*—a Beach-Boys album recorded under the pseudonym of "Carl and the Passions."

"I didn't know it then, but my freelancing days were over. First I spent a week figuring out Brian's home studio, then we did the album. Then we packed up the whole studio and flew to Holland where we set it back up and recorded the album *Holland*. When we got back, the equipment went into storage for about a year before Carl and Dennis asked me to help them put Brother together. Since then it's been a 20-hour-a-day job for me."

Moffitt and Gordon Rudd (of Clover Industries) designed and built the

MAGAZINE

Brother console, then Steve went to work on the monitors with a specific goal in mind: "Most speakers' tone coloration changes drastically as you change volume. This is mainly due to midrange design—say 200 to 5,000 cycles. So, I looked for a midrange speaker that had flat frequency response with no cabinet affecting it. When I found one, I experimented with various enclosures and materials until I was satisfied. The crossover network is pretty unconventional in that it isn't perfect theoretically, but it works with the system. And I think we ended up with monitors that come close to reproducing the signal that goes in, instead of sounding like that signal coming out of a box, which is what most monitors sound like to me."

The Beach Boys have come to respect Steve as an engineer and they do not hesitate to ask his opinion of the music. Brian calls Steve an "efficient engineer who has a stabilizing effect on the group." He adds, "We haven't worked with Earl as much yet, but more and more, recently. I really respect the fact that he doesn't hesitate to tell me exactly how he feels about the music he's recording for us—whether he likes it or feels it could be better."

Like many engineers, Earl Mankey is a musician who tired of life on the road. A former member of the group Sparks, he came to Brother mainly because of his fascination with Brian's production. "The thing about Brian is that he is concerned with the song as a whole, not just with being able to hear a 'hot guitar lick' here or a 'meaningful lyric' there." Earl obviously looks at engineering as a step toward producing, and he can often be found in the studio, after hours, doing numerous overdubs on his own material.

Earl and Steve have very different ideas about drum-miking. Steve likes to close-mic the drums in order to minimize leakage and maximize his control over the balance and tone of the set. Earl leans toward distant mikings, especially if the set's natural sound is right for the song.

Several days earlier, Dennis (who plays most of the drums on the album) was out with a sprained wrist, so Brian called in premier studio-drummer Hal Blaine. Moffitt says that he was very surprised that he could not get a full drum sound on Blaine's drums. "They had a sort of this cardboard sound that I couldn't get rid of." On the other hand (or microphone), Earl liked Blaine's drums and on "Blueberry Hill" he miked them with a pair of Neuman KM84's overhead, a Shure SM56 on the snare and a Neuman U-67 as the more distant room mic.

"A lot of times when you get into close miking you have to spend a lot of time taping or padding the drums to get rid of the ring. Then you've got to EQ the hell out of them to restore some of the sound you've taken away with the tape or pads. If the drums sound good anyway, then I'd rather leave them alone—mic them from a distance, and live with the leakage."

The group is due back from the photo session and the studio personnel are just starting to get a little impatient when Tricia Roach, Brother

Studio's Girl Friday, announces that "The Boys just called and they won't be in because the photo session was sort of a hassle, but they'll be in the usual time tomorrow."

But they cancel again the following day, and the next day only Dennis comes in for a short session. Over the course of the next two weeks, the Oldies sessions continue to lose momentum, and the atmosphere at Brother reflects the change. Steve, Earl, Tricia and the rest of the studio personnel are used to these fluctuations in the group's recording habits, but there is still a letdown after the high energy of the previous sessions.

The album is almost finished, however, with most of the tunes ready to be mixed. Although the sessions have definitely slowed down, most days at least one of the Beach Boys comes in to do some mixing, with Carl taking up a lot of the slack. In the past, Steve has worked more extensively with Carl than with the other members, so it goes fairly smoothly. They work well together, with Carl doing most of the EQ, positioning and level changes and Steve handling the outboard equipment. Brian goes for the final sound on each track during recording, so very few effects are added while mixing down, other than limiting the whole mix a little "so that the radio stations don't play with it too much."

Steve says many of the Beach Boys's albums were mixed on this kind of individual basis, and that Carl's and Brian's production techniques are close enough that Brian will probably not have to remix any of the songs. So, it looks like the Oldies album will be wrapped up soon after all—although without the exuberance of the earlier sessions.

It is easy for an outside observer to blame the lull on a loss of interest in the relatively unchallenging Oldies, or on impatience to get into the original material, or on a rebellion against pressure from Warner Brothers to put out an album. But that is all guesswork. The Beach Boys just are not into putting a lot of energy into recording at the moment, and there is nothing that says they have to. They all seem (at least) comfortable financially, so there is no urgency to finish an album on that level. They own the studio, so there is no deadline or heavy expense when they cancel. The Oldies album may be released as initially planned—simultaneously with the presently unfinished record of original Beach Boy compositions—or the two albums may come out in a double package, which was also discussed. Warners might rush the Oldies album out on its own, or perhaps the tapes will sit in the proverbial "can" forever.

The Beach Boys may be rolling again tomorrow, or it may never happen again. They are in the enviable position of waiting until they are ready to go back into the studio. The rest of us will simply have to wait and see whether this kind of artistic freedom makes it too easy for the group to lay back permanently and rest on their laurels—or if it gives them an opportunity to truly explore their potential, free from the usual outside pressures.

The Beach Boys —'100%'

"The Whole World Is Just a Great Big California"

MEL BOCHNER

Brian, Dennis and Carl Wilson, their cousin Mike Love and neighborhood pal Al Jardine are the Beach Boys. They all grew up together in Hawthorne, California. It was Dennis, the sportsman of the family, who suggested to Brian and Mike (neither of whom have ever surfed) that they write a song about surfing. The result was "Surfin'."

"Insiders called their early material 'pimple music'—that is simpleminded sounds for the pubescent mind."—R. Goldstein.

The Beach Boys sing the fun sound. They have "somehow transmuted the sun, sand, sea and sensuality of Southern California into musical terms acceptable all over the world." Some of their early hits include:
"Surfin'"
"G.T.O."
"I Get Around"
"California Girls"
"When I Grow Up to Be a Man"
"Fun, Fun, Fun"
"From San Diego to Malibu, the Beach Boys are as well received as a long rolling breaker."

Of course, some people don't take California-style hedonism seriously. California culture is thought of as pretty artificial.

"People ask me sometimes how I come up with my ideas," reports Brian. "Sometimes I don't know. The feeling you get from going to school, being in love, winning and losing in sports—these are my inspirations. A sociologist might say I am trying to generate a feeling of social superiority."

"Another reason for their normality is the tremendous intelligence within the group, individually as well as collectively. Each member has a balanced view of his place in the scheme of things."

"Says Carl: 'Without each other we'd all be dead. And going way back, without our parents' support we'd never have gotten off the beach.' Which is true enough, and modest too."

BRIAN
Birthdate: June 20, 1942
Birthplace: Hawthorne, Calif.
Hair: Dark Brown
Eyes: Hazel-blue
Height: 6'2"
Weight: 190 lbs.

DENNIS
Birthdate: Dec. 4, 1944
Birthplace: Hawthorne, Calif.
Hair: Brown
Eyes: Blue
Height: 5'9"
Weight: 145 lbs.

CARL
Birthdate: Dec. 21, 1946
Birthplace: Hawthorne, Calif.
Hair: Dark Brown
Eyes: Blue
Height: 5'10"
Weight: 175 lbs.

MIKE
Birthdate: Mar. 15, 1941
Birthplace: Los Angeles
Hair: Blonde
Eyes: Blue
Height: 6'1"
Weight: 165 lbs.

AL
Birthdate: Sept. 3, 1942
Birthplace: Lima, Ohio
Hair: Blonde
Eyes: Blue
Height: 5'5"
Weight: 135 lbs.

Today a widespread re-evaluation of the Beach Boys is occuring. Gone are those "leaping, lilting, bounding, boundless harmonies" of "Little Honda," "Noble Surfer" and "She's Not the Little Girl I Once Knew." The release within a year of two new records, "Good Vibrations" and "Pet Sounds," with the promise of a new album, "Smile," has caused many to sit up and take notice.

Jonathan King says: "With justification, comments are being passed that 'Good Vibrations' is an inhuman work of art. Computerized pop, mechanized music. Take a machine, feed in various musical instruments, add a catch phrase, stir well and press seven buttons. It is long and split . . . analyzed this is A, X, Y and Z (fast), followed by B, C, D and L (slow) followed by R, P and Q (voices or machines made to sound like voices) impressive, fantastic, commercial—yes. Emotional, soul-destroying, shattering—no."

Brian calls "Pet Sounds" (sounds to pet by) an "evening album." The new songs have a melodic yet melancholy air:
"That's Not Me"
"God Only Knows"
"Don't Talk"
"Caroline No"
"Let's Go Away for Awhile"
"I Just Wasn't Made for These Times"

The influence of early electronic music, especially Les Paul and Mary Ford, can be noted in the intricate cutting into and over of separately recorded tracks of voices and instruments.

"Brian Wilson may be a genius; it's hard to say because the meaning of the word is elusive. But it takes a special word to describe the rare, mindblocking, blinding talents of this 24-year-old."

"Good Vibrations" is a three-minute and thirty-five second record. It took seven months to record.

"I've used a lot of musicians on the track —twelve violins, piano, four saxes, oboe, vibes, a guitar with a coke bottle on the strings for a semi-steel guitar effect, also I used two basses and percussion. The total effect is . . . 'Let's Go Away for Awhile,' which is something everyone in the world must have said at some time or other. Nice thought. Most of us don't go away but it's still a nice thought."

"Of course some people don't take California-style hedonism seriously." The Beach Boys. Courtesy William Morris Agency.

MAGAZINE

Entertainment

There's been a change in the Beach Boys

CARL WILSON, youngest of the Beach Boy Wilsons.

By STU FINE

FROM A SURFIN' SAFARI in 1961 to today's realization of the pollution problem, the Beach Boys have scanned the globe but only recently has the world taken heed. The Beach Boys appear tomorrow evening at 8:30 at the University of Rhode Island's Keaney Gymnasium with tickets at the door at 7 for $5.

The original purveyors of good time rock 'n roll, the Beach Boys swept the country in the early 60s providing America with a challenger to Britannia's Beatles and Stones. Although all five were strong singers and no one monopolized the spotlights the band's image was characterized by Dennis Wilson because no other Beach Boy had ever attacked the wild surf.

"They say I live a fast life," admitted Dennis on the liner notes of an early album, *All Summer Long*. "Maybe I just like a fast life driving my Stingray or XKE, playing my drums and meeting so many girls."

Nothing mystical, nothing below the surface, the lyrics told the whole story. Suntanned California girls with French bikinis were the cutest, and we had fun, fun, fun when daddy took her T-bird away.

With *Pet Sounds* in 1966, the music and production of the Beach Boys blossomed into a complexity matched only by a handful of today's studio masters. "The carefree surfer, whose concerns had been limited to the size and the shape of the day's waves, and the size and the shape of the bumps on his feet, and Saturday night dates in his little deuce coupe with his little surfer girl was getting older, and the need for slightly more profound boy-girl relationships was beginning to assert itself," summarized Brian Wilson, producer, lyricist and composer.

Perhaps the first "concept album" of the rock genre, *Pet Sounds* is orchestrated by lively, enriching harmonies, bubbling keyboards and ingenious electronic gimmicks (half a decade prior to the emergence of whiz-kid Todd Rundgren!). Brian fully actualized the impulsive Jon Voight years before the creation of *Midnight Cowboy*. "I once had a dream, so I packed up and split for the city. I soon found out, that my lonely life wasn't so pretty."

The album led to a feud with Capitol Records concerning promotion, and the situation was never rectified, according to a press release from the current label, Brother Records. The following four years gave birth to the nucleus of the current Beach Boy sound. Brian experimented with numerology, astrology, LSD and the *I Ching*. Dennis, incapacitated by a severe hand injury waived the drums in favor of a synthesizer. Carl, youngest of the Wilson brothers, struggled with the draft board while Mike Love and Al Jardine searched for a better way with the Maharishi.

Sunflower and *Surf's Up* confirmed new directions, with moog, avant-garde piano and social criticism. Regarding water pollution Mike warned: "Toothpaste and soap will make our oceans a bubble bath, so let's avoid an ecological aftermath, beginning with me, beginning with you, don't go near the water."

In the past year, two South Africans, Blondie Chaplin and Ricky Fataar, added another dimension to the Beach Boys on *Carl and the Passions-So Tough* and *Holland*. Blondie's vocals reached the highest notes on the live version of "Wild Honey," and his funky guitar launched "We Got Love." Ricky's sparkplug drumming gave the band a solid backbone for the first time since Dennis' accident forced him to throw in his sticks.

The Beach Boys have come a long way since the surfin', partyin' days which is evident on their latest album, *In Concert*. The old classics are revived with maturity, sophistication and instrumental drive; the more recent material is performed with savvy, confidence and studio perfection. Just like a Beach Boys concert.

RADIO STATION SURVEY

KFWB Fabulous Forty Survey

FOR WEEK ENDING FEBRUARY 16, 1962

#	Title	Artist—Label	LAST WEEK
1.	DUKE OF EARL	GENE CHANDLER—VEEJAY	1
2.	THE WANDERER	Dion—Laurie	3
3.	*SURFIN'	The Beachboys—Candix	4
4.	*COTTON FIELDS	The Highwaymen—United Artists	5
5.	THE TWIST	Chubby Checker—Parkway	2
6.	I'M BLUE	The Ikettes—Atco	6
7.	*HEY BABY	Bruce Channel—Smash	9
8.	DREAMY EYES	Johnny Tillotson—Cadence	7
9.	*CRYING IN THE RAIN	The Everly Bros.—Warner Bros.	12
10.	WHAT'S YOUR NAME	Don & Juan—Bigtop	29
11.	LOVE LETTERS	Ketty Lester—Era	15
12.	*JAMIE	Eddie Holland—Motown	25
13.	DEAR LADY TWIST	Gary (U.S.) Bonds—Legrand	10
14.	*PERCOLATOR	Billy Joe & The Checkmates—Dore	22
15.	*SURFER'S STOMP	The Mar-Kets—Union	8
16.	*BREAK IT TO ME GENTLY	Brenda Lee—Decca	11
17.	*TUFF	Ace Cannon—Hi	23
18.	LET ME IN	The Sensations—Argo	34
19.	MOMENTS TO REMEMBER	Jennell Hawkins—Amazon	19
20.	*CAJUN QUEEN	Jimmy Dean—Columbia	20
21.	TEARS ARE FALLING	The Blue Jays—Milestone	27
22.	PEPPERMINT TWIST	Joey Dee & Starliters—Roulette	14
23.	IRRESISTIBLE YOU	Bobby Darin—Atco	35
24.	SMOKY PLACES	The Corsairs—Tuff	38
25.	*SHADRACK	Brook Benton—Mercury	21
26.	*NORMAN	Sue Thompson—Hickory	13
27.	*BABY IT'S YOU	The Shirelles—Scepter	18
28.	MR. MOTO	The Belaires—Arvee	24
29.	*HER ROYAL MAJESTY	James Darren—Col-Pix	37
30.	*MEMORIES OF MARIA	Jerry Byrd—Monument	36
31.	I KNOW	Barbara George—A.F.O.	16
32.	*SHE'S EVERYTHING	Ral Donner—Gone	32
33.	*I'LL SEE YOU IN MY DREAMS	Pat Boone—Dot	30
34.	*CAN'T HELP FALLING IN LOVE	Elvis Presley—RCA Victor	17
35.	CRY TO ME	Solomon Burke—Atlantic	39
36.	*WHEN I FALL IN LOVE	The Lettermen—Capitol	26
37.	*SHE'S GOT YOU	Patsy Cline—Decca	Debut
38.	*DON'T BREAK THE HEART THAT LOVES YOU	Connie Francis—MGM	Debut
39.	*WHERE HAVE ALL THE FLOWERS GONE	The Kingston Trio—Capitol	40
40.	*DREAM BABY	Roy Orbison—Monument	Debut

*RECORDS FIRST HEARD ON KFWB

FAVORITE ALBUMS

1. Let There Be Drums — Sandy Nelson—Imperial
2. Your Twist Party — Chubby Checker—Parkway
3. Blue Hawaii — Elvis Presley—RCA Victor
4. Andy Williams Best — Andy Williams—Cadence
5. West Side Story — MST—Columbia

98 IS GREAT!

PROMOTIONAL PHOTO

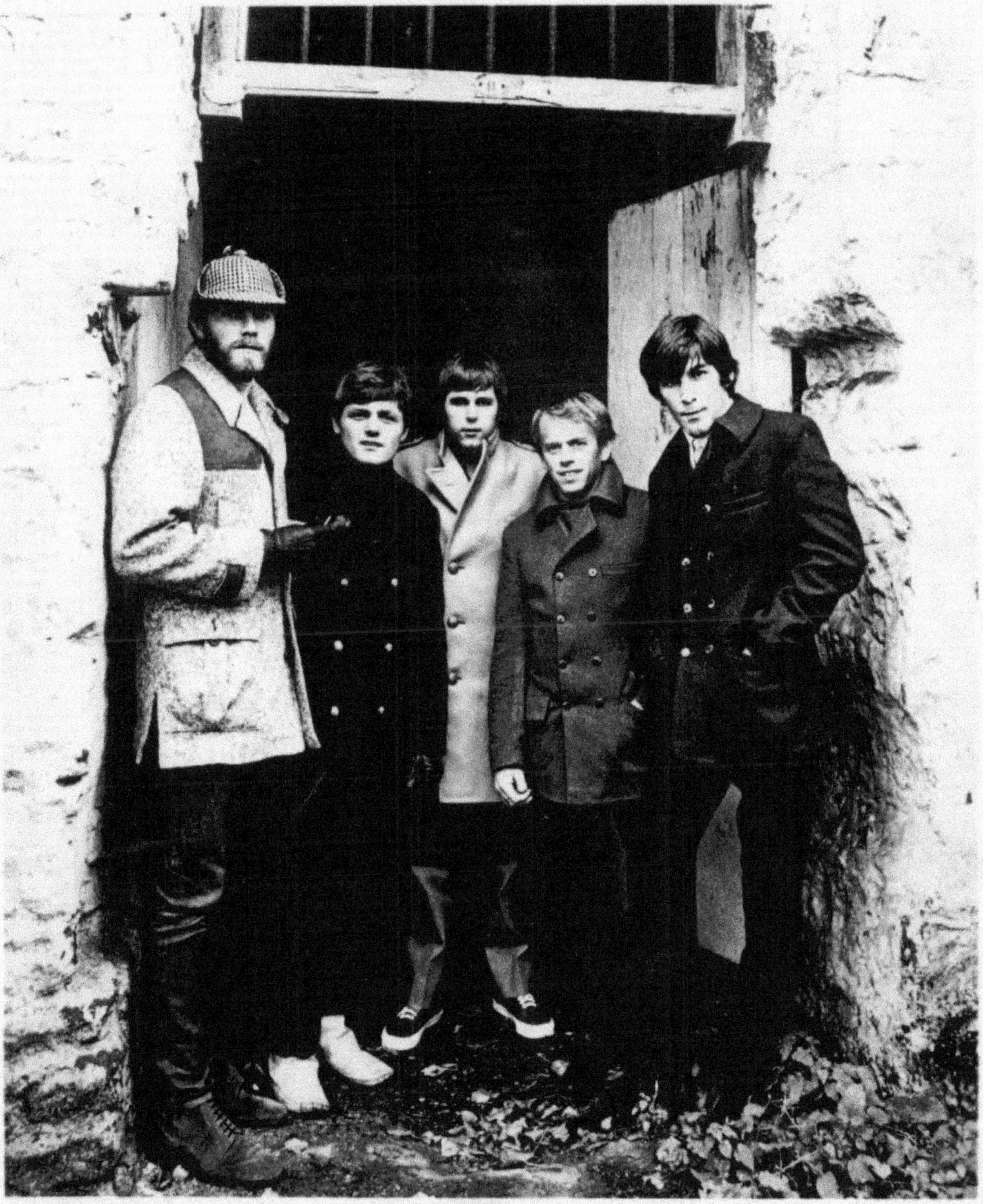

Capitol RECORDS

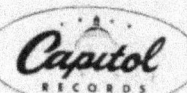

THE BEACH BOYS

International Fan Club
P.O. Box 110
Hollywood, Calif. 90028

NEWS

EARL WILSON
What Happened to Maharishi?

DELAWARE COUNTY (PA.) DAILY TIMES
Monday, May 13, 1968

NEW YORK — There was a mystery here the other day: What happened to the mysterious Maharishi?

Very suddenly the Guru and the Beach Boys from California canceled several concerts. Three reasons were given by various people concerned. The Maharishi got pneumonia. The Maharishi remembered a Hollywood movie contract and flew there. Or, the Maharishi flew back to India, dejected that people walked out. Some folks weren't mesmerized hearing him talking about transcendental meditation while he sat in his white outfit on an antelope skin on a couch holding on to flowers.

The Maharishi promised to rejoin the Beach Boys for a May 17 date in Denver. The Beach Boys, who were advised to sue him for leaving them, declined. They remain loyal and said they'll forever be his disciples.

I may get rich yet. I'm negotiating for the binoculars concession at "Hair."

* * *

All you bald guys who've been writing in about the "linking" system guaranteeing new hair in 2 hours — the Fred Sessler Hair Extension system, 65 E. 55th St., phone 758-7430, is opening and there'll probably be panic. I'm not guaranteeing it as I am only reporting it as an observer. Happy Hair, everybody.

* * *

Has LBJ's appeal against travel abroad collapsed now that Paris'll be scene of the peace meetings? ... Florence Henderson who's going to Europe to vacation, and Paula Wayne, off to London and Germany to make appearances, discussed it at Sardi's. Paula, a blazing blonde, and Florence, a brunette, are constantly mistaken for each other ... Butterfly McQueen'll appear in "Curley McDimple" at the Bert Wheeler Theater

Remember Greek actress Rica Dialina who met a pigeon that bit some good luck beads off her neck? And how she kept the pigeon always near her hoping to recover the good luck beads? Well, the pigeon got away, and she's offering $1,000 reward hoping to get the pigeon back in time for a Merv Griffin TV appearance May 24.

WISH I'D SAID THAT: Remember the good old days, when you'd have to go to a Dr. Kildare movie to find a blazing crisis.

REMEMBERED QUOTE: "Of all the valuable things that money can buy, the most valuable is the man who can't be bought." — Portland, Ore., "Spokes."

EARL'S PEARLS: Lino Lentini heard a woman tell her neighbor, "I always wanted a child with long hair — but I was hoping it would be a girl" Jack Benny says his forthcoming TV "Special" isn't really so special: "It's just a one-hour show. To me, a special is when coffee goes from 73¢ a pound to 58¢." That's earl, brother.

HELEN HELP US!

Beach Boys Bruce gig altered

THE BEACH Boys have changed the date for their upcoming gig at Bruce Stadium from Wednesday November 25 to Thursday November 26.

The concert has been put back because of a difficulty in transporting their equipment north from the second Summer in Paradise concert in Melbourne on November 21.

Their *Good Vibrations Tour* commences on Friday November 20 at the Brisbane Entertainment Centre but the following performances are all outdoors including the North Collingwood Football Club at noon on Saturday November 21, Newcastle, Canberra, Adelaide, Sydney and Perth.

Meanwhile a *Good Times* reader called this week to put to rest claims that the November 26 gig will be the Beach Boys first visit to Canberra.

The reader recalled seeing them at a "half-full" Canberra Theatre in 1970 and said he would bet his Kokomo on it.

Anyone else remember the concert?

Sales for the Bruce concert have been steady and it is expected 15,000 fans will be there.

Nostalgia with the Beach Boys

THOSE sceptics who thought the Beach Boys were long gone should break out the beach gear and head to the Bruce Indoor Stadium on Thursday, February 20.

The night is set to be a beach party with a big competition offering a beach holiday for the most appropriately dressed.

This is the band which created the 'Sound of California' and took it around the world. 'Good Vibrations', 'Barbara-Ann', 'Help Me Rhonda', 'California Girls', 'Surfin' USA', 'Surfer Girl' and 'Wild Honey' will all be relived.

The Beach Boys' most recent album, simply titled 'The Beach Boys', was released in September, 1985. A single from the album went Top 20 in the US.

The Beach Boys line-up will feature original members Brian and Carl Wilson, Mike Love, Alan Jardine as well as Bruce Johnston and the eight-piece backing band.

The Beach Boys will appear at the Bruce Indoor Stadium on Thursday, February 20.

Beach Boys have a better offer

YOU can pack away the Hawaiian shirt and straw hat — at least for the time being. The Beach Boys have, regrettably, postponed their Keep'n Summer Alive tour, due to kick off this month.

It appears the band has been invited to perform during the America's Cup festivities in Perth in February, 1987, and decided to make the tour coincide with that gig.

Those of you who booked early for the February 20 Canberra concert can return your tickets to Canberra Bass in the Jolimont Centre.

During the past ten years, The Beach Boys produced some of their most brilliant and inventive tracks. Now 29 highlights of the past "Ten Years Of Harmony" have been gathered together on this spectacular 2-record set. Rare collectors' items ("Sea Cruise," "San Miguel," "It's A Beautiful Day") are side by side with B.B. classics ("Sail On Sailor," "Add Some Music To Your Day," "Surf's Up").
This is The Beach Boys album for everyone. Featuring the single, "Come Go With Me."
On Caribou Records and Tapes.

Beach Boys want to make world Bicentennial tour

AP Newsfeatures Writer

Mike Love of the Beach Boys would like for the group to go on a world tour during the Bicentennial with Stevie Wonder and another American group. The Beach Boys are on tour now, into July, with Chicago.

"We are so mid-stream, mid-America. No other group typifies that as much as we do, I think. I want to make a Bicentennial album. I want us to sing 'America the Beautiful' a cappella, in four-part harmony.

"I'm very nasty, snide and caustic about America's faults and failings but we're a most positive and creative country." One of Love's criticisms is that, since politicians do what their constituents want them to, the general public hasn't been vigorous enough about insisting on progress to combat evils such as pollution and alcoholism.

"Our albums have always been positive. Our philosophy has been to project good fun, entertainment, good times. I've always been of the feeling people will be attracted to what makes them feel good. Our music in general has grown more positive."

More positive than the original "Surfin"? How could that be?

Love explains that the group went from superficial to meaningful in subject matter, staying positive and growing. "Musically we made the transition in 1965-66. We started singing about other things besides surfing, cars and girl friends. Capitol Records thought we were overstepping our nice Southern California sunny-sideup profile.

"'Pet Sounds' in 1966 was the climax of our new group awareness of more positive and emotional issues. Capitol wanted 'Shut

No collection on holiday

Jackson County Bureau

W.D. Oliver, superintendent of the Jackson County Sanitation Department, announced there will be no garbage pickup in the county on Friday, July 4.

MIKE LOVE

Down Vol. 5.' They released 'Pet Sounds' but they didn't promote it very strongly."

Love considers "Pet Sounds" and "Smile," which never has been released, as the group's two best albums. "We intend to release 'Smile' someday. Capitol wouldn't promote us as a group with an evolving consciousness. In 1968 they were still promoting us as the No. 1 surfing group in the U.S.A."

At present, the Beach Boys' LP, "Spirit of America," on Capitol, is No. 16 on the chart and "Sail on Sailor," on Reprise, is No. 70 on the singles chart.

"Up to 1967 Brian Wilson was overwhelmingly the musical writer and arranger and he wrote a significant amount of lyrics. Now each guy in the group writes songs and is creative individually. It's much broader. Brian still is best at harmonies. He left touring around 1963 or '64. No law states you have to go and be a rock star."

Love's main personal concerns now are diet — he has been a vegetarian around seven years — and transcendental meditation. He learned that in 1967, took training and has been teaching it since early 1968.

"The 'Surf's Up' album of three or four years ago had a lot of stuff to do with pollution and consciousness on it. All of us have learned meditation.

"I figure the main two causes of disease that kill people are tension and stress and inner and outer pollution. By meditation you can gain deep rest and relaxation to support your activity — which we have plenty of."

The Beach Boys play benefit concerts for causes they believe in, one of which is the National Council on Alcoholism. "Transcendental meditation can dissolve feelings of stress that cause some people to go into drinking. If you limit the amount of causes, you can lessen the problem. Alcoholism is a bigger problem in this country than drug addiction." Love adds that he's down on drugs, too. "We played a concert recently and people were smoking hash and blowing out. It bugs me. I hate it. I don't even smoke."

Love also admits that he thinks he has an addictive personality. "When I used to drink, I drank a lot. Now I meditate a lot. If you're going to be addicted to something, it's better for it to be something good."

Gold LPs by the group are all Summer Long," "The Beach Boys in Concert," "Surfer Girls," "Surfin' U.S.A.," "The Beach Boys in Concert," "Shut Down Vol. 2," "Little Deuce Coupe," "Best of the Beach Boys," "Endless Summer" and "Spirit of America."

"The last few years have been amazing," Love says. "The lowest point in terms of popularity — we never had one in terms of creativity — was 1968-71. Things have worked their way back now to where we're doing really well. The attitude at concerts is so positive. I look forward to performing. Everybody has a good time.

"I remember the first show we got paid for as the Beach Boys. It was a Richie Valens memorial. They said all his friends would be there; we'd never met him. It was at the Long Beach Municipal Hall; we'd just recorded 'Surfin'' on New Year's Eve 1961 and the group had got together a few months before that. We got $300. My uncle, our manager, didn't take a cut. We each walked up to the box office and got $60 cash — no mailing it to us later.

RADIO STATION SURVEY

KDWB/63 FABULOUS FORTY SURVEY

WEEK ENDING JULY 25, 1964

		LAST WEEK
1. *I GET AROUND/DON'T WORRY BABY -- The Beach Boys -- Capitol		1
2. *Little Children/Bad to Me -- Billy J. Kramer -- Imperial		2
3. *My Boy Lollipop -- Millie Small -- Smash		3
4. *Memphis -- Johnny Rivers -- Imperial		4
5. *Rag Doll -- Four Seasons -- Philips		5
6. *Dang Me -- Roger Miller -- Smash		13
7. *Can't You See That She's Mine -- Dave Clark Five -- Epic		6
8. *I'm Into Something Good -- Earl-Jean -- Colpix		8
9. *Wishin' and Hopin' -- Dusty Springfield -- Philips		10
10. *Little Old Lady From Pasadena -- Jan and Dean -- Liberty		14
11. *The Grind -- Gregory Dee and the Avanties -- Bangar		20
12. *A World Without Love -- Peter and Gordon -- Capitol		7
13. *Nobody I Know -- Peter and Gordon -- Capitol		15
14. *Hard Day's Night/I Should Have Known Better -- KDW-Beatles -- Capitol		32
15. *Everybody Loves Somebody -- Dean Martin -- Reprise		21
16. *Don't Let the Sun Catch You Crying -- Jerry & The Pacemakers -- Laurie		11
17. *The Girl From Ipanema -- Getz/Gilberto -- Verve		19
18. *I Wanna Love Him So Bad -- Jelly Beans -- Red Bird		24
19. *How Glad I Am -- Nancy Wilson -- Capitol		34
20. *Remember Me -- Rita Pavone -- RCA		9
21. *Don't Throw Your Love Away -- The Searchers -- Kapp		12
22. *I Can't Hear You -- Betty Everett -- Vee-Jay		25
23. *C'mon and Swim -- Bobby Freeman -- Autumn		27
24. *The Mexican Shuffle -- Herb Alpert's Tiajuana Brass -- A & M		29
25. People -- Barbra Streisand -- Columbia		17
26. *No Particular Place To Go -- Chuck Berry -- Chess		30
27. *I Want You To Meet My Baby -- Eydie Gorme -- Columbia		Debut
28. *Yesterday's Gone -- The Overlanders -- Hickory		16
29. *Farmer John -- Premiers -- Warner Brothers		18
30. *The World I Used to Know -- Jimmy Rodgers -- Dot		38
31. *Peppermint Man -- The Trashman -- Garrett		40
32. *She's the One -- The Chartbusters -- Mutual		Debut
33. *Mixed-Up, Shook-Up Girl -- Patty & The Emblems -- Harold		Debut
34. *Hey Harmonica Man -- Stevie Wonder -- Tamla		22
35. *Love Me Do/P.S. I Love You -- KDW-Beatles -- Tollie		23
36. *(Just Like) Romeo & Juliet -- Reflections -- Golden World		26
37. Today -- New Christy Minstrels -- Columbia		28
38. *My Guy -- Mary Wells -- Motown		31
39. *Ain't She Sweet -- KDW-Beatles -- Atco		Debut
40. *Where Did Our Love Go -- The Supremes -- Motown		Debut

*Records First Heard on KDWB

FAVORITE ALBUMS:

1. Hard Day's Night -- KDW-Beatles
2. Little Children -- Billy J. Kramer
3. New Girl In School -- Jan and Dean
4. Beatle Song Book -- Hollyridge Strings
5. Dave Clark Five Returns -- Dave Clark Five

This survey is compiled each week by radio station KDWB, St. Paul, Minnesota. It is a true, accurate and unbiased account of record popularity, based upon sales reports, distributor accounts and all information available to the music staff of KDWB.

RADIO STATION SURVEY

Young Adult WYYY Music Power

TOTAL RADIO 1470 — Kalamazoo, Michigan

For the week of July 5, 1969

TITLE	ARTIST
1. IN THE YEAR 2525	ZAGER & EVANS
2. Love Theme From Romeo & Juliet	Henry Mancini
3. Spinning Wheel	Blood Sweat & Tears
4. Ballad Of John & Yoko	The Beatles
5. But It's Alright	J.J. Jackson
6. Doggone Right	Smokey Robinson/Miracles
7. Sweet Caroline	Neil Diamond
8. My Pledge Of Love	Joe Jeffrey Group
9. Ruby, Don't Take Your Love To Town	Kenny Rogers/First Edition
10. Color Him Father	The Winstons
11. My Cheries Amor	Stevie Wonder
12. Put A Little Love In Your Heart	Jackie DeShannon
13. The Girl I'll Never Know	Frankie Valli
14. Good Old Rock 'N Roll	Cat Mother/All Night Newsboys
15. The Days Of Sand & Shovels	Bobby Vinton
16. Pass The Apple, Eve	B.J. Thomas
17. On Campus	Dickie Goodman
18. What Does It Take	Jr Walker/All Stars
19. First Hymn From Grand Terrace	Mark Lindsey
20. Break Away	The Beach Boys
21. Abraham, Martin & John	Smokey Robinson/Miracles
22. Saint Paul	Terry Knight
23. I Can Remember	Peter & Gordon
24. Along Came Jones	Ray Stevens
25. I'd Wait A Million Years	The Grass Roots

POWER PIX

What About You?	Billy Preston
While You're Out Looking For Sugar?	The Honey Cone
Workin' On A Groovy Thing	5th Dimension
Yesterday, When I Was Young	Roy Clark

POWER LP's

I Can't Quit Her/The Letter	The Arbors
Yesterday, When I Was Young	Roy Clark

WYYY is the Young Adult station. This music list reflects the most popular music in Kalamazoo County of those over 18 years of age, as determined by record sales, requests to the station and our opinions of audience appeal of the records.

1470 GET IT ON!

MAGAZINE

MAGAZINE

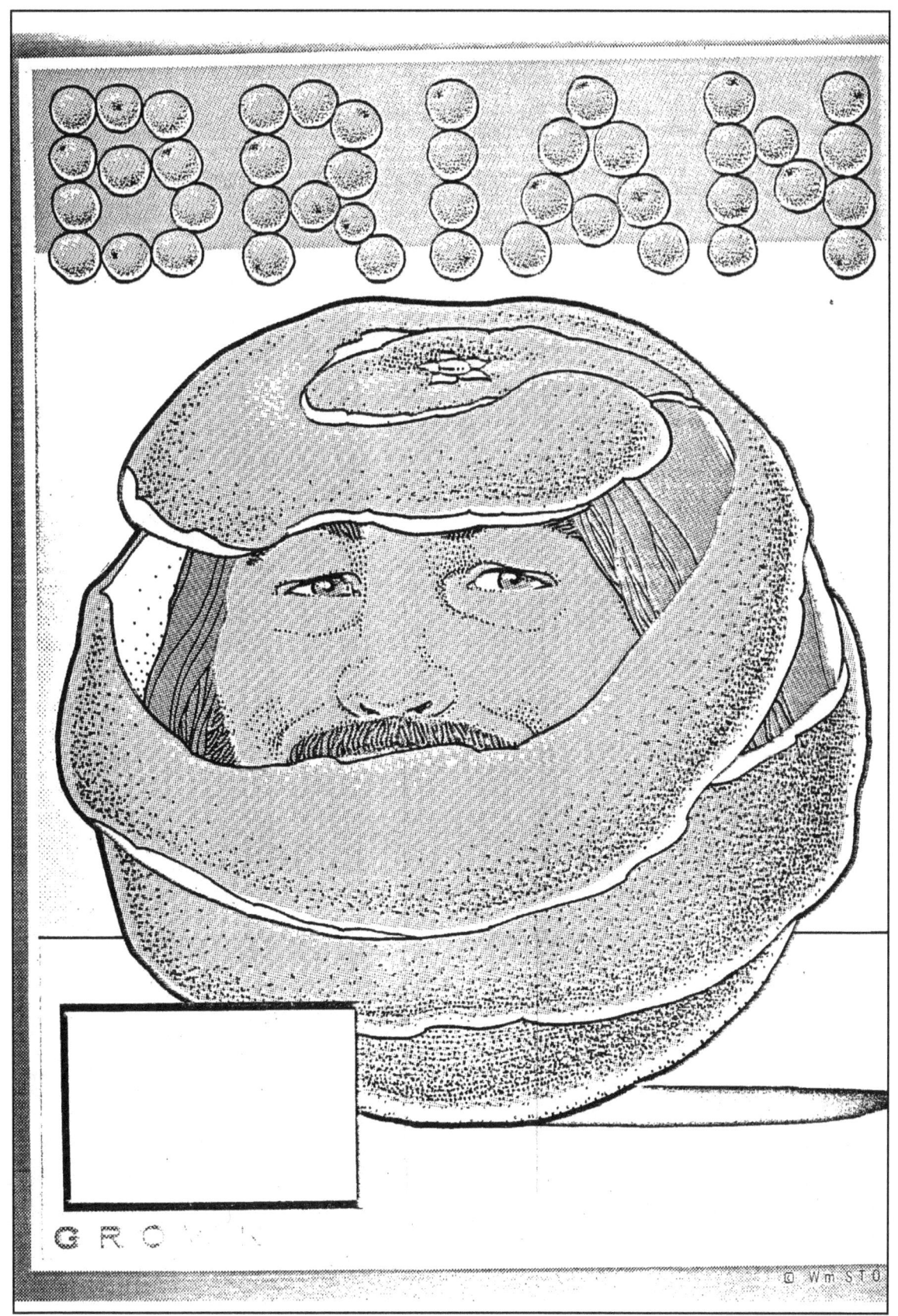

A BOMP EXCLUSIVE!!
BRIAN WILSON
TELLS JIM PEWTER ALL ABOUT THE EARLY DAYS!

Everyone loves Brian, but for an interviewer, he's not the easiest person to make talk. Jim Pewter is one of the few who've been able to establish a genuine rapport with Brian under interview conditions. One of the true pioneers in the field of 'oldies' broadcasting, Jim has interviewed Brian several times, going back as early as 1966.

This interview, presented here for the first time in any magazine, provides a fascinating insight into the background, musical influences and early working methods of Brian Wilson, while avoiding the kind of sensationalistic exploitation of his personal problems that most articles have dwelt too heavily on. We feel this material is a timely complement to the renewed interest in the Beach Boys that has helped make 1976 a banner year for rock & roll fans.

JP: Brian, let's talk about your first record; I believe that was in '62?
BW: Oh, I forgot we were doing an interview! I was looking at the picture over there.
JP: That's Groucho.
BW: Oh, hi Groucho.
JP: He's on a surfboard...
BW: I've forgotten what they look like....
JP: The first hit was "Surfin'", back in '62. How did you decide to tie the whole surfing scene up into a song, how did that come about?
BW: My brother Dennis came home from school one day and said something about how surfing looked like it was going to become the next big craze, and we should write a song about it. You see at that time we were writing songs for friends and school assemblies. So it happened that we wrote a song about surfing due to Dennis' suggestion.
JP: I talked with you on the phone about a month ago and asked you to pick out some of your favorite hits from the past for me to bring along to the interview, and you mentioned a record by the Cadets. Was that "Stranded in the Jungle"?
BW: No, that's Kenny & the Cadets. I was Kenny and the other guys went by the name of the Cadets. This was back in '61 and at that time we were just getting going with a publisher and this guy had this great song, his name was Bruce Morgan, so my mother and I and a friend of mine did this demo... hey, this could get to be a long story!
JP: You were telling me earlier about the way you write songs. How you get down a pattern on the piano and lay down some rhythm tracks. When you went in to cut tunes like "Little Deuce Coupe", back in '63, was it all live or did you lay down a rhythm track first?
BW: Sometimes. It varied, depending on how lazy we were feeling. Like sometimes we had the music but no words. Let's use "Little Deuce Coupe" as an example. We'd do the background track for it in the chord pattern and then when we'd listen to it, we'd be listening and suddenly go Wow! I got an idea! I'm hearing these kinds of words. And all of a sudden we'd be in there writing words to that track. I mean, we'd have a feeling to work with and sometimes that was all.
JP: With the car songs like "Little Deuce Coupe" the lyrics were written by Roger Christian, and then there was a song that came out about a year later which has really become a classic: "Don't Worry Baby".
BW: Roger and I spent so many evenings sitting up. He was really kind of a guiding light for me. He'd get off at midnight, he did a night show from 9 to 12 on KRLA, then we'd go out and get a hot fudge sundae and we'd sit there for hours talking, writing lyrics and all of a sudden it was like I'd written 15 songs!
JP: Did Bill Haley's "Rock Around the Clock" affect you in any way?
BW: "Rock Around the Clock" shocked me, I mean I was so electrified by that experience. Some of my friends came over and said I had to hear this new record, so we went out and bought it and took it home and put it on. We were screaming, that song was really it.
JP: Brian, besides writing and producing all these tunes you developed a style of singing in a falsetto that has been your trademark through the years. How did you develop that style?
BW: There was a group called the Four Freshmen. I used to listen to their records all the time. I'd come home from school and lock myself in my room and listen to this group and I practiced the high parts. I wanted to see if I could get as high as he could so I practiced until my range went up. So I trained my voice to the point where it was easy for me to hit that falsetto.
JP: What instrument were you practicing with while you were developing this style?
BW: An organ and piano, usually those two, though actually I didn't use an instrument much at that time. I'd just sit there on a chair and sing along with the high part...
JP: You wrote the lyrics to "Surfin' USA" didn't you?
BW: Chuck Berry wrote that song. It was called "Sweet Little Sixteen". When we first got going Mike was sort of a Chuck Berry fan, so we took Chuck's song and turned the lyrics into a surfing song.
JP: Do you get a shock when someone mentions "Be True to Your School"? What kind of memory does that bring back?
BW: Oh that fries my brain! I mean, that brings back some heavy memories...
JP: The lyric about the cheerleader...
BW: Now that's one lyric that I wish everyone would pass on and just listen to the music.
JP: One of the tunes you picked out as an all time favorite was one by the Crystals, a song called "Uptown." That song was produced by Phil Spector. You were an admirer of his work, weren't you?
BW: Of the works I remember; it's hard to remember them all, but that was one of my favorites, along with "Be My Baby" and most of the Ronettes songs. One of my favorite Beach Boys records is "I Can Hear Music" which was by the Ronettes originally. That was Carl singing lead on that one, as a matter of fact he produced it too.
JP: You recorded "Help Me Rhonda" in '64 didn't you?
BW: Yes, in the middle part of that year. That's somewhat like a Phil Spector approach and it has the harmonica part like that record "Fannie Mae."
JP: Who was playing harmonica on that, do you remember?
BW: I don't remember. I think it was some musician we hired, not one of the guys. None of us could play harmonica.
JP: Regarding your earlier sides, did you have a favorite studio that you liked to use, or did you experiment with different studios around town?
BW: We went to at least ten of the studios around town. I preferred Western Recorders at 5000 Sunset Blvd. It seemed to have the best echo chamber for what we liked to do vocally. It had good balanced echo, a really fat echo. RCA had a good studio too, and Sunset Sound was great.
JP: When was the last time you were on a Honda, Brian?
BW: Let's see, well, ah, a few years ago when I crashed my Honda.
JP: Did you have a helmet on?
BW: Yeah, I didn't get hurt real bad. I ran into a palm tree and fell off the bike. I haven't gone riding since.
JP: Where did you grow up?

MAGAZINE

• Young Brian the songwriter.

• With Jim Pewter

• On stage, 1965

BW: In Hawthorne, about three miles from the beach. It was a little town and it didn't have any sidewalks until after we grew up. It was really weird, we'd mow the lawn and the lawn would taper down into the street.

JP: You were a close family, weren't you?

BW: Yeah, I guess we were. You know my father mixed all our early surfing records, he was like our producer in fact. Yeah, that's what he was. He'd produce our records though he really didn't get credit. He'd tell us to tighten up a bit, offer us discipline, and if we didn't do it he'd get really mad. It was almost like a pep talk: "Okay you guys, you're slacking off now, tighten up a bit" and sure enough we did.

JP: When the records started getting played and becoming hits, did that change your life in any way?

BW: The guys were in high school, hadn't even graduated yet, and we were on the national chart. Now that's quite a change for a kid! So that tightened things up for our family quite a bit. We realized that we now had a chance to go places so we had to tighten up. Our first record, "Surfin'" made it, and when "Surfin' USA" made it on the national charts everybody was kind of in shock, so we tightened up our attitude and just got more serious about music.

JP: The *Beach Boys Party* album was really the first thing of its kind, wasn't it?

BW: Yeah, I guess it was. We just got everybody together and had some fun. We had no idea Capitol was gonna put "Barbara Ann" out as a single. We thought they were crazy! We weren't even sure it was gonna be an album. We just invited everybody over and turned on the tape machine. Did you know that was Dean Torrence singing that high part on "Barbara Ann"? Yeah that was old Dean, we invited him over and sat him down in a chair and told him to sing, and he did. And we had all these girls come by, it was pretty hectic that night. And then Capitol pulled "Barbara Ann" off the album without telling us, completely snuck that one past us.

JP: I bet that surprised you.

BW: It shocked me. It did very well, and we didn't expect that to happen. I think that was in November of '65 when they released that. We had potato chips and dip and other stuff around for the atmosphere. Box guitars, a standup bass, and drums. Whew!

JP: Brian, what kind of dip do you like, do you like onion?

BW: I love onion. French dip, that's the best. French onion dip or bleu cheese. Do you like Fritos or that kind of stuff?

JP: I don't like dip with Fritos as much, I'd rather have a big potato chip with onion dip on it.

BW: I love that, God I love that....

WHO PUT THE BOMP

ARTIFACT

SITE OF THE CHILDHOOD HOME OF THE BEACH BOYS

IT WAS HERE IN THE HOME OF PARENTS MURRY AND AUDREE THAT BRIAN, DENNIS, AND CARL WILSON GREW TO MANHOOD AND DEVELOPED THEIR MUSICAL SKILLS. DURING LABOR DAY WEEKEND 1961, THEY, WITH COUSIN MIKE LOVE AND FRIEND AL JARDINE, GATHERED HERE TO RECORD A TAPE OF THEIR BREAKTHROUGH SONG "SURFIN'." THIS MARKED THE BIRTH OF THE ROCK GROUP KNOWN WORLDWIDE AS THE BEACH BOYS, AND THE BEGINNING OF AN HISTORIC MUSICAL LEGACY THAT WOULD CHANGE THE RECORDING INDUSTRY. THE MUSIC OF THE WILSONS, LOVE, JARDINE, AND FRIEND DAVID MARKS BROADCAST TO THE WORLD AN IMAGE OF CALIFORNIA AS A PLACE OF SUN, SURF, AND ROMANCE. BRIAN WILSON WOULD BECOME A LEGENDARY PRODUCER, ARRANGER, AND SONGWRITER.

CALIFORNIA REGISTERED HISTORICAL LANDMARK NO. 1041

PLAQUE PLACED BY THE STATE DEPARTMENT OF PARKS AND RECREATION IN COOPERATION WITH THE CITY OF HAWTHORNE, MAY 2005.

ARTIFACT

NEWS

December 3, 1966

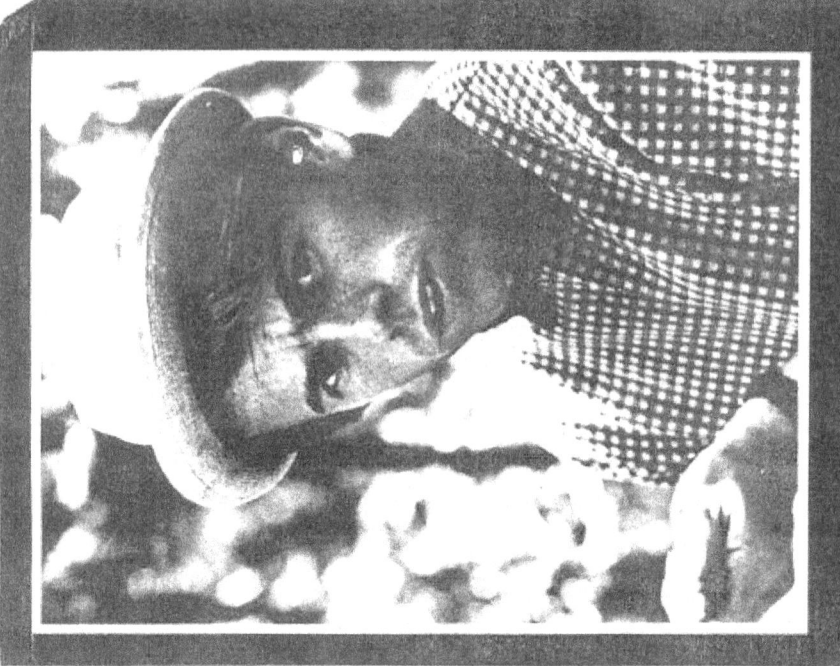

POP THINK AL IN JARDINE

OF THE BEACH BOYS

'The English invasion gave us time to think. We sat down, analysed the situation, and took off in another direction'

LOS ANGELES, TUESDAY

BILL HALEY

Haven't read an article on Bill Haley for ages. I think I must have bought every bloody record he ever made. When Haley was happening was about the time I first got involved in music.

I'd pay a lot of dollars to be able to see that guy work. Here and now! In the rock and roll bag he is undoubtedly fantastic. Whatever bag he's in, it's fantastic. When I think of Haley I don't just think of him but the whole group. That bass player and drummer. He has a group image.

CALIFORNIA GIRLS

"California Girls" the song? My concept of what most people feel the Beach Boys are or should be. That is, a nice compromise between the sophisticated and the simple-heads. Everybody loves it because it's completely passe—and outdated by Brian Wilson's standards. Easy to sing and to identify with. Everything was there.

RONALD REAGAN

That makes me think of

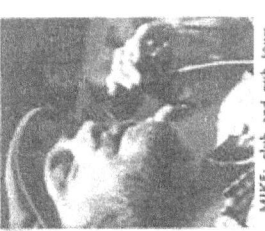

MIKE: club and pub tours

HOW THE BEACH BOYS REMEMBER BRITAIN

THE Beach Boys will return to England when the leaves are green again in Hyde Park. They could never have expected so much warm success from their first British tour.

Maybe it's good that they didn't fly in with heads bursting from inflated anticipation—the lasting depth of their personal achievement is due not to "Good Vibrations" but to their attitude which was neither the "your policemen and double-decker buses are wonderful" down-home nonsense which so irritates the British, nor the other American pose "we're just here for kicks" which is even worse.

NEWS

other American pose we're just here for kicks" which is even worse.

Audiences, clearly starved of musical substance and newness in contemporary tours, were everywhere thrilled and delighted by the Beach Boys. The sustained and concentrated welcome in Britain was extremely generous and it will not be easy for the Beach Boys to settle down to the more scattered US pop scene.

While the Beach Boys were in Europe, Brian Wilson was ceaselessly busy here in Hollywood preparing each of the twelve tracks for their new album "Smile", due for release no later than March. Wilson-willing. He put in a dozen hours work on one track alone, "Heroes and Villains", scheduled to be the follow-up single to "Good Vibrations". Prepare for more pop upheavals when you hear this one.

The group themselves are still touring, fulfilling massive concert engagements in the East of the US. When they return here mid-week they will have a few days at home and then move into the recording studios to lay down the vocal tracks.

Brian Wilson's mystique is heightening as a result of his non-appearance in England with the group. This is not a studied thing; it is simply that once he gets into recording he is like a badger unearthed. Expect him, however, to make a furtive visit to Britain within three months. Probably without the group; maybe with one of his brothers.

Happiest tour memories for the group for Dennis, the rapturous welcome from the fans and the delights of the Portobello Road. For Mike Love, island pipe-smoking "Beach Man" excursions around the clubs and pubs watching how the old world lives. For Al Jardine, idling by the Thames and wandering up Fleet Street to St Paul's. For Carl, everything is wonderful and new; he has an innocence which is enviable and beyond price. For Bruce Johnston, his most joyous recollection was his acceptance by audiences to whom, formerly, he had been substitute Beach Boy.

RONALD REAGAN

That makes me think of the last campaign speech of Governor Brown, who was governor of California, held in a very small park near Manhattan Beach before about three hundred people. I was sitting on the bank watching this guy — a real professional politician — and thinking, "what is it all about?" And now Ronald Reagan is the governor. I was very surprised to see Reagan had won. Surprise is the best description I can think of for my reaction.

BOBBIES

Very sharp. Very good. I have a good impression of your cops. Clean, well-kept, well-organised look about them. Amiable on the whole, none of that ego thing—hey man, I'm a cop!

BIG HEADS

Definitely something that's easy to acquire when you've sold twenty million records. I think we've managed to keep our senses. This was partly due to the Beatles who suddenly swept up in America. The retaliation of the Beatles and English pop music came just when we were beginning to get very big in America. The mystique of everybody's attention, the English groups distracted everybody's attention when we heard rumours about this group—the Beatles. Man, when we heard "I Want To Hold Your Hand" we thought somebody was puttin' us on! Anyway the English groups cleaned up. Even our records didn't sell as well as usual—although I must admit they weren't as good as they should have been. The thing is, the coming of the English invasion gave us a chance to look at ourselves and reflect. I now feel our success is completely legitimate. If we'd got the Beatles hit America — or waited until years after—our true position as far as popularity was concerned may have been false. We had time to think. Brian realised the position and had time to develop musically. He grew while all the English things was happening — and sometimes I'm still amazed we ever survived it. When the disc we issued flopped midst all the English records we sat down and there took off in another direction. That was when Brian decided to give up touring because he wasn't writing like he should have been. I think the whole thing quite well. There's more to say — have you got space?

pages about this. The tragic result of our urbanisation and lack of city planning—which is a cop-out for what it really is! The obvious aspect either of the white or the Negro, to want, or to need, better education and/or better housing. Basically one of the laws of nature is the need to survive and adapt. Something that exists in everyone. I don't think the Negroes have adapted. They have got to maintain themselves at some point —like, the Jews, Russians, Japanese, anybody.

HI-LOS

Something I never really got in to. Never got into their sound at all. Not like the Four Freshmen anyway. The Hi-Los are a little bit too high. Brian and I, when we started, used to listen to the Freshmen, but the Hi-Los were a bit too far out for us.

IVY LEAGUE

In the terms of on-the-campus and all that I just think immediately of the fantastic acceptance of the Beach Boys. The campus thing is one big college—a big fraternity sharing their studies, books, space, booze, love, drugs, cars and clothes.

THROATS

Ours must be the most critical in the country. The trouble is our fans are also the most critical and now the audiences must sit there dead silent. One could always rely on some shouting and screaming to give us time to relax our voices for a moment but now they're taking up listening. One goof and you're dead. If we make a mistake on our harmonies we try to hit back quickly with the force of the number and usually the audience forgets your goof. But man, At the inside all the way you die. inside all the same. we played in Tooting I remember the audience was dead silent, cool, and listening to every little thing. You think of the Beatles, they don't have to worry because they've got this onslaught of noise all the time and their performance can relax off every now and again and the crowd won't notice. Somebody told me that George Harrison started playing "Woolly Bully" on the guitar in the middle of something else—but, like, nobody heard it. If the audience are cool and listening you have to be cool and listening otherwise you might goof. You can't let yourself go on attentive audiences. So it's quite a strain being a harmony group.

WATTS

Just talking about that the other day. I could go on for

NEWS

BEACH BOYS' BLAST

BEACH BOYS: turning their attention to the movies.

IF you think "Barbara Ann" is indicative of the real Beach Boys scene today, you can forget it. It's not. "It wasn't even a produced record," Brian Wilson, Beach Boys leader told me on the phone from his elaborate Beverly Hills home.

"We were just goofing around for a party type album and that was just an old rock and roll hit. Somebody in Boston started playing the track in the album and this just started it all off so they had to put out a single. I don't know how to explain it. That kind of rock and roll is just timeless I guess.

"But that's not the Beach Boys. It's not where we're at at all. Personally, I think the group has evolved another 800 per cent in the last year. We have a more conscious, arty production now that's more polished. It's all been like an explosion for us.

by REN GREVATT

Album

"For myself, I don't go out on the tours at all now. I just work on production. I've spent five months working on this new album and I think this album and the batch of new singles I've been working on, well, it's like I'm right in the golden era of what it's all about. It's all just coming out like breathing now.

"I give a lot of credit, a lot of it for everybody's success, to the Beatles. They've had a tremendous, universal influence. That 'Rubber Soul' album was a great new contribution. It helped them reach a new plateau.

"The Byrds, well, they represent a certain projected attitude. They've got a place too, no doubt of that. I still give Phil Spector credit for being the single most ... influential producer. He's timeless. He makes a milestone whenever he goes into a studio.

Romantic

"The folk thing has been important. I think it has opened up a whole new intellectual bag for the kids. They're making 'thinking' records now. That's really what it is. Everybody is saying something. We got into a romantic rut. It was all boy-girl, crying records with everybody kind of screwed up.

"Suddenly, Dylan comes along with a cold, intellectual, philosophical thing. He's a protester and his message pertains to society in general.

"I predict all this protest-

ing will become highly personal and pertaining to a person's own hang-ups and his ego. The lyrics will be more introspective. There'll always be love records, of course. There's no stronger single theme. But you'll find plenty of thinking records too.

"Sure, all this has helped the Beach Boys evolve. We listen to what's happening and it affects what we do too. The trends have influenced my work, but so has my own scene. I've got this terrific house in the hills with a tremendous view. It's stimulating and it's helped me mature. I may even get married.

Image

"I remember when I used to think marriage was a hang-up to the image. That's no more. The Beatles have brought so many things to the industry, like Lennon's being married right along.

"His being married was so perfect, so beautiful, because it enabled so many artists to be married and still be considered an artist. Marriage has no bearing on a girl fan's adoration for an artist anymore. Two of our guys, Mike Love and Al Jardine are already married.

"They live down on the ocean at Manhattan Beach (California). They both have houses there. My brothers, Carl and Dennis, also have their own houses, here in the hills above Hollywood. I've been working on this especially, since I'm here at home while Bruce Johnson takes my place with the boys. A lot of new things are already recorded, including our next single, "Sloop John B," so we're turning our attention to the movies. I think we've done great on the personal appearance trail and the boys have done terrifically overseas, especially just recently in Japan and Hong Kong, and we think now the obvious next step is pictures.

BOOM! barry fantoni

Giannini
Classical & Fingerstyle Guitars

A new standard is brought to classical and fingerstyle guitars by this new range from Tranquillo Giannini, guitar makers since 1900.

Designed and built by dedicated craftsmen, each model is extremely sensitive and will produce an outstanding tone. The superb overall finish includes: lightweight woods, slightly arched backs, finely carved neck, and smooth rosewood fingerboard.

Seven models from 10 to 59 gns. — there is a Giannini to suit the requirements of every player from beginner to professional.

Visit your Selmer dealer and play a Giannini today.

Write for full details of Giannini Guitars

If Beach Boy Carl is drafted...

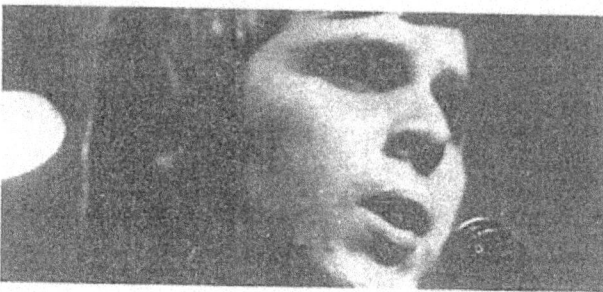

THE burning pop business topic of the moment is the threat hanging over the Beach Boys' Carl Wilson—released on 40,000 dollar bail from the Los Angeles court where he was charged with evading the US military draft.

As the person most concerned, Carl is in the difficult position of not being able to discuss the problem at any length until the court has decided his fate. Which makes him a little reluctant to talk to reporters—just in case the topic should arise.

But he did tell me he will not be drafted into the armed forces.

"I am an objector on the grounds of conscience," he said in Manchester last week. "I have to make them believe me, otherwise the only alternative is jail—and in America it is usually for a term of three years.

"But I have feelings about these things—and I feel absolutely certain that the worst will not happen. I only hope I'm right!"

I asked him if, should he be jailed, brother Brian would rejoin the group in his place.

"I just don't know — but what is more than likely is that the group will stay put in Los Angeles and not travel until I am able to rejoin them."

Dubious and reticent he may have been, but Beach Boy Bruce Johnston was far from reluctant to talk. Bruce is a cheerful, talkative soul who delights in playing himself down.

"When I get back home I'm going to take lessons on bass and guitar," he said. "I wish I was playing piano—I'm much better on that than on bass guitar"—and went on to tell me how he came to be playing with the Boys.

"I was a recording manager and record producer for CBS in Hollywood (he had two single releases with Doris Day's son Terry Melchior as Bruce and Terry) and because I knew a lot of people, Mike Love called me to ask me to find a replacement when Brian decided to stay at home and concentrate on writing.

"I just couldn't find anyone at the time—so to help out I joined the group on piano but this just didn't work out, and after about three dates Mike suddenly threw a bass guitar at me and said 'Here—play that '."

"It was a challenge—so I had a go. So far they haven't kicked me out—and I'm still there after two years. I somehow manage to get by but I won't be satisfied until I can really play the guitar.

"Among the boys I call myself King of the Guitar—but Mike won't have it—says I'm only the Crown Prince. I'll show him . . ."

He may present a flamboyant exterior, but Bruce still cares what people think. He is very disappointed that the record critics have not taken kindly to "Then I Kissed Her."

"I heard it last night on a set with some excellent speakers—and I'm sorry—I like it. They say there is no life in it. That's too bad if they feel that way. It may be different, but I liked it when we recorded it—and I see no reason to change my mind now."

He, too, would not discuss the future of the group should Carl be compelled to withdraw for a time.

"The future is in Brian's hands," he said. "We are far from being puppets, but there has to be a leader and Brian takes most of the decisions. But he is a very flexible guy—always open to suggestions. He has sudden inspirations—often only in the form of a few bars—then he will put it to us—we exchange ideas—then he completes it and teaches us the finished song.

"And very often he gets these ideas and we complete a song at an actual recording session. But most of the vocal ideas come from Brian—we just help out.

"Deep down, Brian, Carl and Dennis, are all good musicians. They get it from their parents who are both musicians. I heard their mother playing piano just recently and it wasn't the corn of the '30s that you might expect. Her playing reminded me of Sinatra's singing. She's good!

"But I wish I could play piano in the group—it is still my favourite instrument."

As to his own future?

"When this tour is completed, I'm going to pack a few things and hitch through Spain until July. I'm a little sorry that my travels around the world so far have been in comparative luxury. Now I want to travel as any other young man without a lot of money, would do.

"I want to try surfing at Biarritz—and I want to take my time and shoot lots and lots of pictures—far away from the screaming crowds and the glamour of show business.

"And perhaps in three or four years (or when and if I get myself married) I shall buy a couple of hundred acres in California for an orange grove and go back to producing records and writing songs."

None of the group appear to be too worried about the cloud that is hanging over them. Let us hope that Carl's "feeling" is right—he is a very sincere young man.—J.D.

NEWS

Brian, pop ge

FOCUS ON BEACH BOY BRIAN WILSON

BRIAN WILSON, leader of the Beach Boys, is a genius, I think. You have to use a very special word to capture the rare, mind-blocking, blinding talents of this 23-year-old whose grasp of popular music is total.

He alone in the industry is full creator of a record from the first tentative constructions of a theme to the final master disc. He is the writer — words and music — performer and singer, arranger, engineer, producer with full control even over packaging and design.

So heavy are the self-imposed burdens of complete control that Wilson has retired from personal appearances altogether, to enable him to meet the mounting challenge from within his inventive musical soul.

If you can imagine the Beatles on stage without Lennon, the Stones less Brian Jones, the Who without Townsend, you have an idea of the sacrifice in visual appeal which Brian Wilson sought from the militant legions of Beach Boy fans in America.

PRIORITIES

Maybe you can imagine also what it means to step from the midst of the group you have formed and nurtured and to hand over the spotlight to a substitute performer, simple because you have re-assembled your priorities.

This was what Brian Wilson did a year ago.

While he and the Beach Boys were battering across the nation, Wilson knew he couldn't spell from his head the tumbling ideas which would give the group a new musical direction. So he quit the road and into his place stepped an unknown 22-year-old, Bruce Johnston, "phantom" Beach Boy.

To Brian's delight, the substitution worked. Fans accepted his reasons for absence.

"Kids were becoming very aware musically. They had started to wonder where songs actually came from. And they come from inside human beings."

So they do. From Wilson's disciplined intensity have poured some incredible sounds, themes, melodies and dynamics in the past five months.

Thirteen of the songs emerge on the Boys' thirteenth album — "Pet Sounds", Wilson's proudest product thus far and a certainty to provide the group with their eighth gold album.

But the fourteenth new song will be the one to send the pop world staggering with wonderment. It is called "Good Vibrations" and it may well be the contemporary song of the year.

Instrumentally the track is quite brilliant; no symphony was ever scored with more inspirational patience and, because Wilson is as much a sound-finder as a maker of melodies, he has used four separate recording studios (each in a different neighbourhood) to build the four-tracked tape into a most masterly record.

What is most amazing about Wilson and all outstanding creative artists is that they are using only those basic materials which are freely available to everyone else.

What exactly is Wilson's story? Here, for a start, is the Beach Boy line-up:

Brian Wilson, at 23, oldest of the three Wilson brothers. The others are Dennis 21, and Carl 19.

Al Jardine is almost a member of the family. Mike Love, 23, is a cousin of the Wilsons.

"Phantom" Bruce Johnston now both tours and records with the group.

They started, with no great seriousness, by making a record called "Surfin", while they were still at school at Hawthorne, on the Californian edge of the Pacific.

It altered the course of contemporary music in the USA, this one slight song recorded in two hours in Hollywood, on a single-track tape system with little Jardine playing a standard double-bass twice as big as himself, 14-year-old Carl Wilson on acoustic guitar, Brian himself standing up using brushes on drums and Mike Love singing the vocals with a severe cold.

EMOTIONAL

The record sold more than 40,000 copies in the dying weeks of 1961.

In the US as a whole, the record reached 75 which is no bad thing for a first disc by schoolboys reflecting the spirit of an ocean which is as remote from most Americans as the Tibet is from the good people of Nelson and Colne.

The Boys started to perform locally, then nationally, and by 1963 they were a prosperous national touring group and massive hitmakers, in a period when, otherwise, American pop music was in a dead faint.

To date they have passed through single sales exceeding 15,000,000 copies, twelve albums, every town and city in the Union, most European countries, Japan, and the Orient, Australasia and Canada.

Now? Says Brian Wilson:

"I know I'm a creative man, musically — from early days I believed there were ideas waiting to be dumped out if I had time. Now I know it and it's a good feeling.

"People are part of my music. A lot of the songs are the result of emotional experiences, sadness and pain. Or joy, exultation in nature and sunshine, and so on . . . like 'California Girls', a hymn to youth.

"I can write through empathy with others. The surf songs are a simple example of that — I have never surfed but I was able to feel it through Dennis, who is a fine athlete.

"I find it possible to spill melodies, beautiful melodies in moments of great despair. Good, emotional music is never embarrassing. But emotional prose sometimes is.

"Music is genuine and healthy and the stimulation I get from moulding it and from adding dynamics is like nothing else on earth.

"If you take the 'Pet Sounds' album as a collection of art pieces, each designed to stand alone yet which belong together, you'll see what I was aiming at.

"I sat up in the house (by the house Wilson meant his $220,000 mansion, exquisitely furnished, in Beverly Hills), for five months, planning every stage of the album. I didn't mind people being around

enius!

—there are visitors up there most of the time — so long as there weren't too many and provided I could cop out and sit thinking.

"I have a big Spanish table, circular, and I sit there hour after hour making the tunes inside my head.

"Or I go the piano (A Bechstein Grand) and sit playing 'feels'. 'Feels' are brief note sequences, fragments of ideas. Once they're out of my head and into the open air, I can see them and touch them firmly. They're not 'feels' any more.

"I think that on 'Pet Sounds' the track 'Let's Go Away For a While' is the finest piece of art I've ever made. Does that sound like I'm bigtiming? It isn't meant to. I just believe it. It all worked perfectly."

HARMONIES

Talking about "Good Vibrations", Brian says: "I tried to make a pocket symphony out of this record. If that isn't overstating the thing, and I don't think it is.

"I write and think in terms of what the Beach Boys can do. Not what they would find it easy to do, but what I know they are capable of doing which isn't always the same thing.

"I have a governor in my mind which keeps my imagination in order because idiot ideas are just a hang-up. But I don't like to be told 'it can't be done' when I know it can. It mostly can be done.

"My greatest interest musically is expanding modern vocal harmony — this goes back to the early days when I worshipped the Four Freshmen, those great guys. That groovy sectional sound!

"The Beach Boys are lucky . . . we have a high range of voices; Mike can go from bass to the E above middle C; Dennis, Carl and Al progress upwards through G, A and B. I can take the second D in the treble clef.

"The harmonies we were able to produce gave us a uniqueness which is really the only important thing you can put into records — some quality no-one else has got into.

"Jack Good once told us, 'You sing like eunuchs in a Sistine chapel,' which was a pretty good quote.

"I'm very aware of the value of speaking through a song. This is why I get so much kick out of bending electricity and recording techniques to make them work for us. They're there to be used — maximum. Top maximum.

"I love peaks in a song — and enhancing them on the control panel. Most of all I love the human voice for its own sake. But I can treat it, with some detachment, as another musical instrument.

"I don't put out anything I don't respect. And I know for sure that the Beach Boys brought something new into rock'n'roll."

Don Traynor

NEWS

Brian Wilson's

Do the Beach Boys rely too much on sound genius Brian? ALAN WALSH finds out...

ARE the five touring Beach Boys merely puppets of sound genius Brian Wilson?

The question is prompted by the vast blast of publicity which has proclaimed Wilson as the complete architect of the Beach Boys recorded sound. Are they just the instruments which BW uses to paint his pop pictures in sound — like the marvellous moods of "Good Vibrations" and the precedent-setting "Pet Sounds" album?

The five touring Beach Boys (minus BW who stayed at home in California to dream up more surrealistic sounds) arrived in Britain from Stockholm on Sunday afternoon.

"No, we are not just Brian's puppets," said BW's brother Carl, who plays lead guitar and is the occasional lead singer for the group. "Brian plays the major creative role in the production of our music, but everyone in the group contributes something to the finished product. It's not like an orchestra translating the wishes of the conductor. We all have a part to play in the production of the records.

"Brian works out the basic arangement before we ever go into the studio. We run through it a few times and there are often suggestions made about changes or improvements. Everybody contributes ideas. We all give something, although I agree that Brian contributes the major part."

Carl didn't think that Brian would ever rejoin the group as an active, touring singer. "I can't see that ever happening now," he said. "He's writing and creating all the time now. You only have to look at him sometimes to see that he's got something going inside him."

Did Carl think that the time spent by the Beach Boys—and the Beatles—on retakes, new arrangements, sheer hard work, was setting a trend in the pop record world?

"It's not a trend. If you spend that amount of time in a studio, the end product has to be something special. We work hard to produce an end product of a high standard. It takes us a long time. If other people can do it in a short time, that's fine. But a lot of people aren't doing this. They aren't prepared to go into a studio and work. And it shows. You can tell from their albums which artists are really working on their records."

Carl felt strongly that criticisms of the group for not producing a "studio sound" on stage were unjustified.

"It's idiotic to get hung up not being able to reproduce the sound. We know we can't and I think it's wrong for people to expect us to."

How do the group's voices stand up to a long tour such as the one they are on at the moment?

"Pretty well, although you have to watch it a bit. Travelling is the worst thing. For example, we come off stage pretty hot and if we have to travel straight off somewhere, there's danger of catching colds, particularly if the weather's very cold. But the voices get plenty of exercise on stage and we rest them at other times. So it works out all right."

The Beach Boys have progressed tremendously over the past few years. What of their future—how did Carl see them progressing over the next two or three years?

"We have to broaden ourselves musically. How? Well, we have a few ideas about increasing our musical scope. But they are still tentative and we can't say too much about them at the moment."

Looks as though the Beach Boys' vibrations are going to be very good for quite some time to come.

NEWS

NEWS

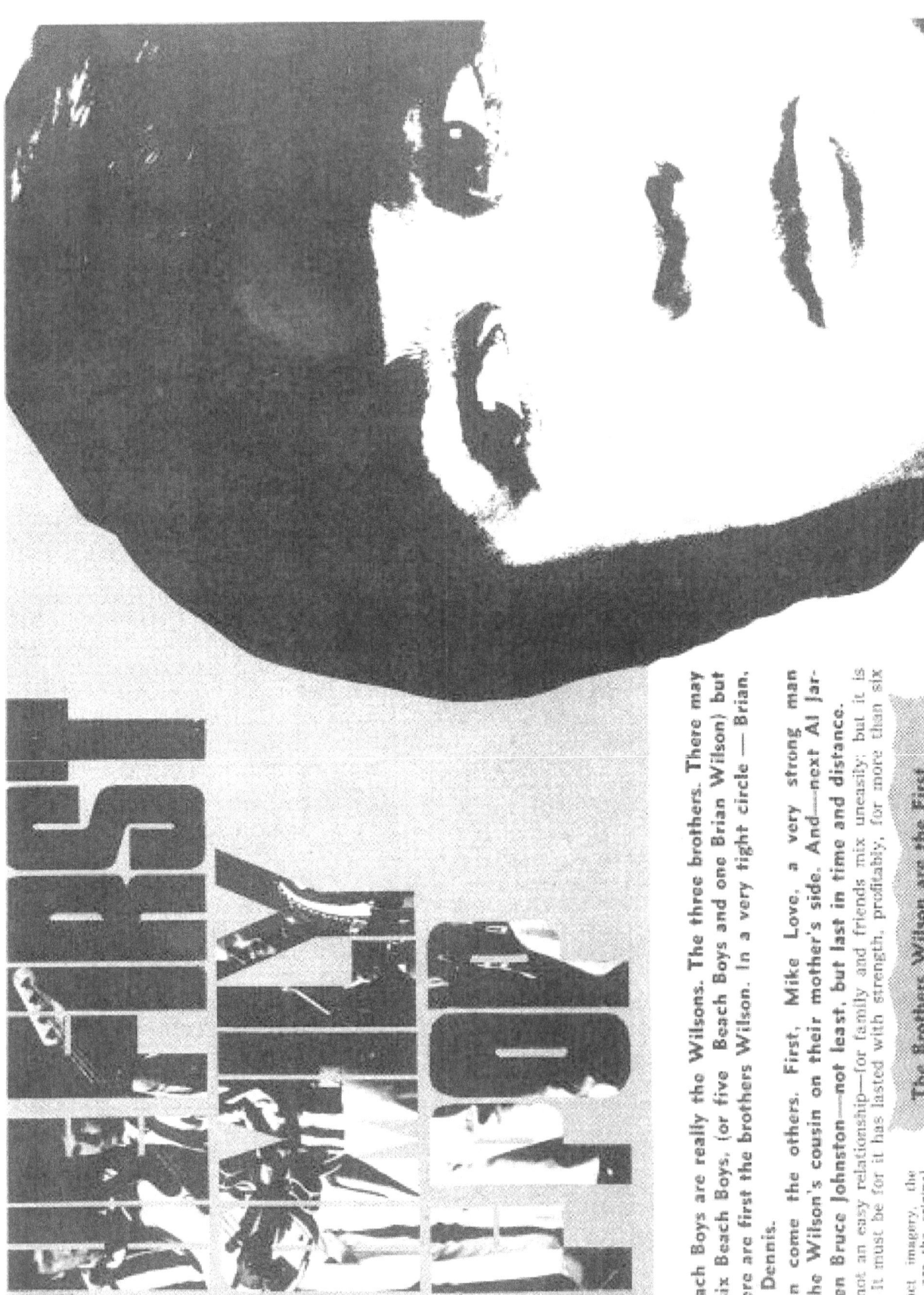

THE FIRST FAMILY OF POP

THE Beach Boys are really the Wilsons. The three brothers. There may be six Beach Boys, (or five Beach Boys and one Brian Wilson) but really there are first the brothers Wilson. In a very tight circle — Brian, Carl and Dennis.

Then come the others. First, Mike Love, a very strong man who is the Wilson's cousin on their mother's side. And—next Al Jardine. Then Bruce Johnston—not least, but last in time and distance.

It is not an easy relationship—for family and friends mix uneasily; but it is workable. It must be for it has lasted with strength, profitably, for more than six years.

In abstract imagery, the Beach Boys are the original five Brian, Carl, Dennis, Mike and Al—the schoolboys from the Pacific coast, young and scrubbed, American and new, white-trousered, springing from the the sub-cultures of

> The Brothers Wilson are the First Family Of Pop. But is it a happy family? How do the other Beach Boys feel about this family domination?

NEWS

How 'special' is a SPECIAL RELEASE?

Wait till you've heard "Then I kissed her"

The BEACH BOYS

C/W Mountain of Love
Capitol CL 15502

EMI

E.M.I. RECORDS (THE GRAMOPHONE CO. LTD.) E.M.I. HOUSE, 20 MANCHESTER SQUARE, LONDON W.1

MELODY MAKER EXCLUSIVE FROM HOLLYWOOD

surfing and fast cars.

In Brian Wilson's subconscious mind, Bruce Johnston will always be the phantom Beach Boy, even though Bruce was Brian's nominee as his replacement when Brian decided not to perform anymore, preferring to remain at home writing the songs which fuel the group engine.

However, in terms of stage performance, physical charm, personality, vocal range, musicality, and personal appearance, and respect from fans; and from the other Beach Boys he has gained friendship and admiration and support, for they knew that it was a very rough spot for Bruce to replace a brother, a leader, a musician and a very exceptional personality all in one.

But he knows that melody forced him to join — he is a Beach Boy because he wants to be and because the others want him to be. No one is forcing anyone. That's healthy.

Now Al Jardine is a horse of an entirely different hue and cry. "In" at the very beginning, he is now stronger than ever, and immensely in favour with the Wilsons and Mike Love who have admitted him to their financial corporation as a participating partner, able to vote, to draw dividends, to share secrets, to be in on the ins, and never out on the outs.

This was not always so. For years, it was "good old Al" and "great little Al," but not Al the insider. Wrongly, but maybe be understandably (remember the power of family ties). Al was always OK for singing, for playing and for anchoring the group's stage-line-up with his strong, cheerful presence. But when the decisions were made, the intriguing whispers exchanged and home-truths driven

home, Al went quietly to his own home by the sea and thought his own thoughts.

But last year, because of his immovable, powerful loyalty, because of his unending cheerful mien, and his very important musical contribution, he was led to the comfort and warmth of the family hearth. Brian Wilson gave interviews which made it clear that he greatly admired and valued Jardine's rock-like support, his uncanny talent for interpretation, his devotion to the Wilson music.

This year, AP's stature increased — Brian was quoted as saying: "He is our anchor, his goodness and strength now through the microphone, along the wires and on to the tapes."

When, the other day, Paul McCartney the Beach Boy-admiring Beatle went to a Wilson recording session, it was Al Jardine who was despatched to the sound-proof booth to add the vocals to a new Beach Boy track.

BLOOD

Now to Mike Love, sophisticated beyond his years, wise, witty and largely without fear. He is in the group because he always was and always must be, as long as they are boyish and beach-like enough to remain Beach Boys. He has known his cousins since earliest childhood and there is nothing about them he has not spotted, comprehended, known, loved, hated, despised, forgiven or forgotten.

More than either Bruce or Al, Mike has had his "outs" with Brian, Carl and Dennis. And they with him.

But the blood relationships, the good times, the interdependencies, the economic advantages, plus a sublimely wry sense of humour empower him to cope with all the whims and demands of group life which is not the easiest way of earning a living, contrary to what you may have heard.

Mike is older than his cousins, he is slim, tidy, redhaired, inclining to baldness, shrewd with money, immensely practical, all of which sets him apart from the Wilsons who

are none of those things.

He is a fine counter-balance to the eccentricities of Brian who is careless with money, incorrigible about time, happily over-weight, shaggy-haired, night-creature who acts on impulse without relating to any known behaviour pattern.

Brian and Mike are very fond of each other because each recognises the other's strength.

DELICATE

They have a very subtle understanding of each other's moods — in carefree moments their cross-talk has an uncanny facile speed and the humour is extraordinarily interchangeable giving the impression of two voices from one head.

Each feels in grave responsibility to keep the group free of the beast Brian for the musical direction, Mike for the concert tours, curtailment of expensive industry geared to fickle teenage spending which means so much to you and how you feed on any given day.

Mike is less concerned than Brian with the subtleties of musical growth — he is as happy with his old Beach Boy standard songs as with the delicate intricacies of the new Wilson music which is highly competitive. The new music is aimed as much at adding something to contemporary arts as at the charts.

Dennis and Carl, devoted as brothers and worshippers to Brian and incredibly patient with him, feel some of Brian's musical pain.

Dennis, wild, physical, and prone to swift mood changes, believes Brian to be the ultimate young genius as well he might be. Carl, youngest of the brothers, feels a strangely paternal protective thing towards Brian — a need to shield him from reality and to put up this barrier against the world. Carl will employ anything, white lies, in general, the Beach Boys cope well. But it is not easy. It needs unusual fortitude. One trusts it can continue. The odds are that it will.

HEALTHY

Sometimes Bruce regrets the group's imprisonment of his individual spirit — the constriction of his desire to shine on his own, the suppression of his will to be himself in his own right.

NEWS

beach b inside-o

That is, the five we saw by their

Dennis Wilson

CERTAINLY Dennis Wilson is a teen idol. He is, by now, used to it and he responds to the title because it is implicit in the call of rock 'n' roll duty. But when the Beach Boys are not on tour, he sheds the image and becomes a day-to-day citizen and a true muscular son of California.

He really does surf, swim, race, hunt, fish and he hurls himself into countless other outdoor activities like bareback riding, raising otters, salvaging stray dogs and nursing injured birds back to a full life.

On Sundays he drives a Cobra too fast for comfort, almost on the threshold of pain, and now and again, beyond the bravest man's margin of safety.

He sings very well. He is kind and gentle, unless he's put out, in which case he can become furniture-breaking angry. Passion and emotion and impulse rule the blond, gladiatorial middle Wilson.

Dennis is not always easy to be with—his temper is sudden, swift and, he would admit, sometimes unreasonable. He can be nervous and unable to sit calmly. Though not, in years, the youngest, he is often treated as if he were. This, quite naturally, infuriates him.

Musically, he enjoys the Wilson flair for singing and he, too, has toyed with songwriting. A wild and enthusiastic drummer, he seems born for this lonely, frenetic profession.

Carl Wilson

OF the three Wilsons, Carl is the oddball. He lacks the impatience, quick and hot temper, nervousness, intensity and easily hurt feelings that characterize his brothers.

When Dennis stomps out of a recording session after one of Brian's blistering tirades on his inability to sit still, Carl can assuage the bruised ego of the one and calm the boiling temper of the other. Years of living and working with the two more violent Wilsons has given him an insight into human nature that ministers and social workers could learn from.

Though he entered the infamously corrupt and cannibalistic music biz at an early age (14), he remains clean and pure, his material appetite satisfied long ago. His protective and watchful comrades have helped—he has always been babied. But he was so very young and they needed his guitar and soft, clear voice.

"Without Carl, we wouldn't have stayed together for two months," claim the Beach Boys.

"Without the Beach Boys, I wouldn't be here," he replies, in his expensive monogrammed shirt, expensive foreign car, expensive Beverly Hills home. But he would be happy without it all.

Mike Love

IT takes a lot of guts to be the stage leader of any group. It takes a lot of quick-wittedness and confidence. It takes a deaf ear when the crowd boos and sharp eyes when the stage is so small you can hardly move without falling off. It takes a special type of person. All groups need one—few have a really good one. The Beach Boys do. Mike Love.

The tall, red-bearded, oldest (25) Beach Boy describes his humour as "heavily based on sarcasm". Whether he started the West Coast's trend to this brand or it started him, no one knows. But even now that Southern California has interests other than surfing, the quick and sharp tongues of the "surfers" and of the Beach Boys lingers on.

Mike's humour is not put away with the white tennies—it's an integral part of him.

This dryness is often mistaken for bitterness, disconcern, contempt, any number of misconceptions. But it is none of these things. Says Mike:

"The only time I'd rather not be MC is when I'm tired or upset. Then I start thinking, why me? Why not one of those idiots. But then, when we get out on stage, the crowd turns me on and I wouldn't give it up for anything.

"Sometimes I really get burned at the others. One will decide well he's the lead singer and my part isn't important. Then he won't sing into the mike or he'll tie his shoelace. To me every voice is vital—we're a group."

Mike is very Beach Boys. He lives at the beach ("to keep up the image"). His reddish beard may not be "boyish" but the innate talent and polished skill is ageless.

Al Jardine

IT'S difficult to find the one word which embraces the qualities of Al Jardine—

oys out!

friend HARRY PULES

like, for Mike it's "witty" or Carl, "serene". To most people he's just "nice", but that implies a blandness which isn't fair to Al.

The attributes which stand out the most are his wide, open smile, his level-headedness, his small neatness and the blondness of his hair. Al is midway between wild Dennis and peaceful Carl. He's never really late, but then he's usually not exactly on time.

Most of the time he's settled and eager to get the job done—whether it's recording, performing or any of the tiny time-consuming things required of an artist. But he has been known to rebel, never without good cause, he would claim, and he may be right.

Even in his moments of temperament, Al differs widely from the others. His is not the sudden, explosive rage of Dennis or the calm, sharp meanness of Mike or the swift, table-banging exasperation of Brian. He's just quietly, but inexorably angry.

Because of Dennis' enthusiasm and Bruce's extravagant bounce, some people consider Al shy. He isn't. He's not even particularly quiet.

But his words are weighed. He rarely corrects himself and he knows whereof and of whom he speaks. There is no waste about Alan: in words, weight, hair (always well-trimmed) and money, he is self-contained; very tidy, well cared for.

Like the other Beach Boys, Al is funny; not as dry as Mike, nor as obvious as Bruce, but the humour is there all the same. He has a knack for explaining the subtle BB jokes to casual observers without presupposing their ignorance. He laughs with immense noise and abandon.

The Wilsons, Love and Johnston respect the small, married Boy. He talks sense and can make them see his way without putting them "uptight"—a difficult task. His honesty has earned their admiration.

Bruce Johnston

BRUCE JOHNSTON does not look like a Beach Boy; a college boy, yes. He trots around Hollywood in casual slacks and shirts (with an occasional turtleneck), wearing tennies and carrying a small leather attache case.

In a way, Bruce has been a "student", living, working and learning all about pop music for the past 11 years.

He fits in musically with the others, on stage and in the recording studio. His voice can handle the high falsetto that Brian made famous and fill in around tenor on harmony. At performances he is as active and personable as the four originals.

Most importantly, the Beach Boys like him. He is friendly, pleasant, congenial, even-tempered, humorous, as good a listener as a talker. Without being obvious, he endeavours to make everyone feel at home and comfortable. Along with Dennis, he is the handshaker. Always eager to please and meet anyone from the youngest fan to the oldest grandfather.

Bruce seems the most active Beach Boy—eternally going somewhere, writing songs, recording. Brian does everything sleepily, the others take their time, but Bruce is a hustler in the best sense of the word.

He must have faults. Yes, he must—everyone does. He has the infuriating knack of insulting you so pleasantly and with such an innocent face that you're about to say, "Oh, thanks" when you realise what he has said. And he refuses to lose his temper violently. There's nothing more annoying when you've lost yours and are red in the face and throwing things and stomping the floor. He's standing there grinning.

Now THAT's a fault.

NEWS

BRIAN WILSON

PEACE
Relative peace must be nice in New York.

FEAR
Not knowing what to expect is the only reason for fear.

DRUNK
I don't know anyone who gets drunk. In fact, I haven't been drunk myself for three years. There's no point in it. It isn't really fun. Why bother?

HONESTY
It's great and groovy and kicks all rolled into one big mind-blower. No one should be without it.

SUICIDE
It only makes things worse. You can't solve anything by killing yourself. I mean, things can always get better, but if you're dead, they may not.

WATTS
It's only four miles from my original home, where my mother still lives. We didn't panic — she just didn't go outside the house.

CRIME
Very consistent.

POLICE
They're nice men, I think.

KOREA
I was about 11 years old and primarily concerned with baseball.

JUVENILE DELINQUENCY
There seems to be a trend toward non-violence today. More and more kids are thinking love and peace and friendship, instead of hate and spite.

SCHOOL
I wonder how much longer school will be compulsory? Very soon, I think, education will not only be free-form, but free for the taking or leaving.

TIME
Time is fine when it's in cadence.

STEREO
I can't enjoy stereo much. I'm deaf in one ear.

EAR
The right one.

DRUGS
An underground train.

PATRIOTISM
Beer and brass bands.

HYMN
I think I can write one someday.

ORGAN
My dad gave me a pipe-organ for my birthday—that's what I'll write the hymn on. Or at.

DOOR
The door has been opened to a whole universe of experience for me.

NEWSPAPER
I don't read the newspapers too much because they depress me.

SWIMMING POOL
I have just rediscovered the delights of swimming. I'm completely turned on to swimming pools again. For a while, they bored me. Now I take a swim once a day and I'm completely healthy.

ALBUM
Our next album will be better than "Pet Sounds". It will be as much an improvement over "Sounds" as that was over "Summer Days".

NEWS

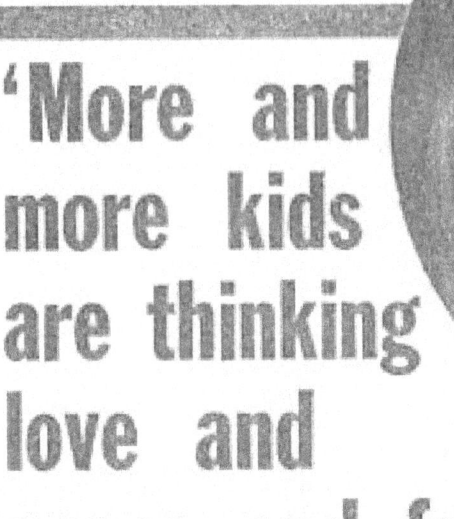

'More and more kids are thinking love and peace and friendship'

RECORDING STUDIO
My recording studio has become a castle, with a wing for everyone.

TELEVISION
Someday I want to make commercials for TV —with a new twist.

DRUMS
Someday I want to write a symphony for drums.

HOLLYWOOD BOWL
The sound men at the Bowl are not rock 'n' roll sound men. I would advise people who want to play there and sound good, to change their plans or plan their changes.

SURFING
It's a very challenging sport. I've never been able to meet the challenge.

LYRICS
Let's make them all free form, so we don't get hung up on making rhymes.

DRUG SONGS
There are myriad drug songs on the pop music market today. I don't know which they are.

MIRROR
Have you tried the mirror technique of the subconscious? I'm reading a book about it—I'm fascinated by the mind and hypnosis and things like that.

CAR
One day everyone will sit up in his car and fall out to the groovy sounds of cartridge tapes. Do I sound like a commercial?

SUCCESS
Came very easily to me, professionally speaking.

GLASSES
I would recommend that everyone who gets eye strain when they read go to an optometrist and get reading glasses so that they can read more and longer. This is what I did, and I really do think everyone should do it.

RAIN
It's purifying. It cleanses the earth and help things grow. It's spiritual, too.

AUTOGRAPHS
I would suggest to every girl who collects autographs that she has them analysed. Amazing revelations.

THE MOON
Funny you should mention that—I've been reading a book about moon deities and about how the moon affects women's personalities. Fascinating.

PUBLICISTS
Professional wordsmen.

CARL WILSON INTERVIEW

interview with carl wilson

1973

If we can pick up the story, Carl, at the beginning of Brother Records. What was the motivation to actually start your own label?

Freedom from... er... limitations and restrictions. Working with Capitol Records... they're a very big company and it was difficult to sort of get the ideas across and have them be receptive to what we wanted to do. It goes back to the old thing with Pet Sounds... you know... being different from the things we've done and... er... I think some of the people there didn't... erm... think it was commercial or something so....

What, the Pet Sounds album?

Yeah, so that direction was... er... I don't know... they were resistant to it, so that sort of led to a... you know, a sort of dissatisfaction... it brought the whole thing round... it seemed like a fun idea... you know... something to do....

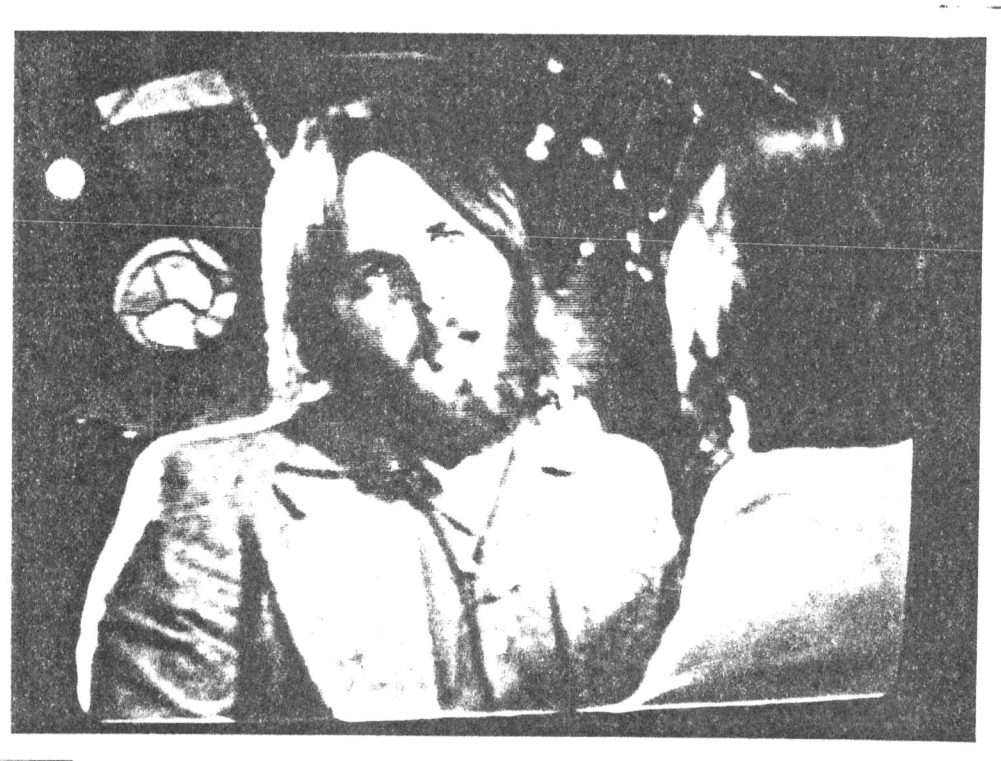

'Cos there was one record meanwhile between Pet Sounds and Sunflower that was on Brother Records - wasn't it...?

Yeah, well let's see, the first one was Smiley...

Right.

And then we were still with Capitol and it was just a different er... I think it was just restructured somehow... the business

CARL WILSON INTERVIEW

part so we were still with Capitol essentially... you know... so we had it released on the Capitol label and then when we signed with Warner's... we did the whole thing and... er... we haven't... er... we haven't developed a label in as much as getting... er... other artists to join us up in... along that line... we've been trying to work on our own things... to get our group... you know... tight as we can....

'Cos Sunflower seems to me to be such a relaxed album after all the pressures that you'd had at Capitol. Was it an easier album to make?

Oh, it was a <u>lot</u> easier than trying to do Smile. It never came out 'cos it was too difficult so... there was so much... er... it was just very difficult, so... oh, Sunflower was really a snap, you know, as far as ease. We didn't do it quickly, it just sort of had its own flow. We recorded more things than we released on it and... er... just, you know, decided to release it when we had that particular collection of songs....

CARL WILSON INTERVIEW

'Cos many people have said that some of the Smile things eventually surfaced on the Surfs Up album and two on the Sunflower album, I think...

S'See, Cool Water was for - was it? - yes, Smile and ended up on Sunflower. Yeah, so that stuff has come out - a good deal of it. And Heroes and Villains hasn't all come out - that's quite long, you know, with all the parts of it. See, we did things in sections, there were just... might be a few bars of music or a verse or a particular groove or vamp, whatever you call it so they would all fit, you know, you could put them one in front of the other or arrange them in any way you wanted and... er... we would tape the sound out of the amps. We just started doing sections and then we'd make taped copies and so Heroes and Villains, when it came to the verse... the tracking goes just the verse... to make other verses you just made a copy of that and sang to it... really strange way of doing it you know 'cos usually you just do the song... you know... the tune... and thats it, you know, just straight, it was sort of like making films, I think... a little bit...

So what about the live album, then, Carl, 'cos you did spend a lot of time on that In Concert album?

CARL WILSON INTERVIEW

Yeah well it... we didn't really spend a whole lot of time on it...it took a long time 'cos we started in winter '72 to record it and we didn't like, you know, most of the things we did and so we recorded again in summer...this last summer so we spent about oh..what we did spend a long time on it, we spent about 3 months...Wow wait, January? We ended up in March with that and then we decided we didn't like it at all, that was funny, and then erm- we just finished the stuff we did in the summer...we finished...I don't know a few weeks before it came out.

CARL WILSON INTERVIEW

I think that was right it had to be January, December...we must have finished it in November -

How much material did you have, Carl?

We had 50 reels of tape and each reel had about five songs, four or five songs, so it was a lot of stuff to listen to - you couldn't tell what you were hearing-

Moving away and coming back to touring, the band has been together really for many years. Is it hard now gathering everybody together and getting them into the studio?

Yeah it's hard to get a rehearsal going really...thats one thing, it takes some doing. I don't know, its like the group has a subconscious life too you know and a lot of times -just -things'll work out and people,you know, er.. we'll all get together, like the various members will get together to work out a new tune or whatever - you know - the thing is, and it wasn't happening anyway, you know... something wasn't happening right about it, so, it just

CARL WILSON INTERVIEW

was really the only time we got a chance to get it going.

How much do you see one another Carl?

Well since Alan and Micheal moved away we don't really see each other as much as we used to but it's nice when we get together...its always good to see each other and..

How is it the band managed to stay together so long Carl? Has any of you felt motivated to go off and do other things?

I think there are probably times when all of us..well we can't have..well you know..well we've had our share you know all the things but..er well we've known each other for a really long time so when you grow up together you except each other..you know as you are and so you know and having that understanding of each other... we just... and it really is great. A great deal of fellowship in the group...in a very cool way.Its just there if it should happen. We've been through an aweful lot you know ..together as people so that type of thing you know makes a bond with people so its you know...so thats part of the reason but the main reason is music ..you know father and family working to it. But you

CARL WILSON INTERVIEW

next couple of years. I think the group will stay tight for the next couple of years. I think the chances..you know of doing things will be more..er..at least clear at that time so we'll see.

Right Carl, thankyou.

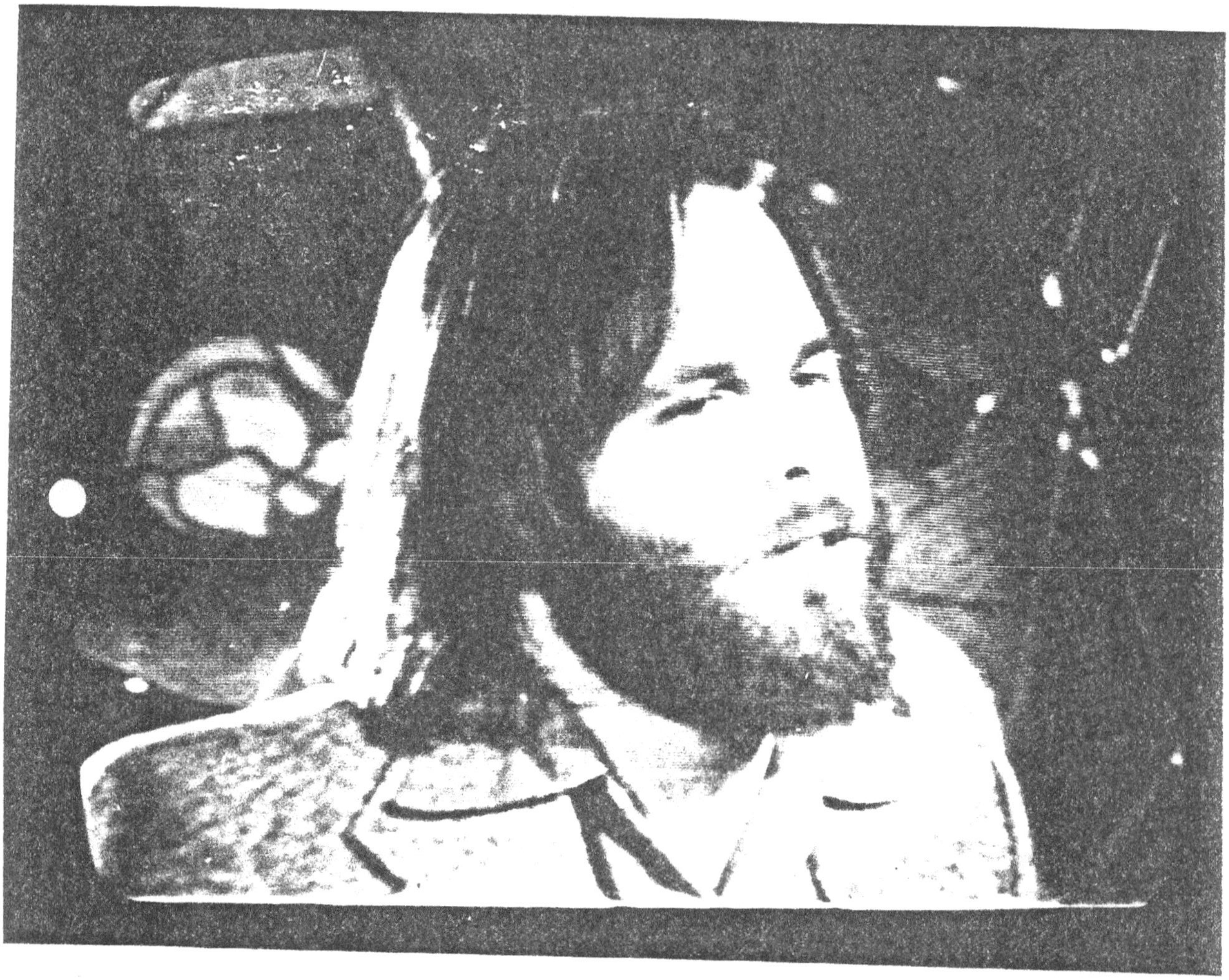

the end

New Beach Board Music From Cal: No Surf-ace Craze To Diskeries

MARCH 30, 1963

"SURFIN' U.S.A." (2:25) [Arc BMI—Wilson]
"SHUT DOWN" (1:50) [Sea Of Tunes BMI—Wilson]
BEACH BOYS (Capitol 4932)

The fellas, who made a tremendous chart splash with the "Surfin' Safari" stand, can come thru once again with this newie. It's a pounding "Sweet Little Sixteen"-flavored rocker, labeled "Surfin' U.S.A.," that the Beach Boys belt out with coin-catching enthusiasm. Terrific instrumental showcase. More top rock-a-teen sounds on the powerful "Shut Down" pairing. Can be a double-header.

MARCH 9, 1963

SURFIN' U. S. A.

BEACH BOYS, CAPITOL 4932

SHUT DOWN

"SURFIN' U.S.A." — The Beach Boys — Capitol ST1890
The Beach Boys, who struck paydirt with their click single, "Surfin' U.S.A.," cash in on the built-in sales acceptance of the deck to tag this initial Capitol LP outing. Despite the waves of surm' LP's flooding the market, this one seems destined to go the hitsville path. With momentum-gathering rhythms, smooth vocals and solid musicianship, the boys unleash their talents on such tunes as "Misirlou," "Honky Tonk" and "Noble Surfer."

APRIL 27, 1963

Her Heroes

LOS ANGELES—16-year-old Jodi Gable of Burbank, California, is national president of the Beach Boys fan club. Miss Gable met the Capitol recording stars when they appeared recently at Los Angeles' mammouth annual teenage fair. Almost 200,000 teens visited the annual fair, which this year featured the Beach Boys, who are currently riding the charts with "Surfin' U.S.A." and "Shut Down." Standing (left to right) in the above pic are Carl Wilson, David Mark, Dennis Wilson, Mike Love and Brian Wilson.

MAY 4, 1963

California, the land of fruits and fads, is sending forth its latest craze: surfing music, and experts believe it is gaining surf-ficient momentum to make a strong dent in teens, to say nothing of their market.

Indie firms on the West Coast have been oozing countless singles and LPs inspired by the sea sprites and their aquatic antics, with majors now expected to follow Capitol Records' new lead in acquiring and nationally promoting Dick Dale—who has the album, "Surfers' Choice."

Last year Cap got started with the surf sound via The Beach Boys and their 45er and LP, "Surfin' Safari." And it is now prepping another Beach Boys LPackage, "Surfin' U.S.A."

According to those in the know, surf music is little more than rock 'n' roll with all accompanying factors revolving around the surfing motif, its exponents merely teens who have exchanged the hot rod for the surf board. White levis and parkas are the official garb.

Surf music, apparently headquartered at California's Balboa Beach, is reported to have started in Hawaii, is next expected to strike big in Florida from where it should move up the East Coast as the weather gets warmer.

Other major diskeries about to brave the briny include RCA Victor, with a tune called "Bonzai Pipe Line" in a new Henry Mancini LP, "Uniquely Mancini"; Dot's just plain "Pipeline," the single by the Chantays; Decca, with "The Birds," by the Surf Riders; and the Dolton LP, "Surfing" by the Ventures. Epic is also planning a plunge.

Nevertheless, the Coast still has a big edge on the new fad. Capitol had to buy Dick Dale from Deltone, a label still big on the surf sound. The Bob Keene-headed diskery has four surfy albums on tap: "Surf Rider," by The Lively Ones; "Surfers' Pajama Party," by Bruce Johnston; "Wipe Out," by the Impacts; "Big Surf," by The Sentinels, and "Battle of The Surfing Drums," the latest set featuring 12 different surfing groups. The Lively Ones also have a new one for immediate release and Keene also has four more albums on the matter due this month.

Also Coasting along are Vault Records with "Lloyd Thaxton Goes Surfing With The Challengers" and "Surf Beat," by The Challengers; plus "Surf Crazy," by Bob Vaught and The Renegades on Crescendo.

Boarding should certainly keep the record industry from being bored for the next few months.

EARTH MAG - 1972

SAN FRANCISCO—"Everybody wants to know about Dennis and Manson. Dennis picked him up hitchhiking once. Then Charlie lived with Dennis for a few months. Charlie was just a cat who loved music and loved to write."

"People put us down because they say our songs aren't relevant or topical," said Mike Love at the Beach Boys show. "Fuck them!" yelled a voice in the crowd. "No, I wouldn't say that," said Mike, eyes rolling heavenward. "I'd say they're full of shit." Then the Beach Boys broke into "SURFIN' U.S.A."

Celebrating their 10th anniversary as a group together, the Beach Boys had an impressive reception at Winterland December 10 and 11. Predating the Beatles, their music started the California dream, evoking sunshine and outdoors ambience. Surfing music had kids in Manhattan dreaming of hard toenails, hanging ten. Their hot-rod songs turned people on, because the life of sun, surf, cars and girls was more real and immediate than Watts or elections. Most of all, their music has always been catchy, positive, and innocent. With the total immersion of rock into politics and sociology, it became almost embarrassing to admit to having been a Beach Boys fan. But the 2000 kids at Winterland didn't think so, and sang along with: "We'll have fun, fun, fun / Till her Daddy takes her T-Bird awaay—"

A good many T-Birds have been taken away since that song was written, and the Beach Boys have changed. Gone are the pinstriped shirts and white pants, exchanged for thick beards and overalls. They still have the falsetto voices that used to make the uninitiate cringe . . . "*Those* are boys?"

In front of me at the concert a guy wore a pin on his hat reading, "I Have Balls." Winterboppers were popping flashcubes at Dennis Wilson, still the pretty boy of the group. Introducing one song, Bruce Johnston said, "Let's take a backwards naive look at yesterday."

That's what seeing their show is like—a long, backwards naive look. The Beach Boys' new album, "SURF'S UP," reveals a certain ambivalence: groping at the hard reality of today, and splashing in the foam and fun of yesterday.

They opened the show with "GOOD VIBRATIONS," the top-selling number that proved, to anyone who doubted it, that Brian Wilson is a genius. Then came tunes like "DARLIN'" from "WILD HONEY," "WOULDN'T IT BE NICE," from "PET SOUNDS," the album which, in 1966, influenced many other rock musicians to get into orchestration. "STUDENT DEMONSTRATION" was from their new album. Mike Love plays the theremin and the horn section made it a hard-driving boogie. Screeching police sirens were produced by the electronic theremin. The pounding drums and hard-hitting lyrics, recalling Kent State and People's Park, made this one of the evening's finest numbers. Their tour-de-force was "SURF'S UP," from the album of the same name.

Written by Van Dyke Parks and Brian Wilson, it reflects the Beach Boys' musical development, and in Brian's words, he hopes it evokes "the sound of heaven." The piece was lauded by Leonard Bernstein when he did a television show with the Beach Boys. Said Bernstein, "It is one of the best things I have ever heard in rock 'n' roll." Perhaps, for the Beach Boys, the surf *is* up again.

Backstage before the Saturday concert the mood was quiet. A few backstage hands were working, children romped about, one announcing in an important tone, "Mason Proffit is here tonight." So they were. Also appearing were Stoneground.

The Beach Boys' entourage arrived, and Dennis Wilson and Al Jardine bounded in. I was introduced by Jack Rieley, the manager. "Have some fruit, or some wine," Dennis says. A pale girl named Monica, whose braless breasts sagged heavily in her velour top, was smiling at him. The sex symbol of the Beach Boys, the Steve McQueen of surfing, he has always been the ladies' man. Yet he was, in fact, polite.

When asked where Brian was, he said, "Home. He can't go onstage with his bad ear, it really bothers him." The story goes that Brian is deaf in one ear, from a childhood injury. I suspected personal hassles might be keeping him back, too, since during the Beach Boys' heavy touring days Brian had a nervous breakdown. Bruce Johnston then

EARTH MAG - 1972

substituted as their fifth member. Brian is still heavily relied on as the virtuoso composer, yet it is the youngest Wilson, Carl, 25, who leads when they're on tour.

"We don't really have a leader," Dennis countered. of un-inspiration for a while. I didn't write any of the songs on the 'SURF'S UP' album. I really wasn't into it that much. I'm a little tired of rock 'n' roll. I like blacks. Sure, it was easy to write the early stuff, that's what we were into—A&W

The Beach Boys

"We're equal, you know—brothers. Yes, we've stuck together because we're a family. The four-year period when we didn't do much touring was a result of quite a few things. We had business problems with Capitol Records, then we formed our own company, Brother Records. It was a time of trouble in the sense that we had to slow down, to be fluent with people, to be inspired. It was a period root beer, woodies, sock hops. I'm working on a symphony now, I just got it together a couple of days ago." He leaned over to Monica and said quietly, "It's really going to be great to do." Monica beamed. He continued, "It's going to be like an opera, only without singing LAAA!" And he imitated a Met soprano gargling. "No," he said softly, "it'll be different. It's dedicated to my wife, Barbara, and the first lines are, "Isn't life funny, Honey."

Fred Vail, the former business manager of the Beach Boys, doesn't see their appearance in terms of a comeback. "They never went away," he said.

"Whenever reporters ask me, "Where have the Beach Boys been?" I say, "Where have you been? They've been right here, all along." Pointing to Dennis on the couch, he said, "Dennis is a little loose on wine tonight. Yeah, everybody wants to know about Dennis and Manson. Dennis picked him up hitchhiking once. Then Charlie lived with Dennis for a few months. Charlie was just a cat who loved music and loved to write. He wrote the lyrics to a Beach Boys song, 'NEVER LEARN NOT TO LOVE,' which is on the '20/20' album."

Al Jardine is a gremlin guru. In January he is taking his family to Spain to study with the Maharishi. "We're going with Mike Love's family, too. The meditation has completely changed me, and helped me survive—teaching humility, such an important part of being human. I never feel distant from people who don't meditate, I feel more tuned in to them. I don't say—hey, you're coming on too strong. I can understand."

Mike Love is a mellow man who is into meditation, too, and wants to teach it when he isn't busy with the group. After the show, while waiting as Mike met friends and admirers, I spoke to his brother, Steve Love, who has a masters' in business administration and handles business for the group. Steve asked me, "Do you meditate?" I nodded. "You can tell," he said, "You seem serene." Then he added, "You have small lips. So do I."

Mike was talking with a large, shy fellow who said he had a song he wanted Brian Wilson to hear. "It's about the rise and fall of the Beach Boys."

"Well, bring it over to Brian's sometime," said Mike.

"Oh, I don't want Brian to hear it first, maybe you can hear it first. It might scare him."

"Uh, I don't think it will scare him," Mike said.

The people backstage emptied into the rainy night. Friends rushed out saying to Mike, "See you in Majorca."

"Oh yeah—you going? Great! Be there or be square!"—*Kathy Mackay*.

NEWS

The Beach Boys Impro

By HUGH CUTLER

Nine years ago this April I was looking for my old buddy Steve late one Tuesday eve outside the Wilmington Armory at 10th and Du Pont.

Chances were slim that I'd spot him, but my watch-for-Steve was really only the barest cover for my real mission—checking out the crowd—all 3,500 of them—that had witnessed the Beach Boys in concert in Wilmington.

I mixed outside with suburban parents retrieving their kids, more than a little worried about what sort of orgy they'd allowed their innocent darlings to attend.

They'd read about the suggestive body language CBS wisely saw fit to edit from Elvis the Pelvis' debut on Ed Sullivan's extravaganza, and though they'd hoped this rock 'n roll craziness would pass with the speed of hula hoops, even their pre-teens had begun to nourish a dangerous fascination with Top 40 "jungle music."

Sure, those Beatle boys with the funny haircuts seemed sweet and harmless on TV the year before, but beach boys? Didn't that mean lazily lolling in the California sun, surfing, playing hookey or drawing welfare and just fooling with the beach bunnies? One worried about how it would affect the homework, this local exposure.

Personally, I was a bit concerned myself about the show, for different reasons. Steve was inside, right, but Steve was a guitar nut and might be excused for attending by reason of his instrumental interest. I was a year older, played nothing but harmonica, which the Beach Boys shunned. No excuse.

Sang baritone in the church choir, worked hard making my deepening voice stay changed, and was more than a bit put off by five guys who made a career singing about axle grease and waxing surf boards, singing in those falsetto harmonies like Sistine Choir reject eunuchs.

Somehow, it was important that I not get linked with 1,000 screaming teen-agers inside, who as the Journal dutifully reported then, "stood on chairs and frantically cheered their current No. 1 idols," or that "starry-eyed blonde" in the front row who confessed she'd "never wash it" after vocalist Mike Love touched her outstretched fingertip.

Somehow, too, it was important, if I did find Steve in this exit mob, that I impress on him that I wasn't part of this pop schmaltz and saccharine Beach Boys legion—all striped shirts and chinos and madras and peroxided forelocks. Steve came out, and when we did line up in the crush, talked ecstaticaly of what a great guitar player Carl Wilson was.

I can't remember if I made the point of my nonattendance strongly enough to suit me.

★ ★ ★

Late last month, I attended two Newark showings of the '60s nostalgia flick "American Graffiti" and twice delighted, if not indulged in the revving of engines in the lot outside after the show. I think somebody even peeled out from the gravel. If I'd been hungry, I'd surely have stopped in at McDonald's to check how many moviegoers turned up to make the parking lot scene there.

In the middle of the movie, Big John with baddest hot rod in town, the cat with the Camels pack rolled under his T-shirt sleeve, argues over car radio volume with a too-young teenybopper he's accidentally propositioned to join him on his strip cruising.

Seems Wolfman Jack, the D.J., has slipped on some "Surfin' USA" and Greaser John—like me outside the Armory—demurs from the choice, although his jail bait passenger delights in it.

"I don't like that surfin' stuff," is pretty close to what John sneers at her. "Rock 'n' roll's been goin' downhill ever since Buddy Holly."

You can tell he'll be no Beatle freak either, but the fab four from Liverpool won't hit American playlist until January 1964, more than a year later.

"Don't you think the Beach Boys is boss?" asks his cruise mater, who's already proving herself a pain.

"You would," scoffs John, "you grungy little twerp."

★ ★ ★

I managed to stay away from any apparent Beach Boys interest until sometime in 1967. It was easy to sing along with "In My Room" and "Caroline, No" all alone in my car, radio blasting, and not let on to anybody that I'd been trying to master both the high and low harmonies of their four-part.

But Leonard Bernstein changed all that. Uncle Lennie of "radical chic" and occasional Philharmonic fame brought us closet surf music fans out, staging a TV special to give his blessing to this whole Communist-plot-seizing-the-minds-of-our-kids called rock.

Lennie meant to have the entire Beach Boys gang run through some current hits for the show, but rumor has it that the gang couldn't get it together for the film crew. Then, after the rest of the guys had left leader-guiding genius Brian Wilson's living room and the technicians were packing up in disgust, Brian himself suggested they rewind and do a take of him alone—performing a new piece for which he wrote the music and Van Dyke Parks, a nonmember but capable wordsmith, did the lyrics.

Brian, you should know, is the one who can singlehandedly — or multi voicedly — sing all the harmony parts himself while the guys handle ensemble. Although deaf in one ear, he has another ear which may be among the finest tuned in rock, making him one of the most complex yet subtle studio sound producers in the business. His "Pet Sounds" album project still stands as a milestone in rock production.

And despite a nervous breakdown or two, an arresting brand of avant-weirdness which would make him build a giant sandbox in his living room and open a health food store in L.A., and his refusal now to tour with the

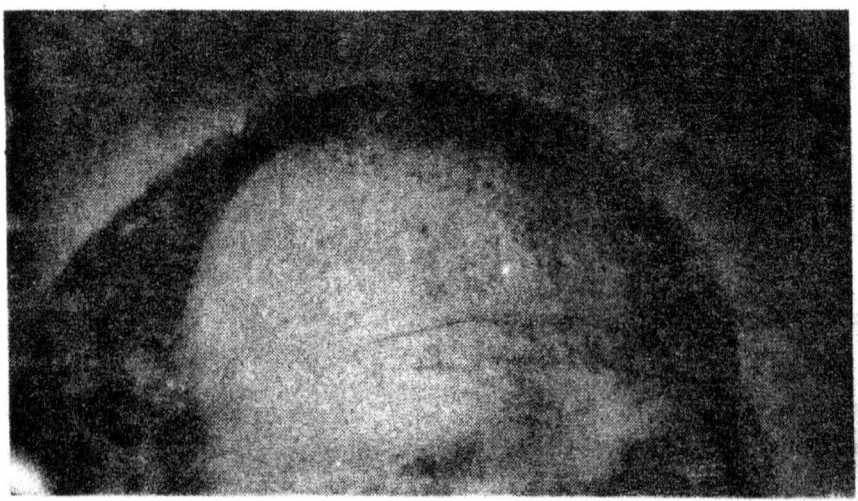

ove With Time

Staff photo by Jodi Cobb

Four of the original Beach Boys are, from left, Mike Love, Brian Wilson (no longer active), Alan Jardine and Dennis Wilson.

And she forgot all about the library that she told her old man, now.
And with the radio blastin' goes cruisin' just as fast as she can, now.
And she'll have fun, fun, fun till her daddy takes the T-bird away!"

Credit those winsome lines to Mike Love. Then set those next to Parks' words for "Surf's Up," which isn't really about waxing boards:

"The glass was raised, the fire rose, the fulness of the wine, the dim last toasting ...
While at the port adieu or die ...
Canvass the town and brush the backdrop; Are you sleeping?"

The way that one poem, sung by Brian, swims in the harmonic wash and shifting rhythms of his music is a beautifully textured experience to mellow the hardest among us.

Only recently have the other Beach Boys transcended their roles as expositers and harmonizers for Brian's tunes.

Brother Carl offers his own music, on the recent and superb "Holland" album, for "The Trader," set around words by one-time road manager Jack Rieley:

"Embracing together, like the merging streams, crying dreams, making it full, begging intently for a slight reprieve, a night of ease, hands to touch beyond the sorrow, on to the force without power, piercing the curse of the tower, reason to live..."

Or take bassman Al Jardine, the only non- without Brian.

They come out in a range of attire now, unlike the stripes-and-chinos fixation of yore. Dennis Wilson, for instance, stands casual but straight out front in what could be a Brooks Brothers three-piece, hands thrust deep in his pockets unless he's cracking a joke or cupping a hand over his ear to catch his proper vocal part in the harmonies.

Dennis is not drumming lately because of a hand injury, and Fataar is subbing admirably as well as switching over for some splendid steel guitar riffs.

Carl's guitar picking is more supple now it seems, and more lyrical, too. And Jardine's basslines drive as much as ever.

Out in the forefront, Mike Love—looking younger than his 32 years, now minus bushy red beard, but still hiding his baldness under a big panama with pick hatband—is stepping high in a belted velvet jumpsuit of matching pink.

Mike has even developed his Mick Jagger parody to absurdity but not excess for the Stones' "Jumpin' Jack Flash," and the band dares to use than one for a show closer.

All the Beach Boys' faves, though, are still there. "Wouldn't It Be Nice?" and "California Girls" and "Surfer Girl," "Caroline, No" and "Help Me, Ronda" and "Surfin' USA," even "Ba-Ba-Ba-Ba-Barbara Ann."

It's almost as much as a kick to see and hear

NEWS

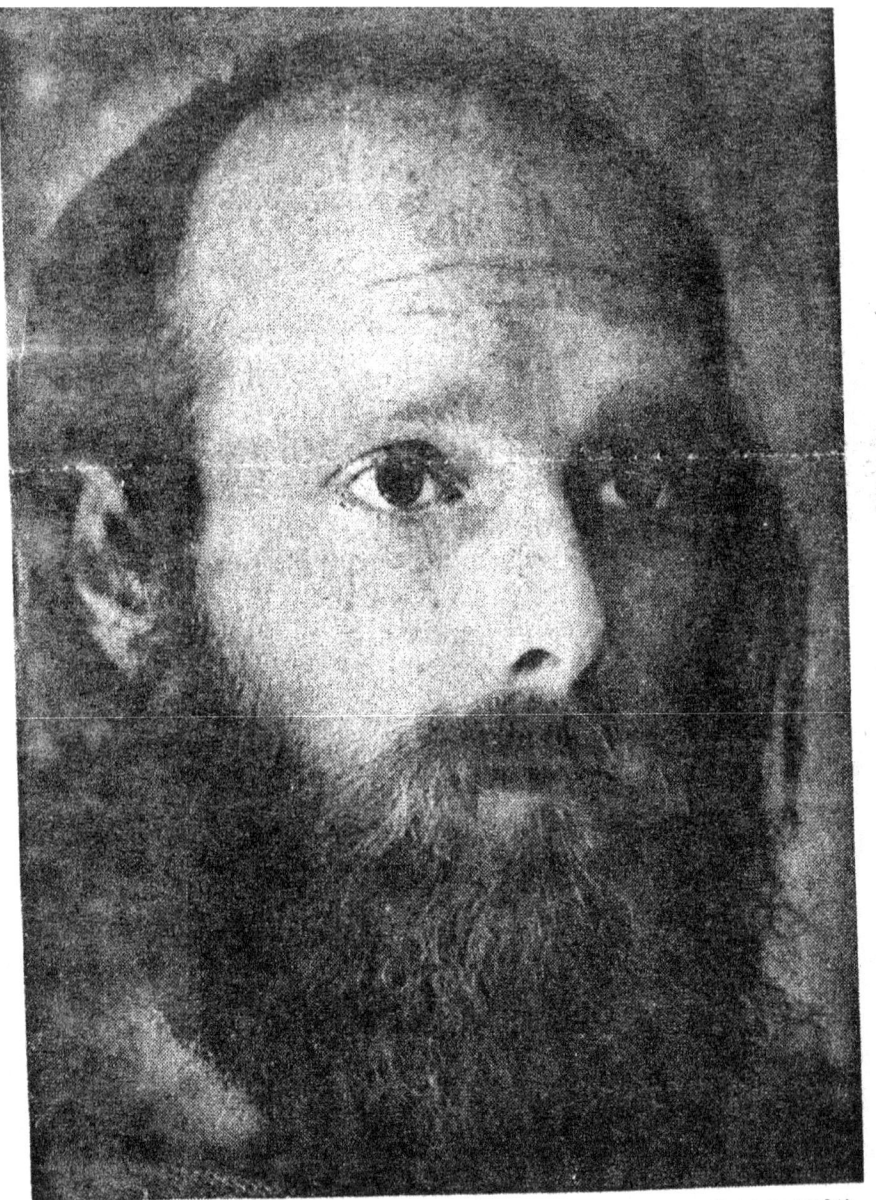

Mike Love

He's Out Front

Staff photo by Jodi Cobb

himself suggested they rewind and do a take of him alone—performing a new piece for which he wrote the music and Van Dyke Parks, a nonmember but capable wordsmith, did the lyrics.

Brian, you should know, is the one who can singlehandedly — or multi voicedly — sing all the harmony parts himself while the guys handle ensemble. Although deaf in one ear, he has another ear which may be among the finest tuned in rock, making him one of the most complex yet subtle studio sound producers in the business. His "Pet Sounds" album project still stands as a milestone in rock production.

And despite a nervous breakdown or two, an arresting brand of avant-weirdness which would make him build a giant sandbox in his living room and open a health food store in L.A., and his refusal now to tour with the group, Brian is still the Beach Boys' essence-- its brains, heart and soul.

Candelabra on his grand piano, Brian made a compelling picture as he barely mumbled Parks' words for the camera, but the tune he played was one of the most inventive and beautiful ever sprung on the rock world — and simultaneous with and equal to the Beatles' epic "Day in the Life" on the Sgt. Pepper album.

That was the first time I heard "Surf's Up" and the last time I would hear its irresistable tune for more than four years. Brian just buried a tape he made of it when he scrapped the breakthrough "Smile" album project for which it was intended, releasing instead the more predictable rhythms and mundane lyrics of "Smiley Smile."

"Surf's Up" didn't resurface until 1971, when Brian was persuaded to dredge up the old tape and squeeze it all on the end of an album bearing the same name — a record which showed the Boys back into the current rock scene and reasserted Brian's genius.

• • •

Although your high school English teacher's taste might not run to the poetry of Beach Boys' songs, especially the faves of old, college sociology scholars may one day study their effect on, and capsulization of, the '60s youth mass psyche. And the harmonies are of course, unparalleled by any, Crosby, Stills, Nash & Young included.

After more than a decade, we can hark back to '62 for this watershed exposition of the generation gap:

"Well, she got her daddy's car and she cruised to the hamburger stand, now—

The way that one poem, sung by Brian, swims in the harmonic wash and shifting rhythms of his music is a beautifully textured experience to mellow the hardest among us.

Only recently have the other Beach Boys transcended their roles as expositers and harmonizers for Brian's tunes.

Brother Carl offers his own music, on the recent and superb "Holland" album, for "The Trader," set around words by one-time road manager Jack Rieley:

"Embracing together, like the merging streams, crying dreams, making it full, begging intently for a slight reprieve, a night of ease, hands to touch beyond the sorrow, on to the force without power, piercing the curse of the tower, reason to live..."

Or take bassman Al Jardine, the only non-family member of the original group before

Carl's guitar picking is more supple now it seems, and more lyrical, too. And Jardine's basslines drive as much as ever.

Out in the forefront, Mike Love—looking younger than his 32 years, now minus bushy red beard, but still hiding his baldness under a big panama with pick hatband—is stepping high in a belted velvet jumpsuit of matching pink.

Mike has even developed his Mick Jagger parody to absurdity but not excess for the Stones' "Jumpin' Jack Flash," and the band dares to use than one for a show closer.

All the Beach Boys' faves, though, are still there. "Wouldn't It Be Nice?" and "California Girls" and "Surfer Girl," "Caroline, No" and "Help Me, Ronda" and "Surfin' USA," even "Ba-Ba-Ba-Ba-Barbara Ann."

It's almost as much as a kick to see and hear lips chapped by a mere 16 beach summers—

ROCK, AND ALL THAT

Brian quit touring—for health and head reasons — to stick to producing. (first Glen Campbell, then Bruce Johnson replaced Brian on the road. Al created the final third of a "California Saga" trilogy on "Holland" that forms an exquisite honorarium for his home state:

"... And have you ever walked down through the sycamores where the farmhouse used to be?

There the Monarch's autumn journey ends on a windswept cyprus tree.

Water, water, get yourself in the cool, clear water...."

Yes, the lyrics have progressed. And so has the show.

• • •

I finally found myself at a Beach Boys concert in mid-December. I would have to say it was a thriller. The fans, though a bit too worldly now to give up hand washing like the old days of idolatry, were as exuberant as ever. The Beach Boys, after all—now with a few extras like Ricky Fataar and Blondie Chaplin, both picked up from South Africa's flame—can still do all those oldies but goodies as well as or better than before.

They even risk recreating the complexities which layers of studio production and overdubs added to songs like "Good Vibrations" and "Heroes and Villains" and pull it off masterfully, although they don't attempt "Surf's Up"

more than a decade younger than the youngest Beach Boy and only preschoolers, some of them, when the California myth from Hawthorne was spreading over the airwaves like a giant curl across 1961 America—to see these lips sinigng along:

"If everybody had an ocean, across the U.S.A.,

Then everybody'd be surfin' like Califor-nye-a..."

The same spark is there, the dozen years in between seeming to drop when you close your eyes; the tight harmonies, the prodding, stomping beat. That warm California sun shines down on Mike, doing the swim on his Ultimate Wave and—delightfully—another new generation joins, hanging ten with the Beach Boys and loving it.

These kids, despite their Alice Coopers and New York Dolls, seem not quite so uptight with such affectations that worried their predecessors. They can laugh at the "grungy little twerp" line in "Graffiti" and be hip to Greaser John's feeling, yet not embrace it.

Now I wish I'd been in the Armory, instead of outside looking in. If only to have smiled the whole next week as I did after that night at Philly's Spectrum last month.

Over-30 family men, their surf boards drying and warping on the racks, maybe—but still, when they start singing, "I'm picking up good vibrations."

ADS

WIN THIS MINI-SURFER!

Customized by George Barris, of Hollywood, this candy-striped Austin MINI-SURFER comes with a Yamaha Campus 60 strapped to the back, a custom surfboard by Con of California cresting the top, a Borg-Warner 8-track stereo tape player, and two giant portable speakers with a half-block of cord!

it's WCFL's BEACH BOYS BIRTHDAY BLAST!

To join in the fun, just look for the Mini-Surfer display and the Beach Boys' newest album:

BEST OF THE BEACH BOYS

Surfin' U.S.A.
Little Honda
Fun, Fun, Fun
Wendy
...and more!
(D)T 2545

It's the easiest contest ever! Pick up an entry blank today!

discount records, inc.
ON CAMPUS
603 S. Wright   Champaign
Phone 352-3822

RECORDS

530 E. Green — "The Mud Below"

HERE ARE THE THURSDAY-MONDAY SPECIALS

MAME with Angela Lansbury
Mono - $3.00 — Stereo - $3.50

All Tiajuana Brass
Mono - $2.10 — Stereo - $2.50

And For All Those Who Crave Andy Williams

DEAR HEART
NEWEST HITS   — $1.50 Stereo

Also, If You Enjoy Junk — THE BEACH BOYS
The Beach Boys Today
Summer Days   — $1.50 Stereo

THE MANAGEMENT (Frank, Jesse, Henry & William) and our stock boy (Stocky Jim Rubovitz) wish to thank our clientele for not bringing their Dads to our hovel last weekend. Did You Ever Try Talking to One? It's like talking to a witless wallet.

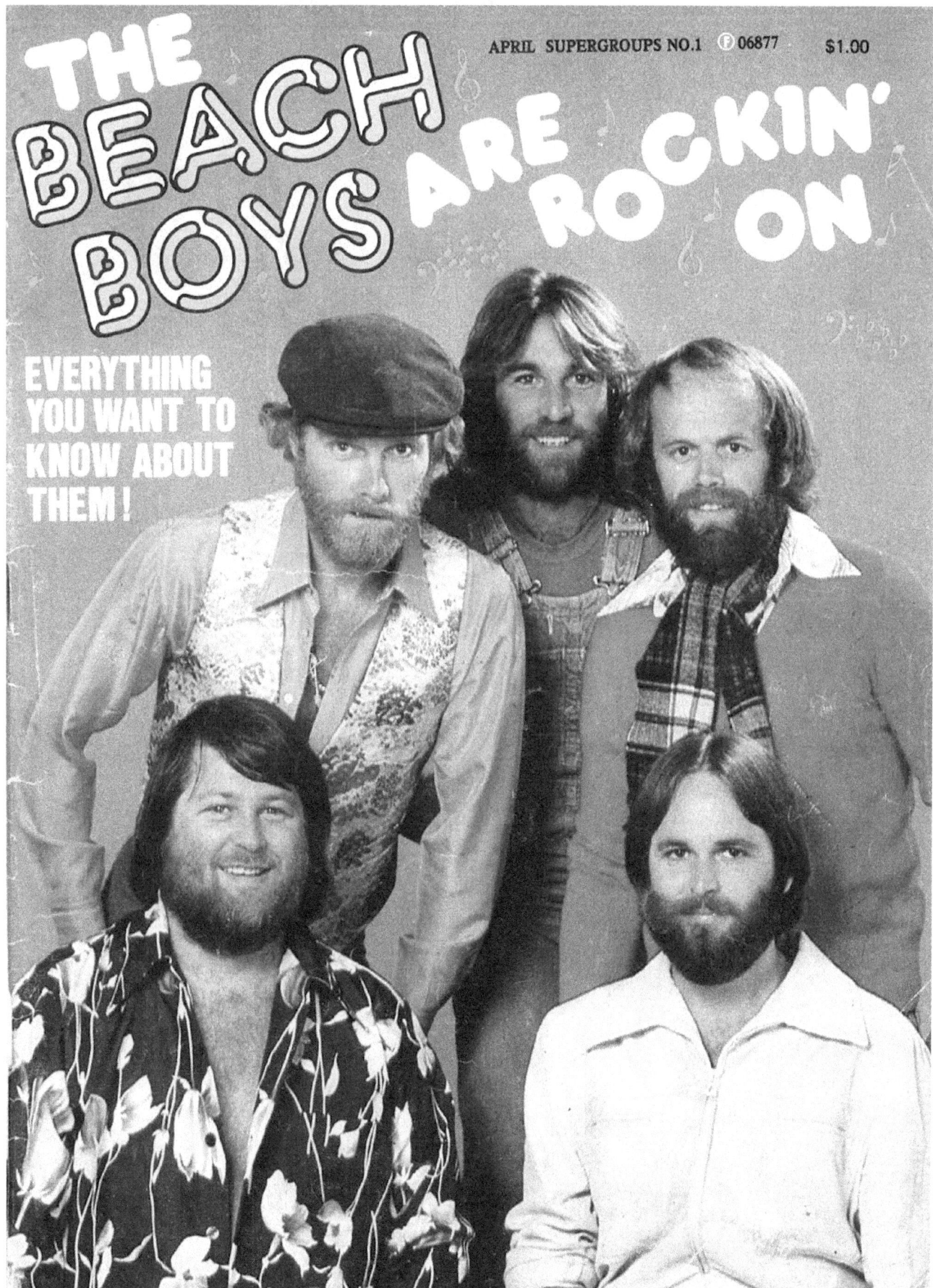

MAGAZINE

THE BEACH BOYS!
Mike Love, Carl Wilson, Brian Wilson
Dennis Wilson, Alan Jardine

MAGAZINE

SUPERGROUPS APRIL NO. 1

- 4 BEACH BOYS: AN AMERICAN DREAM!
- 10 ROCKIN' ON WITH "15 BIG ONES"...
- 14 "BRIAN WILSON *IS* THE BEACH BOYS!"
- 18 CALIFORNIA SAGA
- 23 THE CAPTAIN AND TENNILLE...?
- 24 BUT ONLY DENNIS GOT HIS FEET WET!
- 26 THE BEACH BOYS IN HOLLYWOOD!
- 32 CARL: THE KID BROTHER
- 39 "SUSIE CINCINNATI"—FROM WHEELS TO WAX!
- 42 BEACH BOYS INFLUENCE: CHUCK BERRY!
- 44 AL JARDINE, FROM OHIO TO BIG SUR ON A WAVE
- 46 BEACH BOYS DISCOGRAPHY
- 52 MIKE LOVE: A SUNG HERO!
- 54 SURF CITY, HERE WE COME...
- 62 SUPERSOUNDS!
- 68 WHERE'S YOUR HEAD AT?

RON HAYDOCK	Editor	DON J. ROBERTSON	Art Associate
CHARLES E. FRITCH	Managing Editor	ANITA GAINES	Editorial Assistant
SALVATORE E. SCORZA	Art Director	AL SATIAN	Associate Editor
GLENN H. THORNE	Assistant Art Director	R.J. ROBERTSON	Associate Editor
EDWARD CARBAJAL	Art Associate	HEATHER JOHNSON	Contributing Editor

Cover Designed by SALVATORE SCORZA   FRONT COVER: NBC-TV's "Beach Boys" Special ....

Their tight, high wall of harmony over quietly calculated instrumental arrangements is maddeningly infectious, and their lyrics' promise of an endless summer of cruising wheels, perfect waves, and two bikini-clad beauties for every boy is irresistable.

They are the Beach Boys, prophets of the middle-class American teenage dream.

The story of the Beach Boys and their music begins and ends with Brian Wilson. Oldest of the three Wilson brothers, Brian was quarterback of the Hawthorne High Cougars, while cousin Mike Love ran track and cross-country at Dorsey High, and the weekly youth night at Angeles Mesa Presbyterian Church usually found them harmonizing on **Wake Up Little Suzie** and other Everly Brothers numbers on their way home — where Brian spent many hours at the piano picking out the parts to such Four Freshmen melodies as **Polka Dots and Moonbeams** for further harmonizing with Mike, and brothers Dennis and Carl Wilson. Mike carried the bass line, Dennis the baritone, Carl the tenor, and Brian hit the high notes in a carefully practiced falsetto.

Then Al Jardine, the Cougars' fullback, recovered one of Brian's fumbled pitch-outs, and broke his leg in the effort. But he was an avid folk music fan and stand-up bass player, so his idle hours recuperating from the injury were filled by adding his voice to the Wilson-Love quartet — and shortly "Carl and the Passions" were born.

Carl, the only one of the Wilsons who'd actually learned to play an instrument, became the lead guitar of the new group, while Al Jardine took on the rhythm guitar, and Dennis Wilson the drums. Mike Love played a little sax, and Brian took up the bass. This rather weak instrumental background, though, proved a solid enough framework on which to hang their unique blend of harmonies, and the five of them felt that they just might have a good band here.

by Al Satian

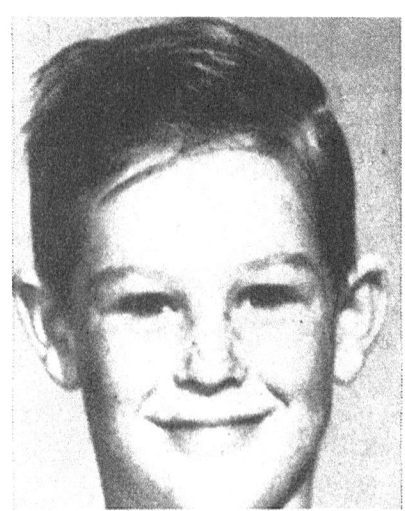

Brian when he was only 9 years old...

Brian Wilson reunited with the Beach Boys for their 15 BIG ONES album...

BEACH BOYS: AN

MAGAZINE

On stage in Anaheim, California, with more than 55,000 fans cheering them on...

Mike Love and the Beach Boys whoopin' it up with Bobby Pickett's "Monster Mash" smash in 1966...

AMERICAN DREAM

MAGAZINE

Dennis Wilson making his debut as an actor in Universal's TWO-LANE BLACKTOP.

costarring Warren Oates, James Taylor and Laurie Bird...

Capitol chose **409** as the most likely of the numbers to hit nationally (surfing, of necessity, being a regional fad), but Brian and Mike's **Surfin' Safari,** the second Beach Boys paean to the watersport, was chosen for the "b" side and eventually won out in radio airplay as the stronger of the two. **409,** however, was not far behind in the charts, and with their first Capitol Record a two-sided winner, the first Beach Boys album followed in short order. Its title was, of course, SURFIN' SAFARI, and surfing in spirit, if not in fact, became a national craze. The striped t-shirts and casual hairstyles of the West Coast surfers were dutifully copied by the rest of the country's adolescent population and surfboards began appearing on the Great Lakes and other inland beaches.

The surf failing, there were still the football games, drag races, drive-in-movies, and the mandatory cruising of the local strips, and succeeding Beach Boys anthems like **Shut Down, Little Deuce Coup,** and **Be True To Your School** (featuring rousing cheerleaders' choruses of "Do it again, Do it again, We like it, We like it!") provided the hymnal for these ceremonies of growing up. Sides like **Surfin' USA** (a revamping of Chuck Berry's **Sweet Little Sixteen)** and the hauntingly beautiful **Surfer Girl** meanwhile kept the myth of youthful summers alive, and the Beach Boys became part and parcel of the American musical diet, sharing highest honors with the Ventures, the Four Seasons, and the unfailingly popular Stax-Volt/Motown "soul" singers.

Then, in January 1964, the unexpected arrived from across the Atlantic in the form of four long-haired Liverpool lads called the Beatles. Their shattering impact on the American pop scene washed the status quo asunder in a tidal wave of musical change that few currently popular recording acts would survive. The Beach Boys, however, proved an endurable institution, competing admirably with the British newcomers for the top of the pop charts with a steady stream of hits like **I Get Around, Help Me Rhonda,** and **California Girls,** possibly the quintessential Beach Boys song of the era.

Continued on page 58

MAGAZINE

ROCKIN' ON!

WITH "15 BIG ONES"

by Joseph Posche

It happened this past spring. It was a long time in coming, but it was most welcome news indeed: the Beach Boys were back in their 24-track Brother Studio in Santa Monica, California, recording a new album, fif-TEEN BIG ONES. And "Big Brother" Brian Wilson was back, recording with them.

Although the past few years have seen a resurgence of public interest in the Beach Boys and their music, with compilation al-

MAGAZINE

Brian at the control panel, recording the Beach Boys...

bums like ENDLESS SUMMER and GOOD VIBRATIONS appearing in record outlets, their last album of new material was HOLLAND, released three years previously.

The Beach Boys having been the first rock 'n' roll band to have full studio control of their product, their absence from the studio had been sorely felt.

Once they got the big studio console warmed up for FIFTEEN BIG ONES, though, they slipped gradually back into their working rhythm, recording and mixing a handful of other artists' oldies, like Fats Domino's *Blueberry Hill,* and Freddie Cannon's *Palisades Park* — the rock 'n' roll they cut their musical teeth on when they were just five guys from Hawthorne, California, thinking about trying to be a band.

Of the few seminal 60's rock bands surviving, the Beach Boys have weathered by far the most agonizing ebb in the tide of their career, but they are still working musicians who remember the roots of their music with an excitement that hasn't dimmed over the years.

"It's bitchin'," Brian would call out from behind the control panel. "Carl, it's just right! Your voice is *perfect* for it!"

He was speaking of *Palisades Park,* for which they had just finished laying down Carl's lead vocal track.

Among the other old favorites included on FIFTEEN BIG ONES are the Six Teens' *A Casual Look,* the Dixie Cups' *Chapel of Love,* the Righteous Brothers' memorable Phil Spector production *Just Once In My Life,* and the Five Satins' unforgettable *I Remember (In The Still Of The Night).* Chuck Berry's anthem to the genre, *Rock 'n' Roll Music,* found its way onto the pop charts this summer with Mike Love doing lead vocal honors and became the Beach Boys' first hit single since the moderately successful 1973 release, *Sail On Sailor.*

FIFTEEN BIG ONES is not solely an oldies package, however. The memories are backed by a fresh assortment of vital new Beach Boys selections, most of them Brian Wilson creations. And, perhaps most significantly of all, Brian is singing for the first time since Bruce Johnstone (and later Blondie Chaplin) replaced him on studio vocals in 1969. Brian sings the leads on *Chapel of Love, That Same Song, Had Ta Phone Ya,* and *Back Home,* for which he also wrote the music. *It's OK* and *The TM Song,* a number endorsing the benefits of Transcendental Meditation, are among Brian's other musical credits on the album.

Al Jardine's *Susie Cincinnati,* originally recorded back in 1970, has been included (and slated for the next Beach Boys single release as well), and Mike Love wrote *Everyone's In Love With You.* Almost everyone is on this last track Darryl Dragon of The Captain and Tennille arranged the background vocal, and wife-partner Toni Tennille joined in the singing. Charles Lloyd played the flute, and Mike's sister, Maureen Love, played the harp.

A most impressive re-entry into the pop field, FIFTEEN BIG ONES is not only the newest Beach Boys album in some years, it's also one of their strongest, both commercially and artistically. When the last track had been mixed, Brian Wilson said only, "This is where I'm at right now."

The critics and fans alike are delighted to see him there. ●

MAGAZINE

Carl Wilson

Born Dec 21, 1946

MAGAZINE

"brian wilson is the b

There's no mistaking it. "Brian Wilson *is* the Beach Boys," brother Dennis assures us, and there is no dispute from any quarter.

The fans, the press, fellow musicians, and the rest of the Beach Boys themselves all agree: were it not for Brian, there would be no Beach Boys.

From the start, Brian was the leader — their bassist, chief songwriter, arranger, producer, and the originator of that unique blend of harmonies that has become the Beach Boys' trademark. His posi-

MAGAZINE

"each boys"

Big Brother is Back, Legend & All..

By Al Satian

tion of undisputed leadership hasn't changed over the years, in spite of sometimes commercially disastrous musical directions, and in spite of his protracted absence from stage and studio.

If anything, his absence and his failures have only further solidified his place in rock 'n' roll history and the legend surrounding him.

Having suffered two nervous breakdowns, Brian was forced to retire from the rigors of touring in 1965. Glen Campbell, and later Bruce Johnstone, replaced him on

MAGAZINE

stage. Left behind when the Beach Boys went on the road, Brian grew increasingly introspective, and it began to show in his music. PET SOUNDS, his answer to the Beatles' RUBBER SOUL, won him almost unanimous critical acclaim (though the album sold very poorly) and stirred the first whispers in the pop world that there was more to the Beach Boys, and more to Brian Wilson in particular, than *Surfer Girl* and *Fun Fun Fun*.

The proof was not long in coming. *Good Vibrations*, the Beach Boys' masterwork, followed a scant five months later, rising straight to the top of the charts worldwide. The 1966 NEW MUSICAL EXPRESS poll in England voted the Beach Boys the Number One World group, breaking the Beatles' long winning streak. Word was out that Brian Wilson was the new genius of rock 'n' roll, and in the plainest show-biz talk, it was a tough act to follow.

Brian Wilson rose to the occasion, compulsively trying to top his own triumph, but turning out very few finished pieces in the effort. Songs like *Heroes and Villains*, which did surface, were praised by the critics but failed to hit the mark with the record-buying public. His magnum opus, SMILE, never made it out of the studio (though portions of it eventually turned up on later albums), and the pressure of measuring up to his past led to Brian's near-withdrawal from the group and the public eye. And, like virtually every prominent rock artist of the decade, Brian experimented with the psychedelic drugs that were so freely available.

Bizarre stories, some of them true, began circulating in rock circles — he had indeed pitched his piano in a giant-sized sandbox he had installed in his den — and the legend grew.

Still, Brian Wilson compositions continued to appear (albeit decreasingly) on Beach Boys albums, and ocasional news stories kept his name and legend alive. This year, however, acknowledging the rest of the group's dependence on him, and, in his own words, "tired of being a failure" (though his track record belies this self-estimation), Brian returned to the studios in his full capacity to produce FIFTEEN BIG ONES, the latest Beach Boys album. Embarking on a concentrated physical fitness program, he managed to lose thirty pounds from his former 240-pound frame, appeared in a NBC-TV special about the group, and made two brief appearances with them during California concerts.

Although his wife, Marilyn, and his doctors continue to keep a close watch on him, Brian Wilson seems well on the way to recovery, both as a person and as a performer.

As ROLLING STONE so aptly phrased it, "Big Brother Is Back," alive, well, and as legendary as ever. ●

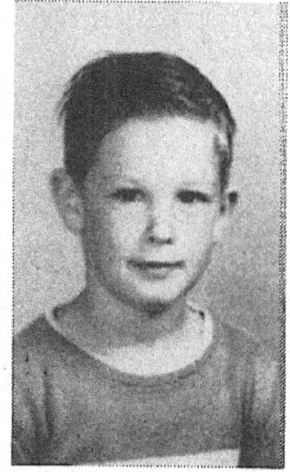

Brian at 7 years...

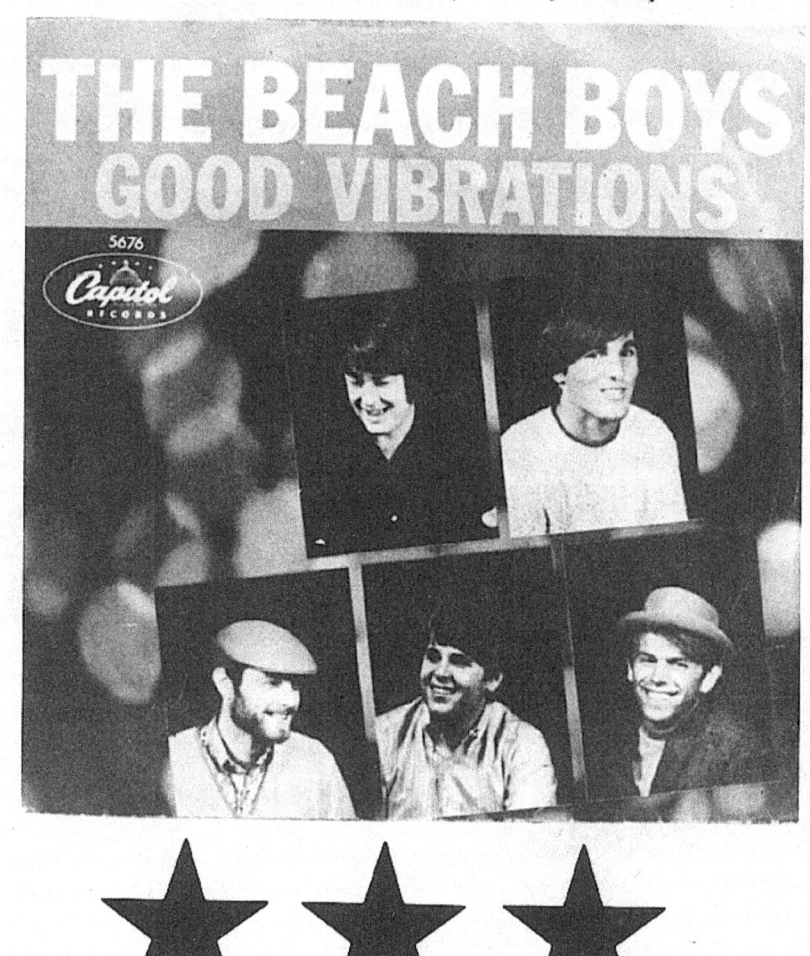

MAGAZINE

by R. J. Robertson

How The Beach Boys, 'those California Girls' & A Surfboard swept the Nation...

CALIFORNIA SAGA

LET'S GO SURFIN'

Everybody may not have been surfing that summer of '62 in suburban southern California, but God, it seemed like it. The whole surfing scene had been building like a tidal wave all year.

"Pray for surf" was inscribed with a pen knife on almost every desk in school. Surfing slang with words like "ho-dad," "gremmie," and "hang ten," and "wipe out" were integral parts of one's vocabulary.

In gym class guys would proudly display their surfing knots (hard calluses on the knees from kneeling on a board all day).

Both guys and girls peroxided their hair for a year-round sun streaked look.

Pendleton shirts, white levis, and sandals were part of the dress code.

The big status symbols were: a surfboard (obviously), a woodie (wood panelled station wagon for carrying your board), and a place to stay down at the beach.

MAGAZINE

Beach Boys (left to right) Al, Brian, Dennis, and Carl. That's Mike seated..

Dennis, 5 years old...

This was the zenith of pre-Viet Nam optimism. Social problems, domestic and foreign, were light years away. Physical fitness was in, and we had a young, virile, president in the White House. Girls seemed to be content to be long of limb and blonde. Surfing, cruising, and making-out were the most important activities of the day.

Sunshine, affluence, youth, mobility, and miles and miles of ocean; it was all here. L.A. was the center of the universe.

MAGAZINE

I GET AROUND

California finally found a sound to match it's life style. Surfing music may have begun with Dick Dale and other local L.A. bands, but these were only attempts to convey the feeling of surfing with musical instruments. In the lyrics of Brian Wilson (along with his collaborators Mike Love, Gary Usher, and Roger Christian) were anthems to not only surfing, but the entire spectrum of southern California activities.

By 1964 the Beach Boys' vision of California had spread to every state in the union. A guy in Oklahoma may not have given a damn about **Catch A Wave,** but anybody, anywhere could relate to **Little Deuce Coupe** A girl in New York might not be a **Surfer Girl,** but she could easily be **Your Summer Dream.**

The California experience was there for everyone to share the minute a Beach Boys' song came on the radio, and we all had **Fun, Fun, Fun** till our daddy took our T-bird away.

The sound of the Beach Boys was as important as

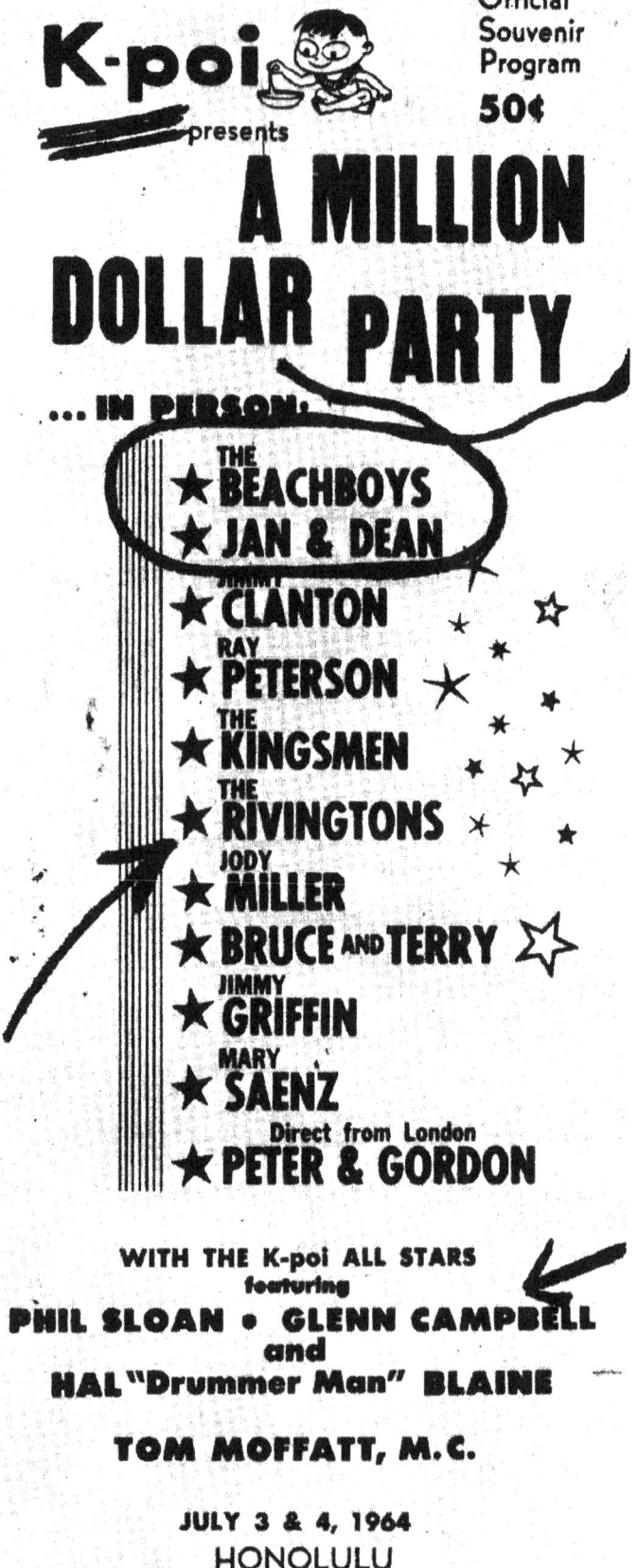

MAGAZINE

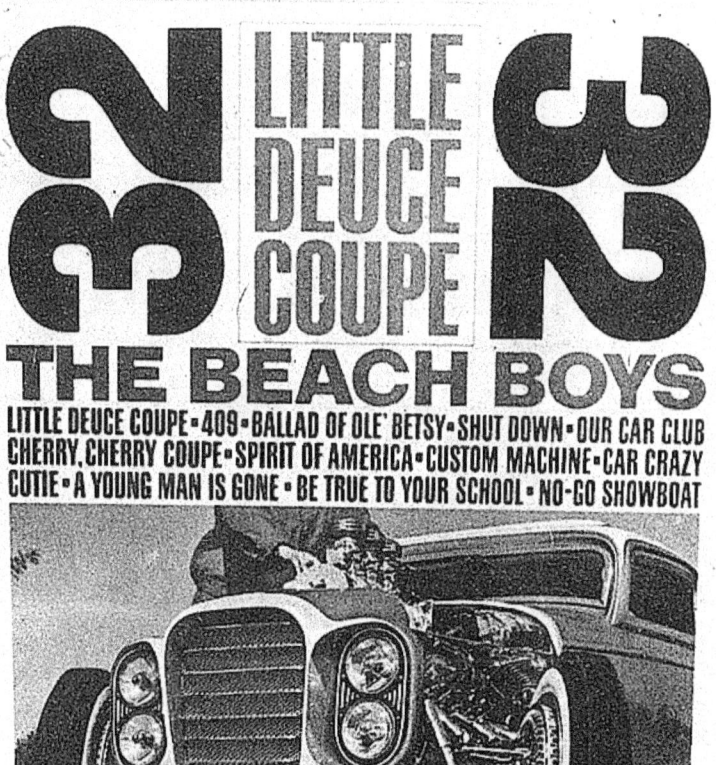

the lyrical content. The opening Chuck Berry riffs on **Surfin' U.S.A.** and **Fun, Fun, Fun** were an unmistakable sign that the Beach Boys were ready, willing, and able to rock. Purists may argue that their sound was too "clean", but the spirit of rock and roll was undeniably present.

The Beatles may have been the leaders of the second rock renaissance, but the Beach Boys were the heralders of its coming.

GOOD VIBRATIONS

As the Beach Boys became a universal phenomenon, their lyrics broke away from social activities and became more concerned with personal problems. **In My Room**, an introspective ode to solitude, was the first. THE BEACH BOYS TODAY and SUMMER DAYS were filled with such domestic traumas as **Don't Hurt My Little Sister, When I Grow Up, She Knows Me Too Well, In The Back Of My Mind, Girl Don't Tell Me,** and **I'm Bugged At My Ol' Man**.

Musically the Beach Boys were developing a more complex, imaginative sound. **California Girls**, with it's unusual keyboard introduction, and **Little Girl I Once Knew**, with it's unexpected stops and intricate melody, were in many ways at least six months ahead of their time.

Folk-rock, exemplified by Bob Dylan and his followers, had become a major influence. Lyrics were more relevant and aware. **Love Me Do** just wasn't making it anymore, so the Beatles responded with their landmark RUBBER SOUL album. Not to be outdone, Brian produced PET SOUNDS a few months later. The lyrics by Tony Asher were intelligent, and the music was as advanced as anything the Beatles had done up to that time.

A few months later the Beach Boys unveiled their monumental super-production, **Good Vibrations**. The lyrics were simple, but who cared? Even on a car radio one could pick up the multi-layered harmonies, the abrupt shifts in tempo, and the incredible complexities of the song. Less than a year later they produced **Heroes and Villains** with many of the same elements. **Heroes and Villains** was not a hit. What happened?

MAGAZINE

Back in the early sixties, when they started it all...

Actually, a lot had happened. The era of **Fun, Fun, Fun** was over. Civil rights, Viet Nam, psychedelic drugs, and free love were polarizing our society. From San Francisco came new sounds by the Jefferson Airplane, Grateful Dead, Big Brother and the Holding Company, and the whole "acid rock," Haight-Ashbury scene.

In L.A. riding the waves was replaced by rushing on THC. AM was replaced by FM. 45 singles were replaced by albums. The Monkees and other bubblegum groups kept the teenyboppers happy, but the older teenagers and those entering their twenties wanted something more relevant.

The Beach Boys tried to keep in touch but nobody was listening. They were irrevocably linked with the good times of the early sixties, and that whole era seemed trivial and out of touch with what was happening in places like Chicago and Watts. In the SGT. PEPPER era the Beatles could be pardoned for **Please Please Me** but the Beach Boys could never be forgiven for **Surfin' U.S.A.** Old Beach Boys records were relegated to the back of the stack. New ones weren't bought.

LET'S DO IT AGAIN

In 1968 the Beach Boys invited us to go down to the beach and **Do It Again**, but it wasn't until the Beatles told everyone to **Get Back** that anyone listened.

The "Woodstock nation" began to fold, heavy drugs were replaced by socially accepted use of marijuana, and the horrendous period known as the "Nixon administration" began.

Continued on page 64

MAGAZINE

Believe It Or Not,
They're Part of The Beach Boys' Story too...

It was early 1965, and Brian Wilson decided to stop touring with the Beach Boys. Brian never had a thick enough skin for that part of the work, and the longer he did it, the worse it got.

Shy, eccentric, creative in ways that wouldn't take a lot of interviewing — uncomfortable in a room with even one stranger in it — Brian finally told the rest of the group that although he wanted to go on composing and producing for them, he couldn't perform anymore.

It was a great loss to the touring Beach Boys, very traumatic for the group, but the show must go on, and so Carl, even though he was the youngest of them all, inherited leadership of the Beach Boys while on the road. His steady temper and accomplished musicianship won it for him.

With Brian gone, though, there were gaps to be filled with the group, and Bruce Johnston, a talented LA musician, joined the Beach Boys to sing Brian's part on tour. Bruce, however, was just one of many good people who drifted in and out of the Beach Boys over the next few years.

Another was Daryl Dragon.

Daryl was the son of composer Carmen Dragon, and he went on to play the keyboards for the Beach Boys for about six years. Then he met Toni Tennille — the only girl who ever toured with the band — and one day the two of them ran off — and became The Captain and Tennille! ●

MAGAZINE

BUT ONLY DENNIS GOT HIS FEET WET!

"We're Here To Entertain..."

Born December 4, 1944

MAGAZINE

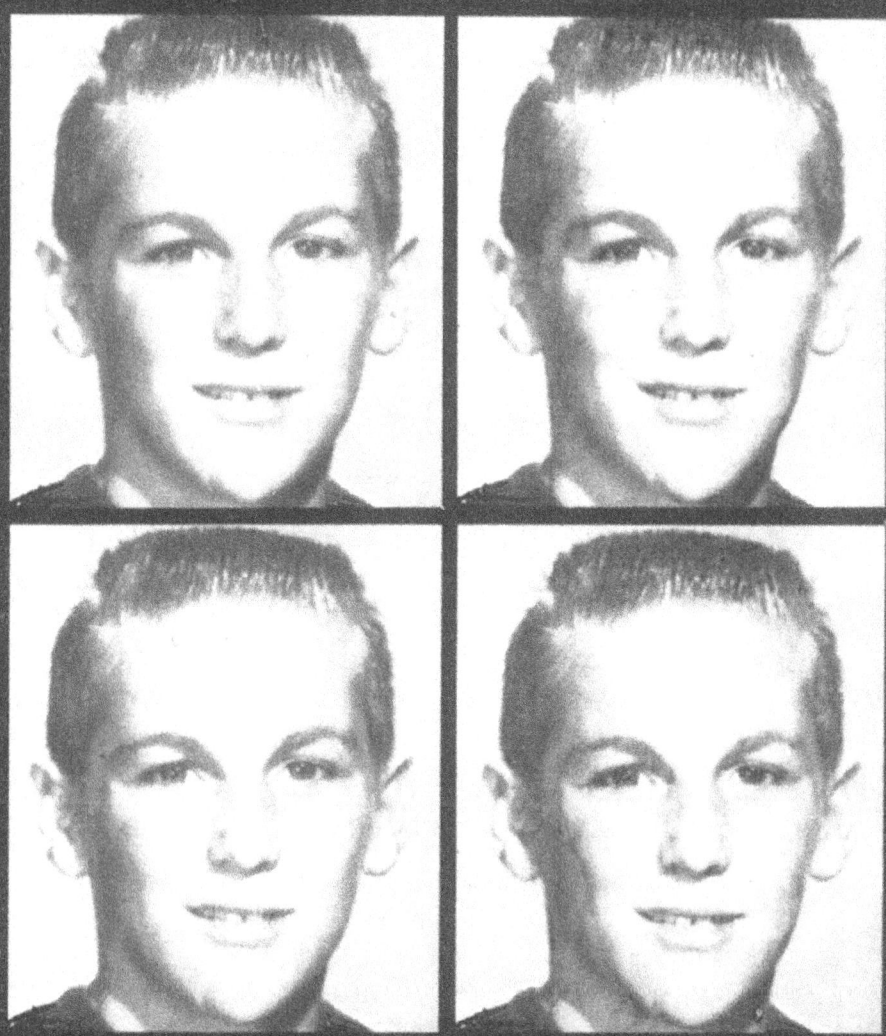

Dennis at 10 years old...

by John Martin

Dennis Wilson, the second of the Wilson brothers, provided the initial impetus for the Beach Boys' "Surf Sound."

The only member of the group to ever actually catch that illusive wave, it was Dennis who came in from a day on the surf in 1961 with the suggestion that Brian write a song about the surfing craze. Brian obliged him with *Surfin'*, which became the first Beach Boys' record and the beginning of their fifteen-year career. That song's title, in turn, inspired the Pendletones to become the Beach Boys.

Dennis became the group's drummer, occasionally stepping down to sing (his slightly flat, but nonetheless exuberant rendition of Dion's *The Wanderer* will be found on the 1964 BEACH BOYS CONCERT album). In 1971 a hand injury forced him away from the drums, and he took on the less-taxing keyboards. His wound now healed, he is currently pounding the skins again with full vigor.

Dennis' musical background has led to numerous original compositions, among them *Steamboat, Only With You,* and *Got To Know The Woman.* He is always quick to acknowledge his secondary role to big brother Brian Wilson, however.

"We all like to get involved in what we put down, but Brian is the leader," Dennis affirms.

Like everyone who grew up in the 60's, Dennis' life has seen many phases, including the customary flirtation with the psychedelic sub-culture. He has only recently managed to live down his brief association with composer Charles Manson and his clan, who were later convicted of mass murder. *Never Learn Not To Love,* a Manson composition, was sung by Dennis on the Beach Boys' 20/20 album.

Nowadays, Dennis continues to surf whenever possible, but is more often seen riding the waves in his sailboat, aptly dubbed the *Harmony.* On shore, he makes his home in a rented beach house with his third wife, actress Karen Lamm. He is currently at work on a film score and studying acting.

"There's a parallel between what we do as musicians and acting," he notes. "What we're there to do in both cases is entertain the audience."

And that, as Dennis himself will tell you, is what he and the Beach Boys do best. ●

MAGAZINE

With Annette Funicello in THE MONKEY'S UNCLE...

HOLLYWOOD

by R. J. Robertson

FEATURE FILMS

"THE T.A.M.I. SHOW" (on-screen title *Teenage Command Performance*) 1964. Released by American-International Pictures. An Electronovision Production in association with Screen Entertainment Co. Executive Producer: Bill Sargent. Producer: Lee Savin. Director: Steve Binder. Musical Director: Jack Nitzche. Running Time: 110 minutes. (Current prints run approximately 90minutes). Performers: The Beach Boys, Chuck Berry, James Brown and the Flames, The Barbarians, Marvin Gaye, Gerry and The Pacemakers, Lesley Gore, Jan and Dean, Billy J. Kramer and The Dakotas, Smokey Robinson and The Miracles, The Supremes, The Rolling Stones.

This was the legendary live concert featuring everybody who was anybody (except, of course, The Beatles) in 1964. The show was performed on October 28 and 29 at Santa Monica Civic Auditorium in front of thousands of screaming fans and three television cameras. The televised image was transferred via Electronovision to motion picture film and rushed into theatres before the end of the year.

The Beach Boys were lost in the shuffle among the eleven other acts. They appeared, did a few of their recent hits, disappeared, and then emerged again briefly during the closing jam. Their straight-forward stage act was easily eclipsed by veteran show stopper James Brown, and the dynamic presence of The Rolling Stones.

Current prints of the film have the Beach Boys sequence removed. Why?

An abbreviated version of the film was shown on a Dick Clark WIDE WORLD OF ENTERTAINMENT television special in 1974 to commemorate the tenth anniversary of the event.

THE GIRLS ON THE BEACH (Paramount Pictures) with the Beach Boys, and featuring The Crickets and Lesley Gore too...

"THE MONKEY'S UNCLE" 1965. Released by Buena Vista. A Walt Disney Production. Co-Producer: Ron Miller. Director: Robert Stevenson. Screenplay: Tom and Helen August. Technicolor. Running time: 87 minutes. Cast: Tommy Kirk, Annette Funicello, Leon Ames, Frank Faylen, Arthur O'Connel, The Beach Boys.

An obvious ploy by the Disney organization to lure teenagers into seeing this moronic comedy. The Beach Boys appear briefly over the opening credits, doing background vocals and performing on their instruments as Annette sang the title song.

The Monkey's Uncle, a real lame number written by Richard and Robert Sherman, was released on Vista records in 1965. The Beach Boys are not listed on the label, but their voices and instruments are unmistakable. Only hardcore fanatics should search for a copy.

―――――――― O ――――――――

"THE GIRLS ON THE BEACH" 1965. Released by Paramount Pictures. Producer: Harvey Jacobson. Director: William N. Witney. Screenplay: David Malcolm. Eastman Color. Running time: 80 minutes. Cast: Martin West, Noreen Corcoran, Peter Brooks, The Beach Boys, Lesley Gore, The Crickets.

In the summer of '65, Paramount released this lackluster teenage comedy in response to A.I.P.'s tremendously successful "Beach Party" series. The only bright spots in the film were the musical sequences which were few and far between.

The title song, available on the ALL SUMMER LONG album, is a pleasant ballad in the *Surfer Girl* tradition. It was better than the film deserved.

It looks like Warren Oates is giving both Dennis Wilson and James Taylor a hard time of it in Universal's TWO-LANE BLACKTOP...

MAGAZINE

MAGAZINE

Dennis Wilson and James Taylor as street racers in Universal's "Two-Lane Blacktop" …

MAGAZINE

Brian Wilson — Born June 20, 1942

MAGAZINE

MAGAZINE

by Heather Johnson...

THE KID

"My family had a lot to do with my early musical life," says Carl Wilson, youngest of the Wilson brothers, and the first bonafide musician of the group.

"During Christmas we would usually gather around the piano and sing carols. My mother, Audree, is a good piano player, and my father, Murry, had already written quite a few songs. They were definitely a big influence on my music."

Carl was just 14 when the Beach Boys began recording, but he had already sufficiently mastered the guitar to become the group's lead guitarist. Though he'd found formal instruction depressing, he had pursued the guitar on his own with the help of John Maus, who went on to become a superstar in England as one of the Walker Brothers. Deriving his style largely from Chuck Berry, Carl's guitar arrangements provided the backbone of the early Beach Boys hits, while his own style of vocalizing on numbers like *Girl Don't Tell Me* added the distinctive Beach Boys touch.

Carl's musical background also enabled him to assume the role of producer in brother Brian's absence on such Beach Boys albums as IN CONCERT and HOLLAND. His original compositions have included *Long Promised Road, Feel Flows,* and *The Trader.*

Carl first attracted national attention during the war in Vietnam, when he refused to be inducted for military service. He was subsequently arrested by the FBI and took his case into court, risking a prison sentence and finally being granted Conscientious Objector status. His alternate civilian service in this capacity included a number of charity benefit performances, and the rest of the Beach Boys participated with him in these endeavors.

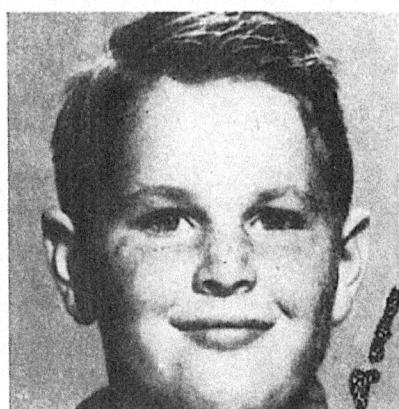

Carl at 8 years of age...

Currently, Carl shares production chores with brother Dennis at the Beach Boys' Brother Studios in Santa Monica, California. His latest recording project is the first album of Ricci Martin, singer Dean Martin's youngest son. Coincidentally, his collaborator on this production is his brother-in-law Billy Hinsche, formerly the drummer of Dino, Desi and Billy. Dino, of course, was Dean Martin, Jr.

Like his fellow Beach Boys, Carl was initiated into Transcendental Meditation in 1967 and calls the experience "a real blessing." More recently, he became a graduate of Werner Erhard's EST training. "It has added a lot to my life for which I am really grateful," he says, recommending both EST and Transcendental Meditation very highly.

Carl, his wife Annie (to whom he has been married ten years), and their two sons Jonah and Justyn make their home in LA's Coldwater Canyon. Their summers, however, they spend in a rented villa on Trancas Beach, still enjoying that seemingly endless summer surf.

In the near future Carl hopes to undertake formal training in orchestration, leaving one to speculate as to the next direction his always expanding musical abilities will take him. ●

BROTHER

MAGAZINE

Mike Love!
Born March 15, 1941

MAGAZINE

SUSIE CINCINNATI WHEELS TO WAX!

by Joseph Posche

 Mike and Al, who was charmed by the real "Susie Cincinnati"......

Arriving in Cincinnati, Ohio, one late September a.m. in 1971, Beach Boys Carl and Dennis Wilson, and Al Jardine stepped into a taxicab at Greater Cincinnati Airport. They were headed for a concert date that evening.

En route to their hotel, Al struck up a conversation with their driver, a thirtyish lady he'd remember as Susie, but whose name was actually Joellyn Lambert. He was so taken by her outgoing personality, and fun-to-be-with air, that he forthwith made her the subject of a song: "Susie Cincinnati's got a groovy little motor car; she lives for the night and her husband's a security guard."

The lyrics, while not 100% biographical (at one point they tell of Susie exterminating her passengers in the throes of a "nicotine fit," while the real "Susie" has never smoked), seemed to fit the lady and the song, and *Susie Cincinnati* was duly recorded upon the Beach Boys' return to California.

The song failed to appear on record, however, until December of 1974, when it turned up as the "B" side of the Beach Boys' Christmas offering, *Child of Winter*. Unfortunately, *Child* arrived a bit too late to fully capitalize on the seasonal market, and *Susie Cincinnati* remained in obscurity until this past year, when it was resurrected for inclusion on the album FIFTEEN BIG ONES and slated to follow *Rock 'n' Roll Music* (a revamping of the Chuck Berry classic) as the next Beach Boys single release.

Seeing a concert date at Cincinnati's Riverfront Coliseum in the offing, the Beach Boys decided to try and locate the bouncy lady who'd inspired the song. They bought newspaper advertisements to announce the search for *Susie Cincinnati,* and finally through Brad Balfour of the Cincinnati Post, Susie/Joellyn was located in Newport, Ohio, now in her early forties and a mother of seven. Her husband, it was further discovered, was in a hospital facing critical cancer surgery, and this news moved the Beach Boys to establish a fund to pick up the whopping hospital bills the Lambert family was accumulating.

So, on the morning of November 22, 1976, Joellyn "Susie Cincinnati" Lambert met the Beach Boys at the airport once again. This time, however, *they* gave *her* a lift — to their evening's concert, where she appeared as their onstage guest.

Even if her name isn't really Susie, in the words of Al Jardine's song, *Susie Cincinnati* is a winner. And so, incidentally, is the song. ●

CARL

MAGAZINE

Along with Gary Usher and Roger Christian, Brian Wilson wrote the theme for MUSCLE BEACH PARTY, the second of American International Pictures' highly successful "Beach Party" series. A version of the theme, sung by Frankie Avalon, is available on U.A.'s GOLDEN SUMMER album...

MAGAZINE

AL JARDINE:

— Born September 3, 1942

ohio to big sur on a wave

MAGAZINE

Al & Mike on stage appearing before 58,000 people at the Anaheim Stadium in California. The concert was filmed & included in NBC-TV's special, THE BEACH BOYS.....

by Alan Arsan

Al Jardine, on-stage rhythm guitarist and vocalist of the Beach Boys, is the only member of the group who is not a native Californian.

Born in landlocked, Lima, Ohio, he moved with his family to Hawthorne, California, where he found himself playing fullback for the Hawthorne High Cougars. Recovering from a broken leg, the result of quarterback Brian Wilson's fumbled pitch-out, he filled the time on his hands harmonizing with Wilson and his brothers. From this backyard beginning, the Pendletones were born.

It was Al who first found someone interested enough in the group to record them at Candix Records. Al's musical roots were primarily in folk music, and the Hootenanny craze was in full swing. The company assumed, logically enough, that they had a budding Kingston Trio on their hands. *Surfin'*, the group's first record, of course, proved otherwise, but it also proved successful. And recording companies have never been known to quibble over success.

It was also Al's folksy background which later led to such Beach Boys hits as their inimitable renditions of *Sloop John B.* and *Cottonfields* during the mid-60's "folk-rock" era. His less-than-reverent version of Bob Dylan's *The Times They Are A-Changing* on the BEACH BOYS' PARTY album is definitely among the "camp" classics of rock 'n' roll.

Also being an ardent fan and collector of early rhythm and blues records, Al's knowledge has proved especially useful in the selection of oldies the Beach Boys have recorded through the years, particularly in the assortment chosen for their latest album FIFTEEN BIG ONES. His original compositions for the group have been many, among them *Looking At Tomorrow* from the SURF'S UP album, five of the songs on their FRIENDS album, and their latest single, *Susie Cincinnati.*

Today, at 33, Al is something of a political activist, lobbying for conservation legislation and keeping his congressmen informed on matters ecological. He and his wife Lynda reside on a spacious ranch in California's Big Sur, where the Arabian horses they raise share their barn with his rustically-styled recording studio. His current lifestyle, he explains, reflects his rejection of the more worldly values of Southern California, though he still makes the drive to LA to rehearse and record with the Beach Boys.

Having settled down, Al has naturally developed a distaste for touring and its myriad demands. His first concern, the raising of his two sons, Matthew and Adam, is at home. The Beach Boys, however, he sees as a larger concern than those of any one of its members, and he fully intends to continue actively contributing to their success.

Al sees no sort of breakup in the offing, so it looks like we'll be seeing Alan Jardine belting out tunes like *Help Me Rhonda* along with them. ●

MAGAZINE

MIKE LOVE: A Sung Hero

MAGAZINE

Blastin' out with "Rock & Roll Music", a Chuck Berry number....

By John Martin

Mike Love, the Wilson brothers' cousin and co-founder of the Beach Boys, has only recently begun to attract the notice of the press through his proselytizing of Transcendental Meditation and Werner Erhard's EST sensitivity training program.

This attention is long overdue, for Mike Love, in his own way, is as nearly responsible for the success of the Beach Boys as leader Brian Wilson.

From the beginning, Mike was the lyricist of most of their hit songs, with the lyrics to such early Beach Boys classics as *Surfin' Safari* and *Fun Fun Fun* among his many credits. And, more often than not, it was Mike's peculiarly appealing nasal twang carrying the lead vocals of these same Top Ten winners.

Lyrics seem to come naturally to Mike, who recalls writing the words to the Beach Boys monumental *Good Vibrations* in ten minutes while barrelling down the Hollywood freeway en route to the recording session.

The most commercially-minded of the group (for which he came under some heavy criticism during the "revolutionary" sixties), Mike managed the Beach Boys' business affairs during their early years, later turning these matters over to his brother Steve. His greatest abilities, apart from those of lyricist, however, were displayed in the Beach Boys' live concert performances. The appearance of Mike Love onstage invariably brought the audience to its feet as he took command of the show. As the group's unofficial master of ceremonies he projected a personality that would make Johnny Carson take notice, and his renditions of such novelty numbers as *I'm A Long Tall Texan*, and Bobby Pickett's *The Monster Mash*, never failed to bring the house down.

In short, Mike Love is a showman, and, "serious" music critics aside, Rock 'n' roll is definitely "show-biz."

With Mike at the helm, the Beach Boys' show went on in fine form.

Now, at 35, he spends most of his time off the road in a house on a bluff in Santa Barbara, California, overlooking one of the area's surfing beaches, where he lives with his fiancee Sue Oliver. Mike having been through three unhappy marriages, he and Sue are proceeding cautiously with their engagement, setting a tentative wedding date for sometime in 1978.

For all of the carefree, good-timey lyrics he has contributed to the Beach Boys' repertoire, Mike maintains a surprisingly austere personal regimen of regular meditation and a vegetarian diet. The Beach Boys met the Maharishi Mahesh Yogi in Paris, where they did a United Nations show in 1967, and Mike and fellow-Beach Boy Al Jardine both became certified instructors in Transcendental Meditation shortly thereafter. Mike has since set up a non-profit foundation for the study and teaching of the art.

"Any group is only as strong as its members," he explains. "I don't think I'd be in the group if it wasn't for meditation. It raises your tolerance for tension and stress. It helps against the fatiguing effects of physical and mental activity."

When it comes to physical and mental activity, Mike Love has contributed more than his share of both to the Beach Boys, and with Mike on the scene, there is no doubt that the Beach Boys' show will go on, as energetically as ever. ●

MAGAZINE

SURF CITY, HERE WE COME...
Or, Striped Shirts Do Not a Beach Boy Make...

by Alan Arsan

"Two girls for every boy..." A most alluring prospect indeed.

Legend has it that Jan Berry and Dean Torrence were visiting the Wilson household when Brian played them *Surfin' USA* on the piano. Their request to record the song was flatly refused, Brian insisting that it was already earmarked for the Beach Boys. Instead, he offered them *Surf City*, which they readily accepted and went right to the Number One spot on the national charts with. *Surfin' USA* came in a close runner-up.

Berry and Torrence, who'd been recording since 1957 (beginning as Jan and Arnie, while Dean completed his military service), had already racked up an impressive record of hits with numbers like *Baby Talk, Heart and Soul,* and *Linda;* light pop ditties featuring the high falsettos and nonsense syllables (un-dut-dit-wa-wa-wa, etc.) in the background vocals that were later to coalesce in the Beach Boys "surfin' sound.' So it was only natural that they, too, would try to catch the wave of the surfing-hot rod musical vogue — and catch it they did, with a vengeance.

Jan and Dean enjoyed a two-year winning streak with such top ten winners as *Drag City, Ride The Wild Surf* (both co-authored by Brian Wilson), *Little Old Lady From Pasadena,* and *Sidewalk Surfin',* cashing in on the inland psuedo-surf fad for skateboarding.

Dead Man's Curve, their elaborately recorded admonition to street drag-racers ("You won't come back from Dead Man's Curve..." wailing over sounds of skidding tires, shattering glass, etc.), proved tragically prophetic: Jan Berry suffered severe brain damage in an auto collision two years later at almost the very spot they'd warned against, and his memory has never been completely regained.

The memory of Jan and Dean lingers on, however, as their records continue to receive frequent AM airplay, and they also make occasional television appearances. Both Jan and Dean were on hand for Dick Clark's special telescreening of THE T.A.M.I. SHOW, a filmed

The Beach Boys at the height of their first popularity in the sixties, sporting the famous striped shirts....

MAGAZINE

concert they hosted in 1964 at the Santa Monica Civic Auditorium; a show which, incidentally, included a performance by a group called the Beach Boys.

A compilation album commemorating their years as Jan and Dean is in current release.

Jan and Dean were not the only ones to ride the musical surf, of course, and even the Beach Boys had their predecessors. Although limited primarily to instrumentals, Dick Dale and his Deltones had already laid the foundation for the "surfin' sound" with such Southern California hits as *Misirlou* and *Let's Go Trippin'* (copping three spots on LA's Top Ten at the height of his popularity) when the Beach Boys began recording. The Beach Boys themselves dutifully acknowledged Dale's parentage, including his biggest hits in their own recording and performing repertoire.

Although Dale failed to make any impact nationally (in spite of hundreds of thousands of dollars worth of promotion by Capitol Records), such subsequent instrumentals as the Chantay's 1963 *Pipeline* and the Surfari's *Wipe Out* carried the fast picking, strong bass lines, and rapid-fire drumming of the Dick Dale style into the national charts.

Vocally, however, there were few chart-making efforts that did not directly involve one or more of the Beach Boys (usually Brian) and/or their close friends and associates in the recording business. Notable exceptions were Tommy James and the Shondells' *Hanky Panky*, which, though recorded in 1964, was not nationally released until two years later, and the Riviera's *California Sun*.

The Hondells' *Little Honda* was Brian Wilson's composition (which the Beach Boys included on their 1964 extended play 45-rpm release), and the Rip Chords' *Hey Little Cobra* and *Three Window Coupe* were the work of Brian's close friends Terry Melcher and Bruce Johnstone (who later joined the Beach Boys as Brian's stand in).

Other groups and records were produced, with varying degrees of local and national success, but rarely did anyone outside the Southern California base reach the charts — and those that did, like the Tradewinds' *New York's A Lonely Town (When You're The Only Surfer Boy Around)*, invariably faded quickly.

The last real attempt to capitalize on the Beach Boys sound was a group called the Sunrays. Managed by Beach Boys father Murry Wilson, the Sunrays copied not only the Beach Boys sound, but their green and white striped shirts as well. After two hit singles, *Andria* and *I Live For The Sun*, however, it became obvious that striped shirts do not a Beach Boy make; in fact, the Beach Boys had long since doffed their striped shirt uniforms in favor of more casual dress on stage.

As always, anything the imitators could do, the originals could do better, and image aside, the Beach Boys are one of a kind. ●

MAGAZINE

AMERICAN DREAM From Page 9

This musical tug-of-war with the English invaders reached its zenith with the Beach Boys' appearance on CBS' ED SULLIVAN SHOW. Determined to meet the Beatles on their own field of conquest, they'd offered to perform gratis.

Early in 1965 the Beach Boys suffered their first real setback when leader Brian succumbed to the excessive pressures of writing, producing, and touring with the group. Forced by nervous exhaustion to retire from live performing, he was replaced on the road by Glenn Campbell, and later, Bruce Johnstone. These two proved to be more than adequate on-stage stand-ins, however, and with Brian free to devote all of his energies to writing and producing, the Beach Boys continued to be a sell-out attraction in concert, and steady sellers in the record bins.

1966, however, saw still more radical changes in the pop world; changes that were to have an even more decisive effect on the Beach Boys' career than the advent of the British rockers.

The Beatles' RUBBER SOUL, released in December 1965, set a new milestone in recording history, signalling the end of the "anthology," or "latest hits" type of pop music album. The Beatles presented, for the first time, a package of all-new songs carefully arranged to make a single musical "statement," or "concept." In the future, single hit records would be chosen from such total productions, rather than being produced individually for eventual album collections.

The Beach Boys' answer to this latest challenge was PET SOUNDS, their most ambitious project to date, and Brian Wilson's masterpiece. A splendid production and easily the equal of the Beatles' RUBBER SOUL entry, it was critically acclaimed a success. Sales however, for the first time in their career, failed to meet expectations, and, in spite of the Top Ten status of the single cut, **Wouldn't It Be Nice,** PET SOUNDS presaged a time of declining fortunes and commercial failures for the Beach Boys.

in concert...

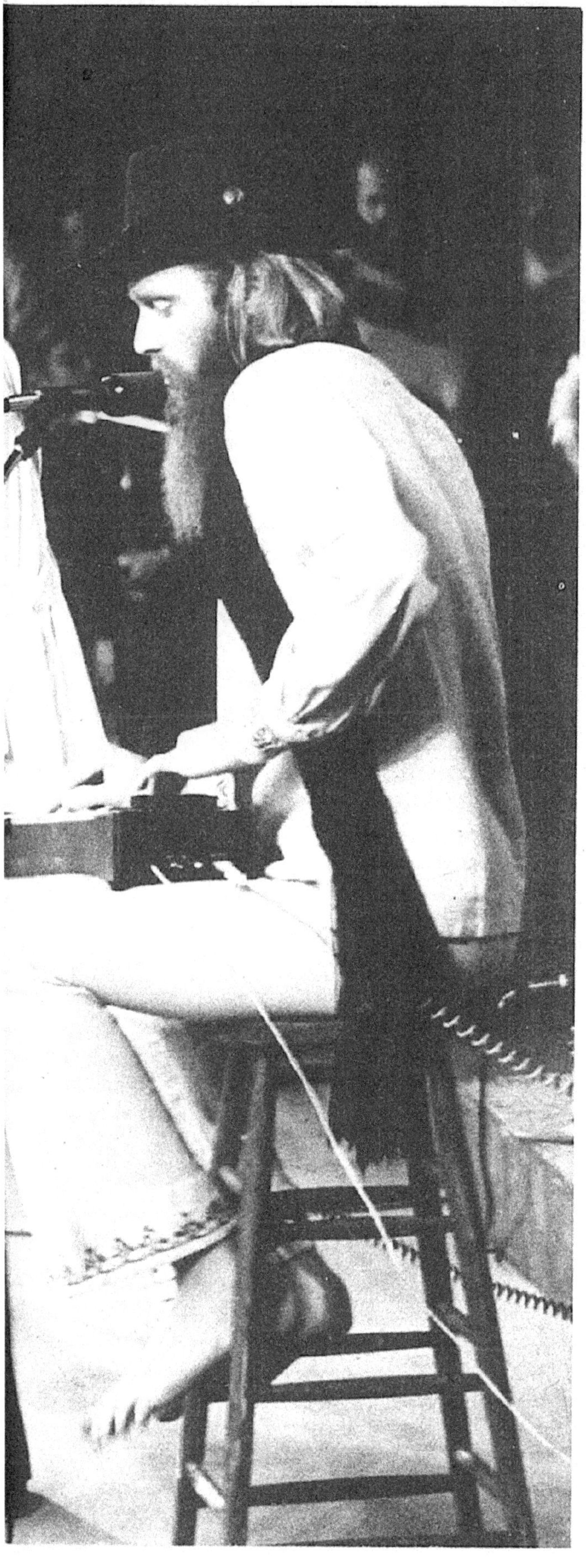

MAGAZINE

Good Vibrations, their next single release, was the monumental exception. A full six months in the making, it was unlike anything the group had produced in the past, yet it was unmistakably the Beach Boys. It stands as one of the most positive musical statements to come out of the confusion of those mid-60's years and the subsequent blossoming of the psychedelic subculture. **Good Vibrations** went straight to the top of the charts worldwide, becoming the Beach Boys' first million seller and netting them the Number One spot on England's NEW MUSICAL EXPRESS poll for Best World Group of 1966. It remains their largest selling record to date.

Sadly, **Good Vibrations** proved an insurmountable triumph, and Brian Wilson's preoccupation with attempts at surpassing it are legendary. SMILE, his magnum opus, never got beyond the studio, and many tracks (not to mention thousands of dollars) were scrapped in the effort. Songs that did surface, like **Heroes and Villains,** though consistently praised by the critics, met with the same lukewarm reaction from the public as PET SOUNDS, and succeeding albums, owing to Brian's gradual near-withdrawal from the group (Bruce Johnstone now became his studio stand-in as well), were disappointingly uneven products.

Although Brian Wilson compositions, in decreasing numbers, continued to appear on Beach Boys albums, the group found itself depending increasingly on their own resources and those of outside collaborators like Van Dyke Parks. Production chores fell to Carl and Dennis, and Blondie Chaplin took Bruce Johnstone's place.

MAGAZINE

The Beach Boys persevered nonetheless, continuing to play live concerts to sell-out stadiums and releasing albums (now through Warner Brothers' Reprise Records) like SUNFLOWER, SURF'S UP, and HOLLAND. This latter album, recorded in 1973 over six months in the country for which it was named, was probably their strongest production during this period. Ambitious in the same way as PET SOUNDS, though more in step with its times, it featured material like the three-part **California Saga** (the joint effort of Mike, Al and Lynda Jardine, and poet Robinson Jeffers), and centered on themes of ecology and mysticism — a not illogical progression from their "surf music" bases.

If nothing else, HOLLAND served as evidence that the Beach Boys, unlike the splintering Beatles, still had ground to cover.

Any doubts that may have existed regarding the Beach Boys' future were cast aside when ENDLESS SUMMER and SPIRIT OF AMERICA, two Capitol Records repackagings of their early hits, went platinum (one million copies of each sold) in '74 and '75. The record buyers' dollars were not to be quarrelled with: the Beach Boys were as viable a commodity on the pop music market as ever.

1976 marked America's Bicentennial, and, in pasing, the fifteenth anniversary of the Beach Boys as well. Fittingly, it also marked the return of Brian Wilson to the recording studios and an active role in the group. The result, FIFTEEN BIG ONES, is an appropriate mixture of favorite oldies like Fats Domino's **Blueberry Hill** and Freddie Cannon's **Palisades Park,** and new Beach Boys material like Brian's **Back Home, That Same Song,** and Mike Love's **Everyone's In Love With You.**

Their version of Chuck Berry's **Rock 'n' Roll Music,** from the album, has already graced the pop singles charts, and Al Jardin's **Susie Cincinnati** has followed it.

Asked by a reporter what the new album would sound like, Carl Wilson simply shrugged and replied, "It'll sound like us. It'll sound like the Beach Boys."

And with fifteen years as an American institution behind them, nothing further about the Beach Boys, and their music, need to be said. ●

MAGAZINE

MIKE

MAGAZINE

CALIFORNIA SAGA From Page 22

American Dream, circa 1965...

MAGAZINE

In the wake of an incredible era of musical and cultural advances, everything stopped, and we entered the decade of "nostalgia".

The first artist to make a dramatic come back was Elvis. At the lowest ebb of his career, due mainly to listless recording material and a series of awful movies, Presley made a phenomenal return as a live entertainer. Soon other artists from bygone days like Rick Nelson, Dion, Neil Sedaka, and Paul Anka began hitting the charts with new material. Veteran performers like Chuck Berry, Bill Haley, and Little Richard enjoyed popularity with a new generation at rock "revival" shows. Multi-album sets of original "oldies" were advertised on television and sold through the mall.

It wasn't until 1974 that the nostalgia craze caught up with the Beach Boys. They had been plodding along with Reprise Records, creating albums of varying quality. One very good album, HOLLAND, even gave them a moderate hit with **Sail On Sailor**. Then suddenly Capitol came out with ENDLESS SUMMER, a repackaging of the Beach Boys' greatest hits from the 1962-1966 period. The two-album set was given saturation television advertising and became one of the best selling albums of the year.

Continued on page 70

SAGA From Page 65

Now, all at once, it was all right to like the Beach Boys again. Their Reprise albums received a boost in sales. Their concerts were filled with fans who brought down the house on the first chords of **Fun, Fun Fun.** Another repackaging from Capitol, SPIRIT OF AMERICA, was almost as successful as the first. The Beach Boys were back.

Well, not quite. Their old stuff was going over well, but their recent material still wasn't clicking. Fans waited for their next studio album. It was a long wait.

In the summer of '76 (how fitting), proceeded by numerous rumors and a lot of hype, 15 BIG ONES was finally released. It was somewhat disappointing. The new songs weren't exactly what was hoped for and half the album was filled with lackluster cover versions of other people's "oldies".

Still, Brian is back taking an active participation in the group's efforts, and maybe the Beach Boys can **Do It Again.** ●

MAGAZINE

THE BEACH BOYS ARE BACK!

An interview with Mike Love
by MIKE DRIPS

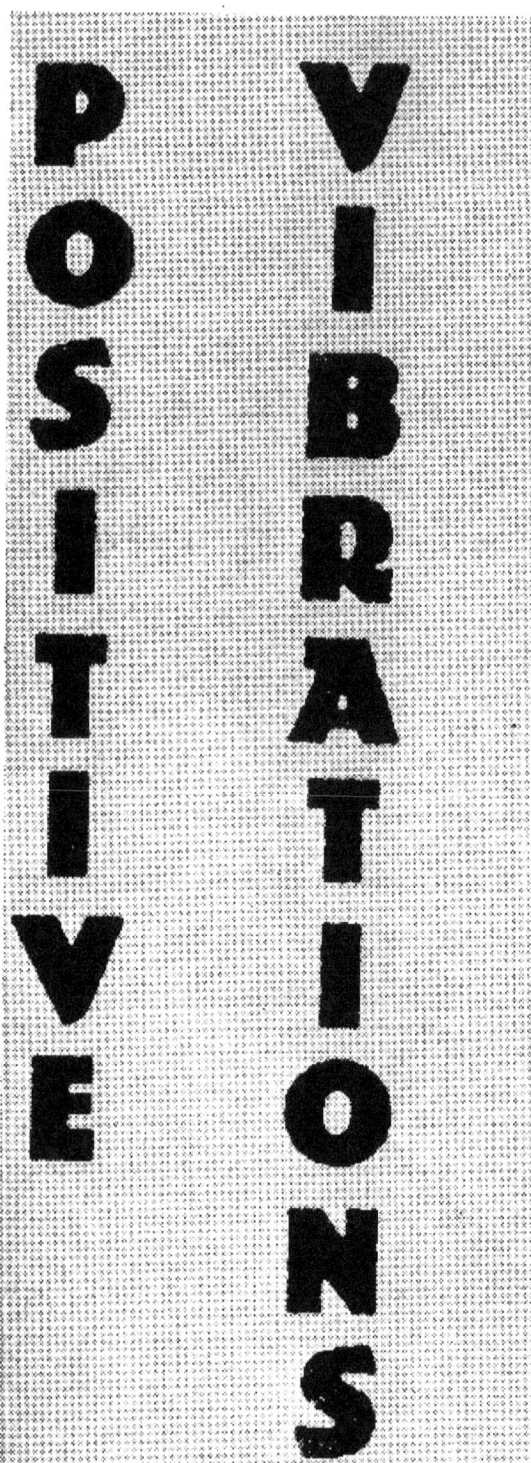

MD: What have the Beach Boys done politically since their performance at the Mayday demonstration?

ML: Just before that time, we had done a Berrigan brothers benefit in Syracuse. We never really did any political type of things except for voter registration; we didn't take a one-sided approach to anything, you know? We encouraged people's involvement in their local and national leaders and politics and so on, but we haven't gotten into campaigning for particular candidates or anything like that, as a group. Mainly because--like any group--each person in the group is likely to have a little different idea of what should go on. So we've just kind of steered clear of that, although we've been very positive about people, trying to erode some of the apathy, you know? So that's about it in terms of political involvement, not in politics per se, but in general atmosphere of being a part of what's going on. That sounds like an answer a politician would give.

MD: Are you considering being a politician sometime?

ML: Never. No, because I think a politician's job is one of the world's worst. By the nature of your job, you have to represent everyone, all of your constituency, and these days the constituency has too many freaks and weirdos and crazies, you know? So I'm not going for that job at all. I like being in the music business; you get to express yourself just the way you feel like, in a nice way that doesn't hurt anybody.

MD: One of the members of the group was quoted as saying, "The Beach Boys will be the group of the Seventies," could you qualify that statement? Do you agree with that?

ML: As far as American groups go, and rock groups and vocal groups, the Beach Boys would probably have to be recognized as being right up there in the running for top honors, just because of the amount of albums we've done, and the critical reviews of our music have always been favorable, you know? I made a statement sometime ago, saying the Beach Boys for the Bicentenial would be the American band. I think that's where it derives from, and I think I said that mainly because our whole track record has been pretty much, uh, we started out singing songs about teenage favorite pastimes and things of ours, and then we grew to where it broadened a little bit, things got more introspective, and we went through a lot of changes everybody else did, always redefining our production and our harmonies and everything. Basically I think, all around the world, like in London, England, we were voted the best group in the world over the Beatles and the Stones, even at like during the late Sixties, when the Beatles and the Stones weren't exactly cold, and so as far as worldwide recognition goes, we stand a chance of being recognized as the American group. You know, by virtue of the fact that we're going into this second decade of music, and we are, if anything, broader-based and more strongly accepted and well-liked than ever before, if record sales and concert sales are my judge.

MD: How do you feel about all these reissues of your old songs by Capitol?

ML: Well, that's kind of a thing where it doesn't do any good to get bugged about it, because they have the contractual right to do those things.

MD: You don't have any control over them doing that then?

ML: Not really. What we did in the case of the **Endless Summer** album last year--which did real well, sold a million and a half copies or so--when I heard they were going to put out an album like, I tried to give them the concept of **Endless Summer**, I tried to work with them on the song selection so it would be more representative of an anthology kind of thing, trying to put in a few songs that maybe

MAGAZINE

weren't number one hits, but were indicative of our abilities on a broad scope musically. So I think as far as creatively, it wasn't a hundred percent what I would have liked to have seen it been, but then it wasn't a hundred percent tacky, either. So I think that on the commercial success side, if you're in the business of recording and selling records and making personal appearances, you can't get too pissed off about an album that goes platinum, you know?

MD: Right. I can understand that completely. I just thought maybe some of the members of the group were kind of irritated that they would haul out old material. I didn't know if you guys were happy or upset or what.

ML: The thing is, that the Beach Boys, we've always had real good success with those songs and people like to hear them, and we have real positive and fond associations, so to speak, with those songs that were number one records of the 1960's. It's not like some artists who get all bummed out about their past or whatever, and they don't like to play their records, thinking that infringes upon their present or something, it's not a true expression of where their heads are at now. Although our heads may not be into surfing, the musical expression and the joy, or the positivity and the fun inherent in a song like "Surfing USA," or "Catch A Wave," or "Surfer Girl" is just as real and positive and uplifting now as it was then. It holds a lot of good feelings for a lot of people, so we enjoy playing them, I enjoy playing them.

MD: Is this twelve-city tour, the only one you plan to do this year?

ML: No, no. We have already done one in the south on our own, and we're gonna do a couple more tours, like one in late August, and a small one in July. We'll probably go out in October, November, and December for a few days each, you know? We'll go to the east coast, we'll do the west coast, and we'll do some, say a college tour in October or something, you know, homecomings and all, so this is by no means our only tour, but it's a very unique tour in that we're combining forces with Chicago, and it's really gonna be powerful, if the rehearsals are any indication of what's gonna go on.

MD: What do you do the other 300-odd days a year when you're not out on tour?

ML: Well, I teach transcendental meditation sometimes. I've been meditating for seven years, twice a day, and for instance, this January, we just went to Hawaii and played there on the fourth, went there a few days early, and I stayed there for five weeks all told, then we came back to the mainland and went to Switzerland for a month to attend a, what's called an SCI course, the science of creative intelligence, which is a course given by Mahareshi International University. It teaches a person the theoretical aspects of what goes on when you meditate, when you do transcendental meditation. So once a year, I usually go to a course of that nature, where I can meditate a couple extra times a day, and watch video tapes on different fields of knowledge, like physics, and all these different kinds of mechanics of nature that are inside the mind and body. This helps to give me deeper rest, and expand my own creative environment, you know, creative processes and everything. Other than that, like when I'm home, I do a lot of sitting on my porch over the Pacific Ocean, up by Santa Barbara, and I meditate there, and I maybe write songs or make phone calls to do either interviews or to the office, you know, odds and ends kind of things. I like to live a pretty quiet life when we're off touring and all that, because what with touring and recording, you know, that's a lot of involvement for me, indoors kind of musical involvement. I like to get outdoors and I like to be quiet mostly, and I like to read and meditate, things like that.

MD: Do you have a new album planned?

ML: We have an album project underway. It's been quite some time since we've been able to get into the studio, let alone enough time to get serious about a project. The last couple of years we've really been touring a lot and also the repackage album. **Endless**

Mike Love, TM teacher and vocalist.

Photo by Vince Rowe

> "We always have a good time singing about prett
> musical and life's philosophy, to sing about thing

Summer, by Capitol, and then this one this April, called **Spirit of America**, it just came out, and just went gold, and then in a month or so, Warner Brothers is coming out with a similar-type package, dealing with the material that's from say, **Pet Sounds**, you know, "Good Vibrations," and "Heroes and Villains," and "Sloop John B." and "Darlin'," and "Sail On Sailor" from **Surf's Up**. They're coming out with another album of that kind in another month, and so really rather than conflict with those kind of reissues, they're doing very well, it seems like. Now a lot of people who are now concert-goers and record buyers are appreciating the Beach Boys probably for the first time in their lives, it's not like a nostalgia thing, so for all purposes, it's a brand new audience, and we've got a double audience--those who knew us before, and those who are just getting to know us through the mass exposure of touring and so on. We haven't really given ourselves enough time in the studio, and yet we've all been writing. There are five of us that have songs to offer to the next album project. I have maybe ten or fifteen songs, Dennis has several, and Alan, and so does Brian. An interesting thing is, what with this collaboration with Chicago on the tour, there's been some talk of getting together and interacting on some

MAGAZINE

Carl Wilson, prime source for Beach Boy original material.
Photo by Vince Rowe

"...much positive things...and that's always been our ...that are positive, fun, uplifting, and harmonious."

songs, so maybe an album will come out of that involvement. Which would be pretty interesting, because they bring a particular style of music to this musical merger--like the horn section obviously--and a lot of heavy percussion, and a particular style of guitar virtuosity and even lead singing that we don't have, but we have the melodic and harmonic expertise, and arrangement of voices to blend with them, and so it really makes quite a fullness when we get on stage, I think. There's some songs that we're doing with them that are really brand new when the two groups do them together.

MD: What's the most embarrassing thing you've ever done on stage?

ML: Well, a couple of times, my pants have ripped out, or something like that. One time in 1964, in Sacremento, I bent down to pick up a girl out of the audience, I did that, I used to do"The Monster Mash," I think I did that, and my pants ripped out. The girl was really heavy, too. My pants ripped out, and I think that was kind of weird. I don't know, I'm pretty much at ease on stage, I don't embarrass easily.

MD: Brian Wilson doesn't tour,...

ML: That's right. He hasn't for years. He's very shy and retiring, and he's very nice and everything. He's a very kind person, he wouldn't hurt a flea and all that, and also very talented musically, and very eccentric sometimes. He does some funny strange things, which I think are hilarious, but sometimes the press, the musical press, picks up on them and makes a field day out of it and all that. Like he had sand in his dining room and he used to play his piano and wiggle his toes in the sand, which sounded like a pretty good thing, until his cats found out about it, and then they had to cancel that program. He had a tent inside his house one time, he's done all kinds of strange things, but he just doesn't like to travel, so it's been that way for the majority of the group's career.

MD: Do you think the economy has affected your success much?

ML: Well, in a strange way, I think it has. The economy and the political and socially negative atmosphere, today, of war and strikes and layoffs and all the things that are wrong, political disappointments and things that have been going on the last couple of years, it seemed to only enhance our careers, for the simple reason that when you go to a Beach Boy show, it's an up. We always have a good time singing about pretty much positive things. The worst thing we'd sing about is maybe we lost our girlfriend or something, but even the loss of somebody you love, we sing a song about the warmth of the sun, right? Still you have the warmth of the sun, you still have the feeling of having loved somebody, so you can have a negative thing, or you can take a positive approach to something, and that's always been our musical and life's philosophy, to sing about things that are positive, fun, uplifting, and harmonious. For awhile there a few years ago, people had enough money to go to shows maybe three or four times a month, five or six times, who knows? They went to every concert coming in. Now they have less money it seems, and so they pick and choose, and when you have to choose, it becomes a survival of the fittest, and people just don't want to go and get bummed out, when it's their only concert of the month. So the Beach Boys, when we play, come through a place once, maybe twice a year at the most. We kind of represent a positive attitude towards life and a good time, and I think even like in the great depression of the 30's, as bad as things were, people flocked to the movies to forget their problems. TV's replaced that quite a bit, but still, people like to get out and nowadays the concert attractions, the musical concerts, the shows, are the big things to draw people out. So, because of our inherent musical and lifestyle philosophy kind of image, or whatever it is we reflect and sing about in our music, and however we actually live, we live a pretty positive life and everything, I think that's reflected into the audience, and people enjoy that. Our success has been going up and up and up, we get more popular everyday.

MD: Maybe you've been asked this many times, but which of your albums is your favorite, and which is your least favorite?

ML: Well, I think that's a very weird question to answer. Different songs are my favorite, for different reasons. Like "Good Vibrations" is a favorite single, because it's so unique and distinctive. "Fun, Fun, Fun" is one of the greatest roll-down-the-windows-and-cruise-to type songs ever recorded, I think, and I could say that the Carl & The Passions album is one of our weakest albums, but then it has one of my favorite songs on it, which is called "All This Is That." You can't hardly judge it, because each song has its own merits, and for different reasons, it may be your favorite.

MD: Right, because there've been different phases you guys have gone through.

ML: Right. I could say, "Well, that was a draggy phase," but on the other hand, it was a phase we went through, and it should be judged just on its merits, on what came out at the time. Similarly, you look at an artist, and you say, well, this is his blue period, and this is his other period, you know, instead of getting uptight and saying, well, that painting was only number ten and it didn't go to number one. I mean it's kind of stupid to look at things that way, and people are so commercially oriented, at least the music business and the radio business are, oriented toward what went over biggest, what sold the most, they're not oriented towards looking at the artist's music as a whole body of work, or something like that, which you can do with the Beach Boys, because you've got enough years and enough albums to gain some perspective.

MD: What do you expect to be doing when you're 60 years old? Still singing?

ML: No, I think that I'll be doing writing, both music and maybe books too, or movies or whatever. I have a flair for words, it seems. I wrote a 160 line poem in iambic septenarius, a couple of years ago. It just kind of flowed out, and it really surprised the hell out of me.

MD: Did you ever have it printed anywhere?

ML: No, I didn't, but I've got copies of it, and I'm just kind of holding onto it for awhile. I'd like to gain a little experience in doing some tv work, maybe some movie stuff, maybe doing a talk show someday, or a tv special series, something that interests me.

MD: What do you think of quadrophonic sound? Have you oriented any material towards that?

ML: Yeah, as a matter of fact, our Sunflower album of about three or four years ago, was quadrophonic. It had a couple of quadrophonic tunes on it, and then Surf's Up was like that too, so we've had quadrophonic oriented albums and stuff. I don't think the switchover to that has taken place too swiftly because it's been a bad time economically to do that, but we've been ready for that for years. We've always been up there in the foreground of whatever changes were going down from a technical point of view.

MD: Do you consider yourself an artist, a musician, an entertainer, or a combination of the three?

ML: I'm not much of a musician, because I don't play hardly any instruments, just a little bit of guitar, but I can understand notes and things like that, and I can sing, I can harmonize just about anything. From that point of view, I'm a musician, but an artist? I never did understand the use of that term in relating to this particular field of rock music, or any kind of singing. I relate to an artist as being somebody who paints. I think it's a pretentious title, but I do think of myself as being an entertainer, because I do enjoy being on stage. I do enjoy that activity of pleasing a crowd, and performing as best I can. So I'm a performer, an entertainer, and somewhat of a musician, mostly a writer of songs and a teacher of transcendental meditation.

MD: Do you have much social contact with other performers and people in the industry? Do you guys usually associate with other members of the group?

ML: Well, we spend so much time together. We live in separate houses, have separate rooms on the road, and we have our separate lifestyles and interests. We do a tremendous amount of work together on stage and in the studios and practicing and things like that, so when we're apart, we enjoy being apart, just as we enjoy being together. I myself don't do too much socializing within the music business, although I enjoy it when I happen to, I just don't seek it out.

MD: Is there a common goal the group is trying to meet?

ML: Just maintaining as high a degree of excellence and quality of our music as we can.

MD: Have you ever felt exploited in your career?

ML: Yes, of course, particularly by our former record company in earlier days. They didn't pay us what they should have, and they didn't pay Brian his producer's royalty. It was quite a drag for quite awhile. It made us think of quitting the business entirely, but then we felt that we still had a lot to say musically, and as people we didn't feel like going down under the oppression of the record company. They were trying to do a number on us, because we were coming to the end of our contract, and if they didn't promote us, we wouldn't sell, and if we didn't sell, we wouldn't be worth as much money to re-sign with. So instead of re-signing, we sued them and split. We've had our ups and downs with the business side of it, and of course because of the pressures of that, we're as subject to the normal pressures of life as anybody is, both as individuals, socially, family pressures, whatever, so we're not sacrosanct from those kind of things.

MD: The company you operate under now, is your own label, Brother Records, right?

ML: Yes, and we distribute through Warner Brothers.

MD: So you're pretty much free anymore as far as...

ML: Pretty much. There's still problems attached to it, but there are less problems than there were before. We're in a better position to deal with them, anyway.

MD: Do you think our society's fadishness has affected the nature of your music any? Like glitter groups...

ML: I don't think so. I think we've been mostly kind of insular, kind of separate and apart. We have our own style, and for instance, right through all those, the two or three years of the psychedelic trip, we never adopted that, mainly because our nervous systems didn't appreciate that too much, you know. It was born out of kind of a blues-dope-negativity kind of thing in a way--a lot of it-- and we were just into...you know, not the opposite of blues, but positivity and harmony which is the opposite of the heavy metal. So, although we appreciated several artists that did that thing well, we never contributed or partook in it ourselves because we just sort of maintain our kind of musical formula, our own kind of bag, and within that, there are a myriad of combinations to play with and experiment with. We just sort of made our own musical track record.

MD: How have you changed in the last two years? Or have you changed in the last two years?

ML: I don't know. I think in the last couple of years, we've gotten more wise to the ways of business, because we've been screwed up enough times now to learn not to attach too much vital importance to the ups and downs of things, and just to put out as best we can on stage and records and however it comes out. You know, don't be too hung up over the outcome, just do your best and all that. I think it's just been a process of planning for the future, and progressing after certain goals and not getting too hung up over past mistakes and the successes.

MD: I know you like your own brand of music, of course that's obvious, but how do you feel about jazz or rhythm and blues? Are there other areas of music like that, that you're into?

ML: Well, like areas of music, it's strange, I relate to people, you know, that make the music. I relate to individuals, and if I find an individual I like the way he expresses himself, the way he lives, or the way he or she, what they feel, or what they do, then I tend to listen to them a little closer, whereas I wouldn't go out of my way to hear somebody just because they played a type of music. Like I have a very good friend, Charles Lloyd, who plays jazz. Now if I didn't know the style of music, like the flute and sax, which is free-flowing, impressionistic kind of a thing, if I didn't know him, I probably would never listen to his kind of music. If I didn't know of certain other people, you know, I may not listen to their music only because I don't go out of my way to buy albums or turn the radio around, because I get so much music in my own occupation, but since I do know some of these people, I find it more interesting to get into where they're at, what they say, and what they feel, and all that, so I approach it, not so much from a musical standpoint always, as from a personal knowledge, or a social standpoint.

MIKE DRIPS is SunRise's Kansas City correspondent and Great Plains field representative. His material has appeared in Screw, Westport Trucker, and Green Groad.

ADS

PANHELL-IFC
Presents
A LOOK TO THE PAST AND AN I TO THE FUTURE
GREEK WEEK '67
APRIL 22-30
WEEK'S ACTIVITIES INCLUDE:

SAT:	8 p.m.	Beach Boys — Assembly Hall
SUN:	2 p.m.	Bridge Finals — 314A Union
MON:	5:30 p.m.	Faculty Dinner — Individual Houses
TUES:	6 p.m.	College Bowl — Union
WED:	5 p.m.	Exchange — Fraternity Park
	7:30 p.m.	House Mothers' Bridge — 275, 277, 279 Union
THURS:	6:30 p.m.	Largest Chapter Meeting — Assembly Hall
FRI:	8 p.m.	Peter, Paul, & Mary — Assembly Hall
SAT:	9 a.m.	Service Project — Downtown
	noon	Parade — Champaign-Urbana
	noon	Sports Car Rally — Streets & Roads
	1 p.m.	Illiolympics — Huff Fields
SUN:	1 p.m.	Awards Banquet — Illini Room C

The Beach Boys

Saturday, April 22
8:00 p.m.
Assembly Hall

Co-Sponsored by
Star Course
and
Greek Week

Tickets Available at
Illini Union and
Assembly Hall

Box Offices to University Students Only, two tickets per I.D.

$4.00, $3.00 and $2.00

ALBUM REVIEW

BEACH BOYS LOSE THEIR BOUNCE

ROCK MUSIC by TONY CATTERALL

15 BIG ONES, the Beach Boys, Brother/Reprise Records, distributed by WEA.

ALTHOUGH '15 Big Ones' represents a song for every year of the Beach Boys' existence it's neither a "best-of" nor a concept album written to trace their history. It's just another Beach Boys album.

Hold on a moment: what am I saying? It's the first "new" Beach Boys album in four years and marks the return to the studio, at least, of Brian Wilson, one of the few men who could elevate pop music into an art form.

And yet, when I first heard the opening 'Rock and Roll Music' (on the radio) I thought to myself, "What is this rubbish". It could have been because I was hardly expecting a new Beach Boys single, let alone that it'd be 'Rock and Roll Music', because it has grown on me.

But it'll never be one of my favourite versions of that song. And, with the exception of 'Blueberry Hill' and 'Talk to Me', that's the way I feel about the other pop classics on the album: 'Chapel of Love', 'Palisades Park', 'A Casual Look', 'In the Still of the Night' and 'Just Once in My Life'.

Brian Wilson can still create studio masterpieces, a full wall of sound (but now using synthesizers and electronic string ensemble) for guitars, pianos, harpsichords, flutes and saxes to bounce off or mingle with.

But his production of '15 Big Ones' has little of the lushness he put into, say, 'Pet Sounds'. He was one of the few producers who could be lush without being overblown.

He's still not overblown but on a song such as 'It's Okay' the "fun, fun, fun" in the "sun, sun, sun" is merely described, not suggested by the music.

Every other aspect of the Beach Boys sound is there, except the bubbling, joyous celebration of life in the overall sound. It's probably why I couldn't place 'Rock and Roll Music' when I first heard it.

It comes close to being recaptured in 'Everyone's in Love With You', 'Had to Phone Ya' and 'TM [Transcendental Meditation] Song' (marred by an amateurish "argument" to introduce it, to point up the benefits of meditation) but along with the rest they suffer from a predominantly droning sound in either vocals or music.

It's difficult to say that one song can make a whole album worthwhile but 'Blueberry Hill' will very likely find its way on to my "desert-island" tape eventually. Following a mournful saxophone opening with the first verse being sung (by Mike Love) over just bass and muffled percussion, with the rest of the backing (including delightful chimes) coming in on the first chorus isn't a new technique, but it works beautifully here.

Add the backing vocals being sometimes mixed so far down into the backing that at times I didn't know whether I was hearing them or just remembering the words to put to the music myself and you have a truly classic version of a classic song.

But although I really wanted to like the album overall. I mean, it is the Beach Boys — I think there'll always be something else in my library that's more persuasive when it comes to playing something just for pleasure.

T SHIRT, Loudon Wainwright III, Arista Records, distributed by EMI.

LOUDON WAINWRIGHT III is a satirist who's equally at home with a rapier or a bludgeon.

Something as pretentious and crass as the US Bicentennial gets the bludgeon in the opening 'Bicentennial' on 'T Shirt': "Hey America's having a birthday. Be 200 years old. Isn't that wonderful. You know it certainly is".

On the other side there's incisive social comment in 'Reciprocity': "If one of them should die, I suppose the other would cry. There would be tears of sorrow and great grief. Or else there would be tears of release and relief".

Or there's a combination of both in 'Wine with Dinner': "Drinks before dinner, And wine with dinner. And after-dinner drinks. Single-entendre, help me Rhonda, look for my cuff links".

And the gem of a satiric "defence" of New York in 'Talking Big Apple 75', which never the less ends, "Ah, but it's not boring".

But Wainwright too often meanders into nothingness (especially in 'At Both Ends') or cheap shots ('California Prison Blues') and there's no musical consistency to the album.

MAGAZINE

AT THE SHORE

•• ATLANTIC AND OCEAN COUNTIES

CASINOS · DINING · MOVIES · NIGHTLIFE

FREE

WEEK OF APRIL 7, 1995

OLD NEWS

Huey Lewis and the News turn to old-time rock 'n' roll
Page 3

Life of Brian: Beach Boys hope for reunion with founder, Page 5

Movies: 'Bad Boys' packs a lot of action, Page 13

MAGAZINE

Fun-fun rumor: Wilson back with the Boys?

Reunited for their silver anniversary in 1987: from left, Bruce Johnston, Brian Wilson, Mike Love, Carl Wilson and Al Jardine. Will these five Beach Boys meet again at Resorts?

Amid reports from within the group that Brian Wilson might rejoin the band he helped create, the ageless Beach Boys kick off their annual summer tour at Merv Griffin's Resorts this Palm Sunday weekend.

The Beach Boys epitomize the sunny sounds of California rock 'n' roll — and with or without Brian — they will bring a string of hits to the casino showroom circuit.

While Huey Lewis & The News have been booked as a last-minute addition at the Trump Taj Mahal (*see story on Page 3*), a few more-traditional casino acts are on the boards of three other casinos. Saloon smoothie Vic Damone is at Trump Plaza. Comedian Alan King and singer Clint Holmes are at the Sands. And country-pop star Kenny Rogers works the Cambridge Ballroom at The Grand.

The Beach Boys at Merv Griffin's Resorts

The last time the Beach Boys worked the Superstar Theatre, Brian Wilson was with the band, but just barely.

The man was a mental mess. The reclusive singer, pianist and songwriter actually tried to perform one night, but played a note or two on the piano and then rested his head on the keyboard for a song or two until he sort of shuffled off stage in a fog. Earlier that day at rehearsal, Wilson, who was still fogged in, accidentally trashed an extremely valuable electric guitar when he knocked it over and stepped on it.

But that's all ancient history. Wilson is reportedly healthy for the first time in years, both mentally, physically and legally. His differences with the band's lead singer, Mike Love, have been patched up, and the two are writing music together for the first time in decades. Wilson was scheduled to make the trip to Atlantic City, according to Beach Boys keyboard player and singer Bruce Johnston (who wasn't sure if Wilson would actually participate in the shows).

Officially now, the band consists of Johnston, Love, Carl Wilson and Al Jardine, who'll be backed up by a well-drilled band that can easily guide the men through their seemingly endless string of endless-summer hits.

Between their own talents and those of the people working behind them, the Beach Boys can work up great and respectable-sounding covers of their own hits and perhaps even throw in — Gasp! — a song the audience may have never heard before.

But this band has always known why people still come out by the tens of thousands to see them, and they rarely disappoint.

(*Show times are 10 tonight; 9 p.m. Saturday; 8 p.m. Sunday. Tickets are $40. Call the Resorts box office at 340-6830 or Ticketmaster at 800-736-1420.*)

NEWS

HOLLAND: AN EXPENSIVE WAY TO KILL A 'DAMNED SURFING IMAGE'

The Beach Boys are the very stuff of which 20th-Century rock and roll heroes are made.

They have never been accorded the 'superstar' tag that falls too easily on too many shoulders these days — and if it happened now, it could only be an understatement.

Individually and collectively they continue to walk tall, as in the halcyon days of *I Get Around* and *Barbara Ann;* producing musical feats of a stature that pales most other bands into insignificance.

'Exhibit A' for anyone in doubt is their latest album — *Holland* — which was made as a result of gouda vibrations in a 'funky old four-track studio' at Baambrugge, in the sleepy, rural Netherlands.

It marks another phase of Beach Boys' development that must surely silence any critics still asinine enough to regard their early surfing sounds as nothing more than the best of California bubble gum music.

ROOTS

Although it was made thousands of miles away from their West Coast influences, *Holland's* most powerful tracks — notably the *California Saga* — speak of the American 'roots' in a manner reminiscent of The Band, who are probably *the* country rock group of all time.

But it is the story of the way in which *Holland* was made — in grandiose American style — that will most likely capture the imagination of both rock fans and recording enthusiasts ughout the world.

it all began with a reaction on the Beach Boys' part to their California image, which had become so powerful that one virtually stood for the other.

Suddenly, last summer, they took off for Holland and went through some half a million dollars settling in and arranging for nearly four tons of flying studio, a prototype for the future, to be brought from America.

Their choice of Holland was, by no means, a random one as their manager, and fellow artist, Jack Rieley explained: 'The idea occurred to us around December 1970. We were booked to do a show in Amsterdam and the morning prior to the gig found us in London. We decided to fly over and spend the day in Amsterdam as the group wasn't due on stage until midnight.

'We got to Heathrow at 11 in the morning but we couldn't leave because of fog. By six o'clock that evening we had virtually given up, but the promoter had hired a jet from Gatwick for us, so we drove down there, boarded the plane and made Brussels by 10 p.m.

'There were 12 limousines waiting for us when we arrived and after the drive to Amsterdam the Beach Boys finally went on stage at 5.30 in the morning — to a completely packed house, not an empty seat in the place.

'It was incredible and we decided there and then that there was something "strange" about the place!'

So impressed were they with their reception that they decided to investigate the country at the earliest opportunity — one which occurred following an invitation to do a Dutch television programme called Grand Gala du Disque.

That resulted in their stopping over for a couple of months, during which time Bill de Simone — an erstwhile

'Oh, Mama can this really be the end?'

Hollywood P.R. man — was employed to find accommodation in Amsterdam for the Beach Boys and their entourage.

The problems he faced in the light of Holland's chronic housing shortage were, in their way, as great as the problems faced by Steve Moffit, who had engineered on the *Carl And The Passions So Tough* album and was commissioned to 'magic' a studio over to Holland.

WHIZ-KIDS

When the group made the initial decision to record in Holland, it was assumed that they would use Dutch facilities. They soon learned, however, that the few existing studios were overtaxed and no way could enough time for an LP be booked.

Their decision to get away from the rush hours, poison air and nerves of Los Angeles stood, however, and it was down to Steve to create a studio from scratch — he was given two and a half months in which to do it.

Leading equipment manufacturers could not come up with consoles in time so Steve called in his friend and physics whiz, Gordon Rudd, and together they designed a real 21st-Century board, one borrowing liberally from the future.

Looking back, Steve says: 'It was a ridiculous task to start with, with only two men working on it — even for a stock model. But the manufacturers were proposing ones twice the size with half the functions. Most of the people who design consoles have never actually had to use them.'

Their job entailed designing and building the board — or console — assembling it in context to make sure it all worked, dismantling it, packing it, shipping it and, finally, reconstructing it in the one-time farm building in Baambrugge, where it sat as a streamlined, multi-coloured anachronism, glowing futuristically in the dark.

The logistics of getting all the equipment to Baambrugge — let alone the Beach Boys — comprised an equally fantastic operation.

When they began shipping, Beach Boy equipment occupied every single flight from L.A. to Amsterdam (of which there are four daily) and, to correct faults, every Amsterdam to L.A. flight (of which there are three daily), for four and a half weeks.

Crates made specially for the occasion cost 5,000 dollars alone. The heaviest single item, racks containing limit-

NEWS

ers, kepexes, Dolbys and the prodigious patch bay, actually cracked the tarmac as it was rolled out to the plane for loading. The gross weight ( ) parts totalled 7,300 lb.

While the shipping was in progress, Steve was busy reshaping the Baambrugge farm building for its new role.

It was a disaster when he found it, having been used only as a four-track studio in which to record the odd Christmas album and commercials.

Outside, it bore the imposing name of BBC 2 — nothing to do with our own BBC 2 — inside, the acoustics were so bad that Steve began his reclamation scheme by having the floor relaid six inches higher, which also served to accommodate the mass of cables required.

Sand was poured between the uprights to avoid resonating, and even the speakers had sand — Malibu sand at that — to prevent resonance. Angles were built into the ceiling, which was covered with spun glass.

The building's delighted and slightly boggled owner ra around taking home-movies and gathering autographs in between looking after the cows, whose faces loomed at the studio windows.

To do a complete breakdown of the equipment that finally made its home in Baambrugge would not only take a small booklet, it would serve only to disillusion those people who think they've got something when taking delivery of half a dozen Dolby systems.

The particular qualities that set it apart from other good systems currently in use give us some idea of the 'goodies' involved, however.

Although it is only 'half' portable — it takes a week to dismantle — its modular construction does allow for individual parts repair and replacement within a minute.

OBSESSION

At the push of a button, all equalisation from the main part of the console is switched into the monitor system.

The peak indicating meters indicate with light, as opposed to needles, so they don't need to be watched so closely.

And its greatest convenience is the 1,000-hole patch bay which acts as a fail-safe system, especially useful for the mix-down process.

Anything can be patched into anything. If an equaliser breaks, you patch it out and patch another one in. It's possible to reassign the position of tracks that have already been recorded, grouping them as you like. You can put a limiter before or after faders, or anywhere you like and Steve said they had occasion to use it all.

It all bears witness to the Beach Boys' well-known obsession with technological advance — whether or not their obsession was justified can be decided by listening to a few tracks on the album.

Material for Holland was written by every member of the band, including the two 'new' boys, Ricky Fataar and Blondie Chaplin. Jack Rieley earned his 'fellow artist' label by supplying additional material, Al Jardine's wife, Lynda, had a hand in the writing too and Jack reports that even his dog, Bingo, made one or two 'contributions' to the overall sound.

Individual reaction to being away from the States is quite clearly shown in the album, Al Jardine for example missed his family and friends in Big Sur, hence his part in the California Saga. Carl Wilson and his wife enjoyed Holland so much they now have plans to take out a dual residency and, as always, Brian Wilson provided the enigmatic touch that keeps fans coming back to the Beach Boys time and again to see just what will happen next.

Getting Brian to Holland in the first place was every bit as touch and go as getting a ceasefire in Vietnam.

'It was a monumental thing for Brian to board that aeroplane,' Jack Rieley told *Beat Instrumental*. 'He just doesn't like to leave his house in Bel Air, but it is getting better these days and I understand he's been travelling to the mid-West and back recently, apparently he's into getting out of L.A. in a big way.'

THE KEY

A journalist by profession, Jack met Brian and Carl Wilson while he was taking a year off to write a book on social and economic affairs in Latin America.

He could be found at gatherings muttering things like the 'Beach Boys', 'damned surfing image' and 'if only they could get rid of it people could concentrate on the music'.

Brian and Carl offered him the chance to do something about it and his immediate reaction was: 'Me get involved in the music business, why, that's absurd.' It certainly was 'absurd', to the point where he finished up as Managing Director of the Beach Boys, lyricist and President of their record company, Brother Records.

That was a little more than two years and several headaches ago, the biggest one of late being the financial aspect of the whole *Holland* undertaking.

'The project, in terms of special cash outlays, personal housing and stuff like that, will end up costing us something in the region of several hundred thousand dollars — and I'm not including the cost of the recording equipment which worked out at about 175,000 dollars,' he said.

Was it worth it? Well, the Beach Boys stand behind the 'experiment' more than pleased with the results and Jack has become so enamoured of Holland that he has set up a permanent office in Amsterdam, an exquisite, 17th-Century house overlooking a mossy, green canal. He quotes Russ Mackie, a friend of his who summed it all up: 'In Los Angeles there's so much more to do and so many things are done; but one is less. In Holland there are fewer things to do, but one is more.' 'That's the key to the whole thing, really,' he added.

Circa '72 Beach Boys, rockin' on!

ROB BARTLETT

Toss a question at The Beach Boys and they all begin scrambling for answers like a water-polo team in a scrimmage. Tanned, sharp-looking, and full of fun, they leap from the serious to the comic with gymnastic ease. Though in some respects they look alike (three being brothers, and a fourth a cousin), each one's response is different, and thoroughly his own.

Naturally, we wondered what "success" could mean to this young group of singers, riding the waves of surfing popularity. So we asked. It seemed a sure thing that their notions of "making it big" would add up to something cool, like money in the bank, names in the papers, and the screams of the faithful. Frankly, we were shook up by what else they said it meant.

Said Brian Wilson, eldest of the three Wilson brothers in the group, "I don't go for being 'in' just for the sake of being 'in.' To sing, whether it's for an audience or in the shower, is an experience that wakes you up spiritually. I don't want to sound puffed up, like making with the words. But I feel a strange thing come over me when I'm singing. It must be the way religion affects some people. Our family was never deeply religious, and as a kid, I wasn't a regular church-goer. I'm growing older now, and I'm at the time when I want to find myself, my right course, my personal direction. I've gotten hung up on philosophy lately, and it's had a sobering effect on my manner of living. Just like a lot of people, up to a few months ago, I'd never heard of 'Subud.' This is not actually an organized religion. It's more of a philosophy, you see. And it helps an individual blaze a path to God. Much of what a young man sees is a mystery and, like the song goes, a puzzlement. Now this is one of the most important meanings success has for me. If I hadn't made it with our group, I'd probably not have found Subud, mainly because I wouldn't have been so pressed to seek peace of mind.

"People who just look at the surface signs of making good, the material advantages . . . well, they tend to forget what a rat race show business can become. Sure, I enjoy the thrill of performing. Who wouldn't, if he's appreciated? But after a while, you have to sit down and make a good accounting. Usually, when you're on the run, making records, going on tours, doing the clubs or TV, you have to give up other things. And some of these things are more valuable than *(Continued on page 62)*

IN SEARCH OF 5 MEN

Counter-clockwise 'round the 5:
Brian Wilson is the boss Beach Boy;
Dennis Wilson is the "most sociable";
Alan Jardine is the happiest guy in the crowd (and the only married one);
Mike Love is the impatient boyfriend;
Carl Wilson is the baby brother who got bugged...and then there's Bruce Johnston, the fill-in drummer whose mom called the police!

BEACH BOYS

Continued from page 39

anything else in life—like putting values in their right perspective, so that you don't get arrogant—or cultivating your faith in God, because there is one blessing religion can give you, even if it can't solve *all* your puzzles and problems, and that blessing is hope."

Brian, twenty-four, recently decided that he didn't want to go on traveling with the Beach Boys. He would like to marry and settle down. Out of this came the decision to recruit young Bruce Johnston to replace him for tours.

"I simply felt I was getting kind of old for all that rush-rush racket," said Brian. "And then one of us had to concentrate on production for Capitol Records. That's a full-time job, and I've always felt I was more of a behind-the-scenes man than an entertainer anyhow. For me, that's the real fun."

The other lads refer to him as "the Boss," but though he is the leader, they take a vote on all issues of importance.

Brian lives in Beverly Hills, a few blocks from his "little brother" Carl. Close as the brothers are though, they each lead separate lives.

Six-foot-two and 190 power-packed pounds, Brian has dark brown hair and hazel-blue eyes. His birthplace, and that of his brothers, is Hawthorne, California. He is still single, "but looking," he grins. . . .

Two years Brian's junior is Dennis, the "middle brother" of the Beach Boys. Eager to get "a word in edgewise," Dennis finally was given a chance to explain his ideas on "the success thing."

Smaller than Brian, Dennis is five-foot-nine and tips the scale at a trim 160 pounds. He is very blond, with intense blue eyes.

"About this success thing, now," he said, creasing his forehead seriously. "For me, the most I get is my appreciation of my brothers, especially Brian. I really mean it. The plain fact is, we didn't get along as well as we should have when we were children. Even in our teens, we weren't exactly united. Too independent, I guess. But after we formed the group and I saw how talented both of my brothers were, and what fine ideas they came up with, I began to respect them. I started to really like them—as people.

"I'm not saying our fights stopped the second we became the Beach Boys. We sure had some brawls. It was a good thing Dad traveled with us and managed us at first. He set the pace and the example to follow. He told us he expected a certain standard of conduct from us, and warned us the public would expect it, too. Dad put us down the moment we got rude, flip or offensive. And we valued him more than anything else. When Dad had to quit, Brian took over as boss. I must admit Brian has kept up the discipline. That's when I became impressed with the ability of my brothers, and their sense of fairness, especially Brian's, when it came to differences of opinion.

"And one thing all three of us got straight: Success is sweet but family unity and love is sweeter yet. We all live alone, but close enough to see each other as often as we feel the need. And the need to see brothers you're fond of can be pretty urgent."

It was from Brian that we learned Dennis was the "most sociable" of the group. Totally outgoing, he loves meeting and talking to people, and after a performance, he will often mix with the audience and go in for a session of bantering. He is also given to bringing his latest girlfriends backstage to meet the rest of the Beach Boys. To this, he observed, "They say I have a temper and I'm sort of far-out. But when I look into the baby-blue eyes of a pretty girl, all I do is agree with everything she says. It's easier to argue with brothers or friends. . . ."

Youngest of the Wilson brothers is guitarist Carl, who will be twenty in December. He took a lighter view of the topic under discussion than the first two. "Success?" He laughed and said, "To me, success is getting my big brothers to quit treating me like a baby. That isn't easy, you know. Their idea of doing me a favor used to be a pat on the head—which was worse than a bang on the noggin. Maybe it didn't hurt as much, but it sure bugged me more. Now we're doing real good as a group, so I've become self-supporting the past three years. I've got my own house which, for a guy of nineteen, is not bad. Every time I look at the house, I say to myself, 'Now I'm a grown man, and beginning to sink some roots.' I know that's kind of hurry-up, but it's how I feel these days.

"Guess what?" he demanded with a grin, half proud, half embarrassed. "My house has eight rooms, four baths and a cottage by the pool. It just occurred to me that maybe, subconsciously, I've been thinking about the future—when I get married and have kids of my own. But for the time being, I do like living alone. It's something we Wilson guys have in common. It puts responsibility where it belongs, on the individual. This is peculiar, a sort of twist, because I learned responsibility first by becoming part of the group. Being on my own, I have to keep the place up, pay my taxes, and deal with all the people from insurance companies to the bank. As a result, I'm getting familiar with handling money, using credit, and the like.

"Success to me is the respect I'm getting nowadays from my brothers, my parents and other people. I'm one of the Beach Boys. That gives me status. The girls give me a higher rating. And you know what? My brothers even ask my advice once in a while. . . ."

That brought us to Mike Love, a cousin of the Wilsons. Born in Los Angeles, he is twenty-five, a tall, lithe lad, six-foot-one, weighing in at about 165. He, too, is blond, with blue eyes, single, and good at track and football. He enjoys beach sports and traveling, which makes him "extra glad to be one of the Beach Boys." Mike is many things to his group, lead vocalist, singing both bass and tenor parts, and he emcees their stage shows. He is by temperament a cut-up, and his practical jokes and capers keep the group, friends, pretty girls and even strange bystanders in stitches. Yet he has a serious side.

Mike has earned the reputation of being a Jekyl-Hyde personality—he can be sarcastic or kind, sympathetic or impatient—he can also show a side that is studious, idealistic and tenacious as a bulldog when it comes to learning new material.

The question of success and its meaning to him brought out the complex duality of his nature. "It's a feeling of comfort—like this beard of mine. I'm the only one of this beach-bum outfit who has the whiskers, and I'm the only one who looks the part of the surfer musician. But why should I shave when I feel so good not shaving? (ED. NOTE: Somewhere, somehow, Mike must have found an answer to that one. Shortly after this interview, the beard came off.)

"Until we hit the big time, though, I couldn't wear the kind of clothes I liked or the haircut I preferred or a beard. It would have looked as if I were putting people on. I used to work as a gas-station attendant, sheet-metal apprentice, bus-boy, all kinds of jobs, but as a Beach

"WHY did it happen to my baby?"

FIGHT BIRTH DEFECTS
Join **MARCH OF DIMES**

Boy, people sort of anticipate a little of the eccentric and bizarre. So I can do what comes comfortably, and not feel self-conscious about it. That's one thing success can do for you.

"I have a steady girlfriend. Guess I'm hooked. But I can't divulge her name. She's not in show business and is a bit shy. She doesn't care to marry me while I'm still on the here-today-somewhere-else-tomorrow route. She doesn't dig it. And the way things are going, it looks like we'll be traveling around for a while yet. I'm not as patient as she is, but she's more sensible. And stubborn. When she says, 'I'll wait till you settle down,' that's it. She means it. What attracts me most to her? She makes me feel real comfortable. Relaxed. Cooled. Know what I mean? Well, if it never comes to marriage, I suppose that's how it was meant to be. But I know one thing, I'll never marry a girl in show business. I want my wife to be just that, a wife, and willing to make that her career."

Pausing to consider another train of thought, Mike's blue eyes grew piercing. He finally said, "I like to be comfortable, sure. But I'm not a lazy character. I like work. When the Beach Boys die out, and that's liable to happen someday, I'll probably go into real estate or use the money I've saved to get into the investment game. Anyway, I can relax for now. Being with the Beach Boys has given me security and freed me from petty worries."

Mike lives in a three-level house in Manhattan Beach, on the Pacific Ocean shoreline. His place is furnished "casually, in the Spanish style. The location is great for my taste. I love the beach, sunning, swimming, surfing. Most of all, I like just sitting on my porch, looking out comfortably at the water washing in on the sand, with that special thunder only ocean waves make."

Mike drives a 1948 MG-TC and confessed, "I drive too fast. It's a psychological thing I haven't licked yet. You'd think with all the traveling we do, I'd have it up to here. But not me. My idea of a bang-up time is to take off for a spin up the coast, or fly to Hawaii for a weekend. I'm usually not recognized, because when you're a member of a group, people don't notice you so much. I love to take long, barefoot walks along the beach. I'm slightly older than Brian—the senior citizen of the Beach Boys. But I don't feel I've found myself completely yet. Maybe that's why my girl feels I'm not ready for the big settle-down. Anyway, when I do get married and quit this entertainment business, I'd like to move to the Carmel area of California, which is as beautiful as any place I've ever seen...."

Alan Jardine put his views on success briefly, clearly and with no attempt to embroider. He said, "The big prize for me was to be able to marry young and support my wife decently. Being so much in the public eye helped mature me." Going on twenty-four, Alan was born in Lima, Ohio, and is rather small compared to the others. He weighs 135 pounds and stands barely five-foot-five. But he's an attractive, dynamic blue-eyed blond, with a resolute air and a manner that invites confidence and respect. His hobbies are many: tennis, bowling, surfing, scrabble, and building model airplanes, some of which are his own designs. "I am, you might say, a folk singer turned dental student," he explained softly. "And a dental student turned swinging singer, rock-'n-roll guitarist and probably the happiest guy in the crowd, as well as the only married one."

Alan's wife, Linda, is a cute and curvy brunette, twenty-one years old and, according to the others, "a livin', breathin' doll." He went on to describe his marriage to Linda as "love at first meeting, when we were at El Camino College. We were both in the same political-science class, but she has gone on with her studies, majoring now in business management. She sure manages me. No," he shook his head, "we don't have any children yet. I'm her only child."

He is often teased by the other Beach Boys for being "our only intellectual." His interests include astronomy, and his first great extravagance was a high-powered telescope.

Al has one brother older than himself and he looks on family relationships as "top value in making for contentment and fulfillment." It is his hope to have a family of his own soon, and he and Linda are saving all they can for that eventuality. They live modestly and serenely in Manhattan Beach, near both sets of parents.

"Success" he said in his calm, concise manner, "is being married to a girl like Linda, not being plagued by worry about the money to raise kids properly, and enjoying your companions and your work. That's it for me...."

Newest member of the group is drummer and pianist Bruce Johnston. He fills in for Brian when the boys go on tour, and also works with Terry Melcher, who is Doris Day's son. He's fast with a quip and he is the sole member of the group who doesn't own his own home. An adopted child (as are his two older sisters), Bruce still lives with his mother. He put it somewhat differently. "I visit with her," he said, adding, "it happens to be a long visit."

Bruce generally works from eleven A.M. to seven P.M. at Capitol, recording with the Beach Boys. Then he walks across the street and records with Terry Melcher at Columbia. He and Terry have

MAGAZINE AND NEWS

managed to do three albums together.

"How would I know what success is?" he said. "Success can be most anything. Get a nice, private-school, well-bred girl and you're a successful Don Juan. Get yourself a slob and you're a flop. I come from a pretty well-to-do family, all very square. Success first came to me when my parents admitted they liked something I played, which was far from square. You know, I started banging the drums when I was fifteen and I used to go at it until two in the morning at a local night club. But my mother didn't see the humor in it and she called in the police.

"I joined the Beach Boys when Brian needed someone to hit the road for him. For me, the height of success would be to write an Academy Award song, and do it before I'm thirty. Then I'd like to produce dramatic films. That's when I'd begin to talk as though I were a success —not before. Meanwhile, I'm having fun, which certainly counts for something, doesn't it...?"

Brian took up the chain of conversation to point out that forming the group and doing surfing songs was Dennis' idea. "He gets the credit for that."

As for the group itself, Brian's view is the long one. "We all appreciate what the fans have done for us. If we are a success, then they are a success because they recognized what we were trying to give them and they took it to their hearts. Whatever good things have happened to us came through the public. We can't thank them enough." —EUNICE FIELD

Nov 22, 1971

March 3, 1971

Beach Boys
(CARNEGIE HALL, N.Y.)

Southern California's pioneer rock band, the Beach Boys, made a rare New York concert appearance last Wednesday evening (24) at Carnegie Hall. Mike Klenfner made his promotion debut with two sellouts.

Though Brian Wilson's presence was missed, the Beach Boys went over big with a mixed repertoire of songs that chronicled their long existence in the rock field. Dividing the show into two segments, the group appeared somewhat tight at first, but soon got it together for a show that highlighted their precise four part vocal harmonies. "California Girls" and "Good Vibrations" stood out, with the former showing that the Beach Boys have always been into melodic rock.

While the group approached the Merle Haggard country classic "Okie From Muskogee" with a touch of satire, the tune showed that if they would direct their energies toward country rock they would be excellent in that idiom. With Mike Love's voice up front, the Beach Boys' harmonies are particularly well suited to country rock. —Jeff.

ONE BEACH BOY COMES IN OUT OF THE DRAFT

Carl Wilson, one of the Beach Boys, ended a five-year fight over his draft status last week when the Los Angeles Federal Court gave him permission to choose a "most unique" alternative to military service. Wilson will be allowed to satisfy his draft obligation by performing with the Beach Boys at prisons, hospitals and orphanages.

Judge Harry Pregerson said entertainment is certainly in the national interest. The singer's attorney, J. B. Tietz, called attention to the Attica tragedy in urging ap-
(Continued on page 54)

One Beach Boy
(Continued from page 1)

proval of the alternate service proposal.

In 1967, Wilson refused to report for induction to military service, saying he was opposed to all war. He was granted conscientious objector status but then refused to report for civilian duty as a bedpan-changer at L.A. Veterans Hospital because the job did not make use of his talent.

Wilson proposed to give performances instead. But his proposal was turned down by the draft board and in successive court appeals until last week's decision.

CONCERT REVIEWS

June 4, 1975

Concert Reviews

Chicago (8)
Beach Boys (9)
(STADIUM, CHI)

The concert billed as the rock event of the summer, had its now-obligatory show-biz frills — most notably two aerial acts performing to strains of "Exodus" and some neat stage lighting — but no amount of glitter could have added to the excitement caused by the arrival for five nights of these two durable groups.

Unfortunately, in the area that counts most—sound—inadequacy prevailed. The Beach Boys, opening with an hour of mostly oldies, found their unequalled harmonies reduced to loud blurbs. Much of the blame belonged to their needlessly intricate nine pieces which turned some songs like "Heroes and Villians" and "Good Vibrations" into extended shouting matches.

But their onstage presence is so strong that the handful of satisfying renditions of songs like "Surfer Girl" and "In My Room" seemed enough. Dennis Wilson, though, gave the show a black eye with his senseless ramblings and horrendously sung encore number, "You Are So Beautiful."

Chicago's homecoming, which drove an SRO throng to the edge of pandemonium, was laced with the same sound problems, but their highly animated set, led by cheerleading trombone player James Pankow, and spirited lead singer Peter Cetera, kept the crowd on its feet most of the time. Again no risks were taken — Chicago played only its hits, with barely any jamming. When it came through clearly, the musicianship was fine.

Following an excellent encore of "Got To Get You Into My Life," Chicago was joined by the Beach Boys for a third set that fared well enough with "Dialogue" and "Darlin'" but ended up reaching deafening heights. Chicago producer James William Guercio appeared as the Beach Boys' tour bassist. —Loyd.

June 15, 1983

Beach Boys (10)
Kingbees (3)
(CLARKSTON, MICH.)

The Beach Boys opened Pine Knob Music Theatre's 12th year of operation with a three-day stand. While most of the songs came from the top 10 charts of the mid-'60s, the crowd responded as if they were current hits, singing and clapping along.

Songs of surfin' and cars for the "car people" of Detroit were put together into two long medleys that received ovation after ovation. High harmonies by Al Jardine, Carl Wilson, and Billy Hinsche were very impressive and tight on classic songs like "409," "Little Deuce Coup," and "Surfin' Safari."

While an album of new songs is rumored to be in the works, the only new material performed was by Carl Wilson, who was promoting his new Epic solo album. His "Rocking All Over The World" had a hard edge to it and was warmly received.

Bruce Johnston was also given a short solo set which began with a surprise short rendition of the chorus of "I Write the Songs" (which he wrote) and then moved on to a nice little ditty, "Disney Girls," that featured Carl on acoustic guitar.

The Kingbees didn't realize until a few days before the show that they would open, but delivered some fine '50s-type music. Their hit, "My Mistake," and a cover of "Bo Diddley" were standouts, but the crowd mostly ignored their set, a Pine Knob tradition for opening acts.

—Kelv.

CONCERT REVIEWS

July 4, 1976

Beach Boys (9)
America (3)
Santana (8)
Gerard
(ANAHEIM STADIUM, L.A.)

The Beach Boys sound and manner at this Saturday (3) marathon were generally familiar. The tone was consistently cheerful. The beat was as uncomplicated as the rhythm of a marching song. And the 55,000 young fans who jammed the stadium, grandstand and outfield grass, jumped and clapped in joyful time from the first number to the last.

It was fine showmanship. It was also the best possible concoction for this audience. The Beach Boys gave out with what they have always presented, a kind of pop rock, and maybe — aside from the emphasis on percussion — more pop than rock.

The other groups were less successful. America stirred the most enthusiasm, and that was pale by comparison with the reaction to the headliners, though this group also did pleasant things. "Amber Cascades" was an exhibition of fine musicianship with a fine arrangement. "Today's The Day," not much on lyrics, was an interesting tune. And so it went, with the old favorite, "Daisy Jane" and a new number, "She's A Liar" and others.

The best thing Santana did was a Latin-flavored opening, a kind of flamenco rock. But the group was soon on a more pedestrian level, and much of it from then on was downhill.

Gerard, a late replacement for Flash Cadillac, was disappointing. The musicianship was uninspired, the music unoriginal and the flavor strictly derivative 1960s rock.

— *May*

Dec 1, 1976

Beach Boys (16)
(MADISON SQ. GARDEN, N.Y.)

The surf was up and so was the crowd at Madison Square Garden, Wednesday (24) as The Beach Boys ran through most of their rock 'n' roll clicks. Performance signalled the first Gotham appearance in many years for Brian Wilson, the combo's key cleffer and producer, but, even in The Beach Boys' early days, a rare performer.

The show, which was added by promoter Ron Delsener when the original concerts Thursday (25) and Friday (26) neared SRO, drew well although there were empty sections behind the stage. Beginning, as usual, with "Wouldn't It Be Nice," the combo, supported by Charles Lloyd on flute and tenor saxophone, and other backup, delivered a string of faves with lead vocals shared by Wilson, Mike Love, Alan Jardine, and Carl Wilson. Dennis Wilson, a third brother, led the cheerleading for the closing string of oldies as he came forward from his usual spot on drums.

Brian Wilson, playing bass guitar for a couple of tunes, was on grand piano for most of the concert, which included a 25-minute intermission. The blended vocals on "Surfer Girl" stood out. Number drew audience singalong as did "California Girl." "Good Vibrations" continued one of the most musical of rockers for the Brother/Reprise disk act. —*Kirb.*

Nov 27, 1968

Beach Boys' Live LP Victim of AFM & British Union

London, Nov. 26.

Joint action by Britain's Musicians' Union and the American Federation of Musicians has killed plans by the Beach Boys to record a live album at the London Palladium on Dec. 1 preem of their upcoming United Kingdom swing.

This is the latest step in the get-tough attitude of the MU toward Anglo-American group exchange, first disclosed by its refusal to okay a London recording of a double album for the SGC label by the Nazz (VARIETY, Nov. 13). If the move is endorsed by the AFM, it will put an end to inter-country recording activities.

The MU doggedly insists that recording should only take place on home territory—and in the case of the Beach Boys it has won the support of the AFM. The feeling here is that the provisions of the exchange agreement should be strictly observed, and this goes for recording as well as performances.

"It is no good. The Americans think they can come here and make records, but when the British act goes to America there is no chance of them getting in the studios," commented assistant MU secretary Harry Francis. "If the reciprocal arrangement is to work, then it must be a two-way thing in all respects."

But many industries, while having some sympathy with the MU's point of view, are saddened that indications of a reversal of the trend of British combos going to America to record should be so severely vetoed.

There is also puzzlement that in clamping down, the MU seems to be depriving its members of work. The Nazz had mapped a month-long project which would have involved a large number of local tooters. The Beach Boys had planned to augment their 12-piece British touring unit by a further dozen musicians for recording.

And to make sure of hiring the best talent available, the Beach Boys had agreed that instead of the usual rehearsal fees, the orchestra would be paid full session rates during the two days of preparation. The full lineup would have been engaged for a second London concert to have been taped as in-

CONCERT REVIEWS

Dec 26, 1973

Beach Boys (11)
Linda Ronstadt (6)

(MADISON SQ. GARDEN, N.Y.)

Madison Square Garden was filled with patrons and "Good Vibrations," Wednesday (19) as the Beach Boys played their first date in the large arena. Even the sound, often a bugaboo in large halls, was better than when they last played New York, which was more than a year ago at Carnegie Hall. The Ron Delsener promotion sold out for a $130,000 gross at a $7.50 top.

The Brother-Reprise act, roused the throng with newer material, but especially with such oldies as "Wouldn't It Be Nice," "Darlin'," "Surfer Girl," "Help Me Rhonda," "Surfin' U.S.A.," and "Sloop John B." Combo now appears to be a septet plus four assorted sidemen. Regulars, including veterans Carl & Dennis Wilson, Mike Love and Alan Jardine, comparative newcomers Ricky Fataar, drums, and Blondie Chaplin, lead guitar, were joined by a keyboard man, who aided vocally.

The vocal blends were exceptional, a key for the old rock 'n' roll clicks as well as the newer stuff. For the "Good Vibrations" finale, a classic rocker, the Beach Boys were joined by Bruce Johnston, a former member of the unit. He remained for the string of solid encores. Banks of small colored lights, which flashed different patterns, backed the Beach Boys, who previously eschewed special effects.

Linda Ronstadt, looking and sounding great, was wasted as the opening act. The Asylum artist, who hasn't played New York in some time, would have done better by going through with projected earlier dates as headliner in smaller halls. The loot would have been less, but the long-range effects would have been more rewarding.
—Kirb.

Mar 29, 1972

Beach Boys (7)
(CARNEGIE HALL, N.Y.)

The Beach Boys, with the addition of two South Africans, gave another of their spirited rockin' concerts before a packed Carnegie Hall Wednesday (22), the last of three consecutive sellout nights promoted by Ron Delsener. The three shows grossed $50,100 at a $7 top.

Of the new members, drummer Ricky Fataar actually had been with the group at their Carnegie dates early in the season as a backup musician, replacing Dennis Wilson, who previously was the unit's drummer. Wilson, whose voice is a key in the Beach Boys' blended sound, played piano in a couple of numbers, but usually just sang.

Blondie Chaplin on bass and electric guitar, was more prominent, occasionally joining in vocally, even on lead, and was an asset. The unit, who can get an audience clapping along without special urging, combines newer material with oldies. In the latter category were "Fun, Fun, Fun," their fourth encore, and "Surfer Girl," their second, which have not been heard around here in some time.

Although the Beach Boys, who performed with about eight back-up musicians, have instrumental virtues, it is in their vocals and tempo that they shine. The different voice blendings of Dennis Wilson, his brother, Carl Wilson, Mike Love, Al Jardine and Bruce Johnston are good fun.

Included were tunes from several albums, especially their latest on their own Brother label, distributed by Reprise, "Surf Up." The Beach Boys' appeal continues to grow.   Kirb.

CONCERT REVIEWS

Wednesday, March 28, 1979

Beach Boys Back On The Road

Jerry Schilling Takes On Management Duties For Combo's Multiple Projects

Hollywood, March 27.

Jerry Schilling, personal manager of Beach Boys member, Carl Wilson, has assumed responsibility for all "creative and business projects" for the group.

With the Beach Boys, Schilling's major task is to serve as a liaison between the group and CBS Records, in the area of touring, promotion and merchandising, among other things. In the area of "creative projects," it was Schilling who reunited the group with composer, Bruce Johnston in an effort to deliver the group's first CBS LP to the label — at the time, the album was already a year and a half overdue; CBS has just released it.

Johnston will be touring with the group as in days of old when a new series of Beach Boys dates begins April 20 in Indianapolis. Brian Wilson, whose personal problems have been widely reported, will perform on approximately 50% of the dates, Schilling says, spending the remaining time working on the second CBS LP, due in late August.

Johnston will also be involved in the new album project. It was his idea to create a disco single on the current LP, using a track from the group's "Wild Honey" album of several years back, called "Here Comes The Night."

The tour sked will be organized so that the group has 10 days on and 10 days off, to permit the members to record while touring. Schilling says Brian Wilson is writing a number of tunes for the new LP. Other creative projects include a proposed Beach Boys tv biopic.

Schilling is also currently studying proposals from merchandising outfits for in-store items which he feels the group has not "really taken advantage of" until now.

Concerts West is handling the group's tour sked, which now has dates firmed through May 20. Dates now set, in addition to the April 20 stand at the Market Square Arena in Indianapolis are: April 21, Miami U. of Ohio; April 22, U. of Toledo; April 23, Southern Illinois U. in Carbondale; April 24, the Murfreesboro, Tenn., Murfree Center; April 25, the Roanoke Coliseum; April 26, the Columbia, S.C., Carolina Coliseum; April 27, the Stokley Athletic Center, Knoxville; April 28, the Rupp Arena in Lexington; April 29, Greensboro, N.C. Coliseum, and April 30 and May 1 at the Capitol Centre in Landover, Md.

Beginning May 11, stops include Cincinatti, Pittsburgh, Rochester, Nassau, Springfield, Mass., Buffalo, Binghampton, Vt., Boston, Scarsborough and Providence.

A Coast swing is being planned for June, followed by a fall tour of Europe and Japan.

CONCERT REVIEWS AND AD

Oct 6, 1971

Beach Boys (5)
(CARNEGIE HALL, N.Y.)

The Beach Boys returned to Carnegie Hall, last weekend and the "Good Vibrations" in the first of two sold out shows carried from the opening number of that title through the six encores. The two Ron Delsener-promoted shows grossed $30,000.

The California quintet (Brian Wilson no longer performs with his group because of an ear problem.), one of the earliest supergroups with surfing songs, is back on top again with a skillful combination of their old favorites plus inventive newer material.

They really went back for their fifth encore, "Surfin' U.S.A.," which hasn't been done by them in some time. Carl Wilson took vocal lead as he had for most of the show aided by some of the finest vocal blending around. This encore followed an updated version of "Help Me, Rhonda," which the Beach Boys had done during a late set jam with the Grateful Dead at Fillmore East last spring.

All of the boys had solos, including a poem recital by Mike Love, pianist, who did most of the talking to the audience. Dennis Wilson played piano instead of his usual drums because of a hand injury.

Kirb.

NOVEMBER 1975

WKBO Does it Again!!

BEACH BOYS

November 20—8 P.M.

State Farm Show Arena
Harrisburg, Pa.
$6.00 advance—$7.00 at door

Available at all Ticketron Locations
Lancaster: Stan's Record Bar
Camelot Music

Mail Orders: Checks or money orders payable to "Beach Boys Concert"—Suite 914—1411 Walnut St.—Phila., Penna. Please enclose stamped self-adressed envelope.

CONCERT REVIEWS

Beach Boys To Sing In Gym Monday Night

The Beach Boys will appear in a two-hour concert in Mayser Gym Monday night at 8:00, SUB President Dennis Riff has announced. Tickets can be purchased in front of the campus house for $2.50, and at the door for $3.00.

The Beach Boys, from Hawthorne, California, are Brian, Carl, and Dennis Wilson, all brothers, Mike Love, a cousin, and Al Jardine, a friend they met at school.

Defiant of Bach

The group began to organize when Brian and a few of his friends, in defiance of their college music instructors, whose praise for Bach and Beethoven apparently allowed little room for popular music, organized several vocal jam sessions in the locker room of the school.

Brian's triumph over his professors was short-lived, however, since he dropped out of school not long after his first experiments. He began to spead a great deal of time with his cousin, Mike, singing and playing the guitar, and before long, found his two brothers and Al joining with them.

ACS Philip Hay, from Somerset, Pa., is also a college scholar. He has been in the Glee Club, and has been a member of the Student Council Curriculum Evaluation Committee.

Another college scholar is Leslie Lenkowsky, from Norwalk, Conn. He has been *Prolog* editor, president of Committee for Social Action, co-chairman of the Campus Chest, and chairman of SWOP. Steve Smith is a college scholar from Harrisburg, Pa. He has been a member of Glee Club and IAESTE

The Beach Boys' first idea for song came when a friend suggested to Brian that surfing would be a great theme for a song. Brian and Mike went to work on the idea and the result was "Surfin'," published at their own expense at a minor California studio

The Beach Boys, for a decade one of the most popular American rock ups, will perform in Mayser Center on Monday night, March 27, under auspices of the Student Union Board. Tickets for students are $4.50 ce and may be bought at the switchboard.

CONCERT REVIEWS

SUB Presents Beach Boys In Mayser Center Concert

The Student Union Board has announced that the Beach Boys will appear in concert on Monday night, March 27, in Mayser Center. This is the second of six concerts which the SUB has scheduled for this semester. Tickets are $4.50 and may be purchased at the switchboard office in East Hall.

One of the most popular American rock groups of all time, the Beach Boys have demonstrated a phenomenal durability. Their initial rise occurred in the early 1960's, at a time when, according to an article in the September 6, 1971 edition of *Time* magazine, "along with hot-rods and sports cars, surfboards had become both means and metaphor for the new, rootless mobility of the American young. In southern California especially, sunning, surfing, chasing chicks, gobbling Cha-Cha burgers, even watching TV became life values worth celebrating."

According to *Time*, the music of the Beach Boys epitomized these "slender but seductive values." It was a "soft, euphonious music—intricate, warm layers of bell-like harmonies over calm, steady rock beats, all of it intended to evoke the rhythm of the ocean. When it came to the message, the Boys never let content interfere with contentment."

Instant Success

The group managed to attain hit status with their first single, "Surfin'," released in March, 1962. According to an article on the Beach Boys written by Ben Edmonds, this song, released on the local Candix label, was not an "especially monstrous hit," but "more a slightly expansive regional hit." Nevertheless, its release prompted a representative of Capital Records to sign them immediately, and they produced a steady stream of successes with 'Surfin' Safari," "Surfin' USA," "Shut Down," and "Little Deuce Coupe." All of a sudden, writes Edmonds, "they were no longer just five guys from Hawthorne, they were full-fledged stars with a well-defined responsibility to their audience and image."

In the ten years since they had their start, the Beach Boys have released 23 LPs and sold twenty million records. The LPs have included "Shut Down," "Surfin' Safari," "Surfer Girl," "Summer Days," "Pet Sounds," and their most recent, "Surf's Up." Their hit songs have included "Good Vibrations," "I Get Around," "Car Crazy Cutie," and "Sloop John B."

Wilson Withdraws

The leader of the group is Brian Wilson, and the other members include brothers Carl and Dennis Wilson, Al Jardine, Bruce Johnson, and the "businessman" of the group, Mike Love. Wilson had discontinued his appearances with the rest of the group in 1965, to devote more time to composing. He helped the others record the "Pet Sounds" and "Surf's Up" albums, but although he had pledged to once again appear in public with the group in a recent Carnegie Hall concert, he did not.

In recent years, the Beach Boys have become increasingly identified with radical politics, both individually and together. Carl Wilson had refused induction into the armed forces in 1966, and eventually won his contested Conscientous Objector status on a technicality. His efforts have not halted there, however. He has challenged that C. O. service should be based on an individual's unique talent (such as music) rather than on random government assignment. If his cause is successful, Edmonds reports that it could "shake the very foundations of the draft system."

Greatest Performance

A March 6, 1971 review of a Beach Boys concert in Carnegie Hall, written by Bob Merlis of Record World, declared, "The Beach Boys came to Carnegie Hall last Wednesday and the aftershocks, I am sure, will be felt around the world. The group offered the audience, who were virtually rapt in awe, the greatest performance I have ever witnessed in Carnegie Hall or any other place where rock has ever been played. Group leader Brian Wilson was not there physically, but his genius could be felt throughout the evening.

". . . . The concert, which ended with three encores, offered many moments of compelling beauty — beauty which words cannot adequately describe. There is no point in cataloguing the songs they sang; suffice it to say everything they did, they did better than anyone could imagine. The complexity of their melodies; the difficult harmonies and the rocking beat they presented were more than a delight to hear. The group, simply stated, is supernatural."

Lee Kaufman, President of the Student Union Board, urges all students to purchase their tickets for the concert before they leave for vacation, as the concert is scheduled for the first day after break.

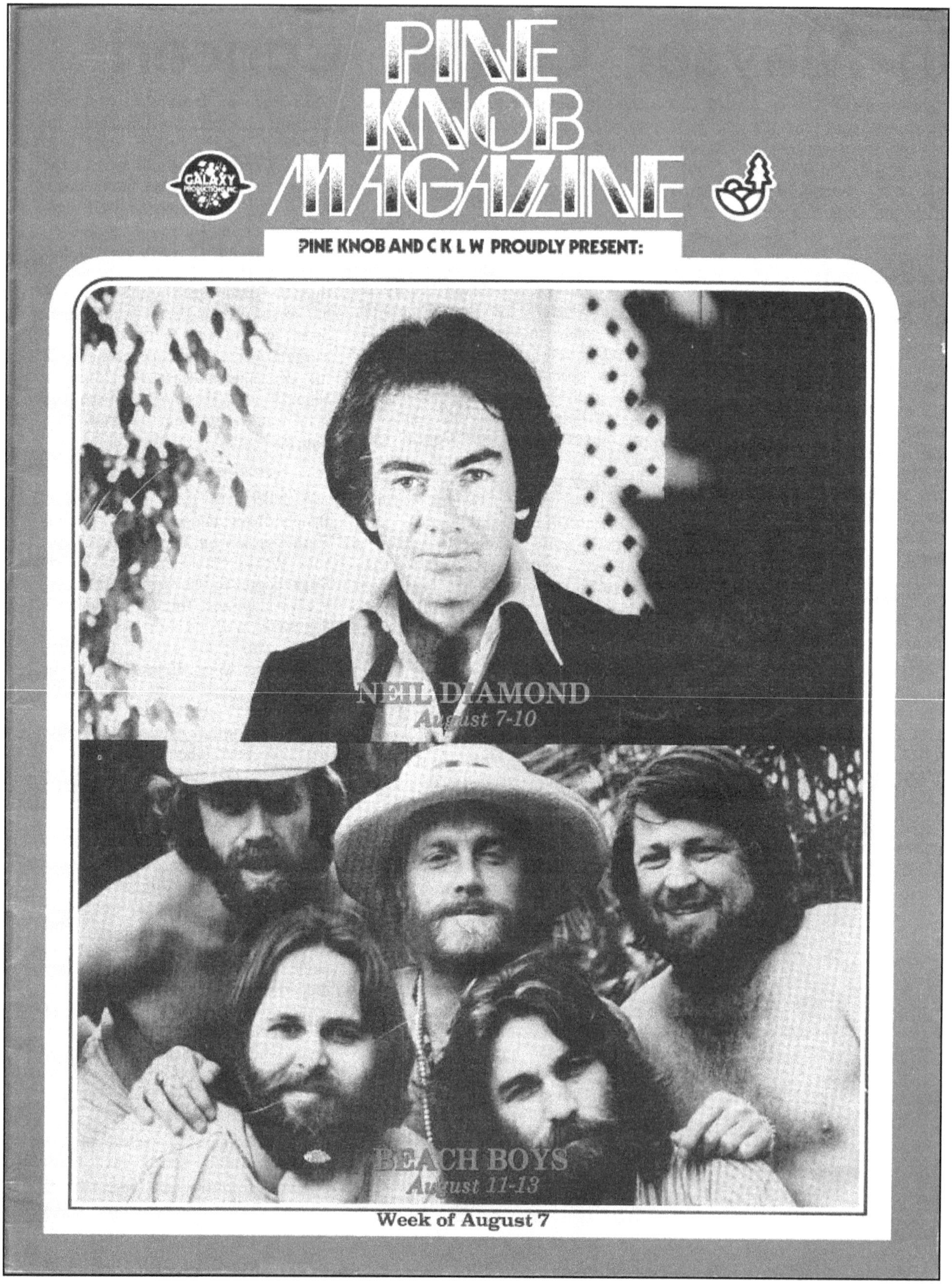
PINE KNOB MAGAZINE
PINE KNOB AND C K L W PROUDLY PRESENT:
NEIL DIAMOND
August 7-10
BEACH BOYS
August 11-13
Week of August 7

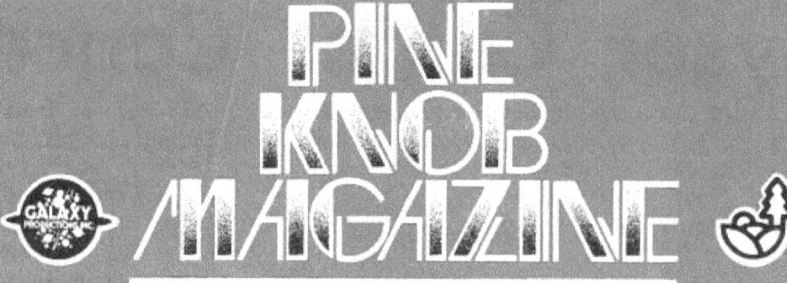

MAGAZINE

'S STARS WITH JACKIE

Jackie Kallen is a columnist for The Oakland Press

the beach boys

The Beach Boys, 1965.
Dennis Wilson, Bruce Johnston,
Carl Wilson, Mike Love, Al Jardine

The Beach Boys were one of the first groups I ever interviewed. They were the top American group in the world at the time and had already accumulated million-selling hits like "Surfin' Safari," "Surfin' U.S.A.," "Surfer Girl," "Be True To Your School," "In My Room," "Fun, Fun, Fun" and "I Get Around."

It was fourteen years ago. We were all teenagers. The Beach Boys represented something that the rest of the country only dreamed about — California living. Surfing, year-round sunshine, riding in open cars and falling in love on the beach. Dressed in striped shirts and white slacks, they captured the imagination of the youth of America.

The first time I met them, they headlined a Winter concert at Cobo Arena that also featured such popular attractions at the time as Jay and the Americans and the Shangrilas. At a party after the show, I got one of my best, most interesting interviews to date.

Not even a year later, the group was back at Cobo again. But this time, Brian Wilson was not with them. In his place was Bruce Johnston, one of several musicians who drifted in and out of the Beach Boys during Brian's absence.

Daryl Dragon played keyboards with the band for about 6 years. He met Toni Tennille, who also toured with the group for awhile, and then the two of them got married and formed the Captain and Tennille. But the Beach Boys rocked on. Glen Campbell played one tour with them, but Brian's touch was always missed.

The mid-sixties blended slowly into the late sixties and then the early seventies. The 1966 album, "Pet Sounds," was not much of success although it did spawn their biggest hit single, "Good Vibrations."

The guys started meditating and Mike Love and Al Jardine became Transcendental Meditation (TM) teachers. Later Carl and Dennis took est (Erhard Seminars Training). They hung together as a group and as a family (Brian, Carl and Dennis Wilson are brothers, Mike Love is their cousin and Al Jardine was Brian's best friend in high school).

In 1973, they cut their "Holland" album. It was their most ambitious project ever and it showed a deeper, more complex side of the Beach Boys. "Sail On Sailor" came out of that album as did the three-part "California Saga."

By 1974, America was hungry again for the happy, positive sounds of the Beach Boys singing simple songs like "Fun, Fun, Fun." Their concerts became sold-out parties. In 1976, they released "Fifteen Big Ones," an anniversary album that marked 15 years in the business. It also marked Brian's return. He got more involved in that album than he had been for a long time. Soon he was touring with the group again after his lengthy retreat from the pressures of the road.

Now, 17 years after it all began in Southern California, the Beach Boys are still one of the hottest acts in the business. Without the strength of a hit single or album, they continue to pack auditoriums and stadiums wherever they go.

The Beach Boys are now an institution. They are a big part of American musical history and they are always welcomed appreciatively by Pine Knob audiences. When the Beach Boys come to town, it's time to party!

Dennis Wilson

Brian Wilson

Carl Wilson

Mike Love

Al Jardine

NEWS

and MUSIC ECHO 9d
NOVEMBER 5, 1966   USA 25c

The city where people stare in horror at hip gear and mini-skirts

BEACH BOYS WEEK! With a big hit on the way—"Good Vibrations"—the toast of the Anglo-American pop scene fly into Britain for a sell-out tour which kicks off at London's Finsbury Park Astoria on Sunday. Pictured in Hollywood before they flew here are (from left, seated): Carl Wilson, Dennis Wilson, Bruce Johnston and (standing) Al Jardine and Mike Love. IN THIS ISSUE: "Hello Britain" and exclusive preview of their act by Wendy Varnals. See page 9.

MOD BRITAIN '67 —SEE PAGE 10

JULY CALIFORNIA CONCERT INSERT

FRIDAY, JULY 3, 1981 *Press-Telegram*

JULY CALIFORNIA CONCERT INSERT

Catch a Wave

Throw me a favor, try the greatest sport around
Everybody tries it once
Those who don't just have to put it down
You paddle out, turn around and raise
And baby, that's all there is to the coastline craze

You gotta catch a wave and you're sittin' on top of the world
Not just a fad 'cause it's been going on so long

All the surfers going strong
They said it wouldn't last too long
They'll eat their words with a fork and spoon
And watch 'em, they'll hit the road and be surfin' soon
And when they catch a wave they'll be sittin' on top of the world

So take a lesson from a top-notch surfer boy
Ev'ry Saturday, boy
But don't you treat it like a toy
Just get away from the shady turf
And baby, go catch some rays on the sunny surf
And when you catch a wave you'll be sittin' on top of the world

—*Brian Wilson*

Eternal sunshine, eternal surf,
eternal song, eternal rock band

JULY CALIFORNIA CONCERT INSERT

By Steve Elders

It was a myth, an idea, a state of mind.

A high surf; tanned, bikini-clad beauties; cruising hot rods just rarin' to go; and year-round sunshine.

Young American radio listeners of the early and mid-1960s grew up dreaming of California's Endless Summer — a season when youth was never out of style, there were always two girls for every boy and life was fun, fun, fun.

While the principal sellers of this dream, the Beach Boys, have changed, both musically and spiritually, the myth hasn't, and it's still alive today; not as strong, perhaps, but still evident especially this time of year.

Likewise, the Beach Boys go on, beginning their 20th year in the music industry.

The group's story begins with Brian Wilson, the first son of Audree and Murry Wilson.

Indeed, just about anything having to do with the group must begin with the multitalented but enigmatic Brian, the group's leader, chief composer, producer and arranger and inspirational force.

Brian, brothers Dennis and Carl, and cousin Mike Love began singing together in their elementary-school years while growing up in Hawthorne.

A heavy influence to 15-year-old Brian was the Four Freshmen. He and the others would spend hours duplicating the harmonies of the quartet.

On Youth Nights at their church the four would perform cover versions of Everly Brothers' songs and other then-current hits.

While in high school, Brian met Al Jardine, who shared the eldest Wilson's interest in music, and

The Beach Boys are still sailing a tide of popularity after 20 years.

JULY CALIFORNIA CONCERT INSERT

Fun, Fun, Fun

Well, she got her daddy's car and she cruised thru the hamburger stand now
Seems she forgot all about the library like she told her old man now
And with her radio blastin' goes cruisin' just as fast as she can now
And she'll have fun, fun, fun till her daddy takes her T-Bird away

Well, the girls can't stand her 'cause she walks, looks and drives like an ace now
She makes the Indy 500 look like a Roman chariot race now
A lotta guys try to catch her, but she leads them on a wild goose chase now
And she'll have fun, fun, fun till her daddy takes the T-bird away

A-well you knew all along that your dad was gettin' wise to you now
And since he took your set of keys you been thinkin' that your fun is all through now
But you can come along with me 'cause we got a lot of things to do now
And you'll have fun, fun, fun now that daddy took the T-Bird away

—*Brian Wilson and Mike Love*

The Beach Boys are still having *Fun, Fun, Fun.*

JULY CALIFORNIA CONCERT INSERT

The Beach Boys are still having *Fun, Fun, Fun*.

soon Jardine was singing with the group, too.

But the Wilsons' father, Murry, was disgusted at their desire to perform rock 'n' roll rather than the songs he himself had written.

Ignoring his father, Brian wrote a song about brother Dennis' latest love — surfing. The song? *Surfin'*. It was pretty simple. Just a few lines about the joys of being out on the waves built around an easy beat.

But the pattern was set. Recorded for the small Candix label, it set the Beach Boys on their way to establishing their image, even though none of the members except Dennis actually surfed.

Surfin' was a local hit and made No. 75 on the national charts, and Murry soon got the group a contract with Capitol records.

The first Capitol single, *Surfin' Safari*, reached No. 14 on the national charts in the summer of 1962, and Southern California became the microcosm for young Americans.

The first album, named after the single, was released later that year, and the group was off.

But the breakthrough song was *Surfin' U.S.A.*, released in early 1963. Sung to the tune of Chuck Berry's *Sweet Little Sixteen*, the song rattled off all the key surfing places in Southern California, then wrapped it up by saying "everybody's gone surfin', surfin' U.S.A."

The song was coupled with *Shut Down*, which helped establish the Beach Boys on their other front — hot rods.

The album *Surfin' U.S.A.* also contained a lot of instrumental filler in the style of guitarist Dick Dale, but one ballad, *The Lonely Sea*, signaled that Brian was seeking some new directions.

That new phase was explored in the next single, *Surfer Girl*. Brian used five-part harmony to tell the story of a male teen-ager's dream of finding a female counterpart to ride the waves with him. On the flip, *Little Deuce Coupe* was another car-bragging ditty, filled with hot-rod lingo.

At this time the group, particularly Brian, became friends with Jan Berry and Dean Torrence, better known as the recording duo Jan and Dean.

One day, just after playing his then-new *Surfin' U.S.A.* on a piano for them, the duo suggested he let them record it.

But Brian declined, saying it was intended for the Beach Boys, so he gave them another song he had finished, *Surf City*.

That song, probably more than any Beach Boys track, best summed up the aura of the land of surf: a place where "there's two swingin' honeys for every guy, and all you gotta do is just wink your eye," and life is just a collection of parties, woodies (wood-paneled station wagons) and surfers.

Apparently, the record-buying public agreed, because the song quickly overtook Beach Boys songs on the charts to become No. 1, a feat the group had yet to accomplish.

There was no jealousy, however, as Jan and Dean and the Beach Boys formed a friendship that saw Brian continue to have a hand in writing the pair's songs as well as having members of both acts sing on each other's records.

Brian received help on most of his lyrics from various writers throughout the Beach Boys' career. His major collaborator at this time was Roger Christian, who composed most of the car-related words.

Just two months after the *Surfer Girl* album, the group released *Little Deuce Coupe*, which featured predominantly car songs, including one, *Spirit of America*, which was sung in a slower pace with harmonies.

While the Beatles crashed onto the American charts and minds in early 1964, the Beach Boys showed that they were still having *Fun, Fun, Fun*, which became their highest-charting single to that date, reaching No.5. Again borrowing from Chuck Berry (the guitar intro is from *Roll Over, Beethoven*), the teen-related story told of a girl who borrowed her dad's Thunderbird to go cruising by the hamburger stand.

Mundane? Sure. Significant? Of course not. A joy to hear? Unquestionably.

The record also showed the increasing importance Brian placed on the sound of Beach Boys music. A high falsetto was mixed in at the end as the group repeated the chorus, "and you'll have fun, fun, fun now that daddy took the T-Bird away."

I Get Around and *Don't Worry, Baby*, the next single, advanced Brian's commitment to sound even more. The first song, an ode to being out with the guys on a Saturday night just having a good time, had an arresting, cold intro: a drum bang and "Round, round, get around, I get around," and there it went. It was their first No. 1.

Don't Worry, Baby combined the lush-sounding love story with a car race. Again, Brian and lyricist Christian found a way to combine the group's chief selling points. It proved to be one of the group's best-ever records.

The resulting album, *Shut Down, Volume 2*, (*Volume 1* had been a Capitol compilation featuring other artists besides the group) was, by contrast, nothing much, but the next LP, *All Summer Long*, released in July 1964, had a gem in the title cut, which was never released as a single.

All Summer Long was a lesson in lush, harmonic counterpoint that seemed to sum up not just the joys of being young in the summertime, but the group's output to that point.

"We've been havin' fun all summer long," they sang, and indeed they had been.

Brian's next single, *When I Grow Up (To Be a Man)*, was an introspection, as the singer, a teen-ager, asks if he'll still want to have fun when he's older, with responsibilities as a father and husband. The song's ending leaves him still wondering without having resolved the issue, hardly the happy note the group's songs were usually promoting.

Near the end of the year Capitol released two albums, a concert recording and a collection of Christmas songs.

But the group's most significant occurrence of 1964 was Brian's nervous breakdown while the band was on tour in Texas. Feeling under pressure from the record label, his father and the music scene as a whole, Brian decided to leave the group on tour to devote his full time to writing and working in the studio.

To replace him on the road, a young studio guitarist of some note among fellow musicians was chosen — Glen Campbell.

In the meantime, Brian began work on the *Today*

Turn to Page 4

JULY CALIFORNIA CONCERT INSERT

Help Me Rhonda

Since she put me down I've been out doin' in my head
Come in late at night and in the mornin' I just lay in bed
Well, Rhonda, you look so fine
And I know it wouldn't take much time
For you to help me, Rhonda, help me get her out of my heart
Help me, Rhonda, help, help me, Rhonda
Help me, Rhonda, yeah, get her out of my heart

She was gonna be my wife and I was gonna be her man
But she let another guy come between us and it shattered our plans
Well, Rhonda, you caught my eye
And I'll give you lots of reasons why
You gotta help me, Rhonda, help me get her out of my heart

—Brian Wilson

JULY CALIFORNIA CONCERT INSERT

From Page 3

album, on which he spent more time with personal themes other than surfing and hot rods. But while his songs began to examine love relationships in a not-always-so-rosy light, the group's lush sound of harmonies layered on beautiful melodies remained.

One track on the album, *Help Me, Rhonda*, didn't sound quite right to Brian, who thought the song, an uptempo salute to a girl who helps the singer get over his previous bad love relationship, needed tightening, a swifter beat and more harmonies.

This he did, and the song became their second No. 1 single, in May 1965.

At this time, Bruce Johnston replaced Campbell with the band on the road. Johnston had been with a group called the Rip Chords, who had a hit in early 1964 with *Hey, Little Cobra*.

Brian went back to the studio, again looking for new variations on one of their old themes — girls.

He found it. The song was *California Girls*, an ode to not just the tanned girls of the Southland, but from all over the country.

Brian used an elaborate keyboard opening as a buildup on the intro, layered on thick harmonies, and the group had what may be its most popular track ever.

That song was the keystone of the next album, *Summer Days (and Summer Nights)*, highlights of which included *Let Him Run Wild* and *Girl, Don't Tell Me*.

A single, *The Little Girl I Once Knew*, in which Brian explored musical time changes, coming to a complete four-beat halt twice in the song, was released next, but it peaked at only No. 20, causing Capitol some consternation and fear that Brian was growing uncommercial.

Well, he was, being hard at work on a major project that included symphonic sounds and a sort of "story album." But to fend off pressure from Capitol the group recorded *Party*, which was the group just sitting around Brian's house singing usually satirical versions of their own songs as well as those by the Beatles and Bob Dylan and some old standards.

But *Barbara Ann*, with guest Dean Torrence on lead vocal, was released as a single from the album and hit No. 2.

Finally, Brian's creation, the *Pet Sounds* album, was issued in March. The lyrics, most of which were written by Tony Asher to Brian's music, had a general exploration of the course of a love affair: the

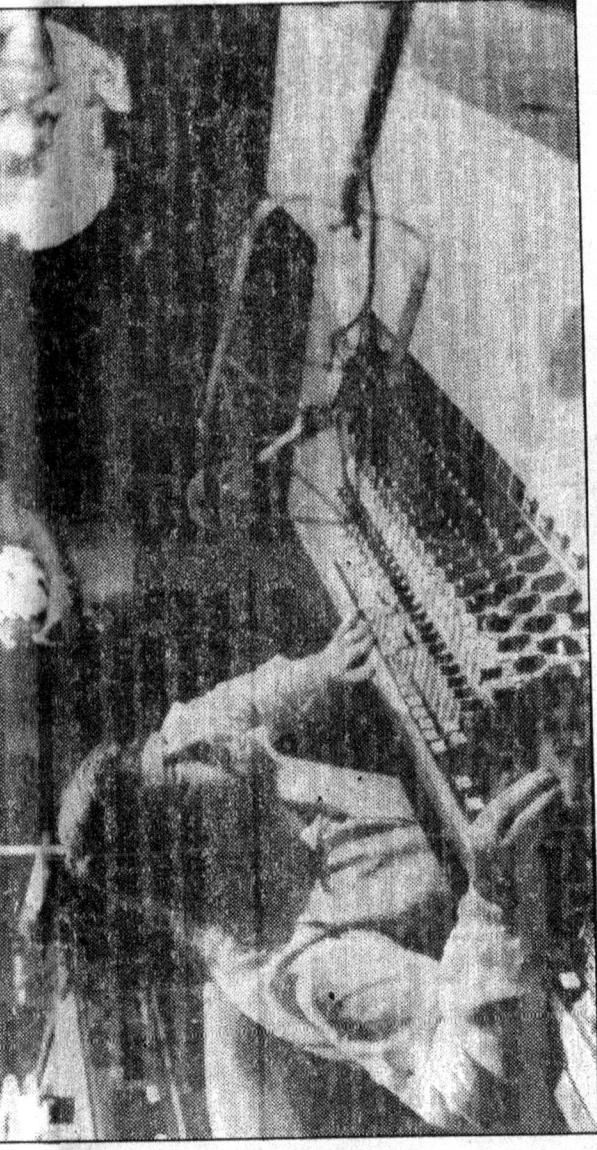

Brian Wilson is the group's chief composer and inspirational force.

sweet, optimistic beginnings (*Wouldn't It Be Nice; I'm Waiting for the Day*), self-examinations (*You Still Believe in Me; That's Not Me*), contentments (*Don't Talk (Put Your Head on My Shoulder)*), love devotionals (*God Only Knows*), signs of trouble (*I Know There's an Answer*), bitter breakups (*Here Today*), self-realizations (*I Just Wasn't Made For These Times*) and bittersweet memories (*Caroline, No*).

To this general story flow Brian added some mood instrumentals and, at Capitol's insistence on a "hit" sound, the group's adaptation of *Sloop John B.*

The critical result? A huge success. The commercial result? A relative failure.

Failure? Well, the album peaked at No. 10, excellent for most artists, but for the Beach Boys, it was their lowest-selling album in some time. The fans, it seemed, just weren't ready to accept the group as anything but sellers of a happy-go-lucky dream.

Despite Capitol's qualms, Brian set to work with complex lyricist Van Dyke Parks on *Smile*, which he conceived as the most thematic album in rock to that point. From the sessions he released *Good Vibrations* as a single. The finished track, actually a combination of several songs, hit No. 1 and Capitol was temporarily relieved.

But Brian's perfectionism — his penchant for redoing take after take — began to wear thin on both the record label's and the group's patience, as the project began to take longer and longer.

To bide time, Capitol released two greatest hits collections, but somehow along the way, the *Smile* project fell through.

Brian had believed he was in direct competition with the Beatles, and this paranoia helped to do him in.

Finally, it had been a year since the last new album, so the group gathered some of the *Smile* fragments and some other doodlings and released *Smiley Smile*.

The next few years brought a flurry of albums — *Wild Honey*, *Friends* and *20/20*. Each had short songs usually woven around pretty melodies and simple, fun lyrics, kind of like in the old days.

In addition, with Brian becoming increasingly

JULY CALIFORNIA CONCERT INSERT

Surfin' U.S.A.

If everybody had an ocean across the U.S.A.
Then everybody'd be surfin' like Californ-i-a
You'd see them wearin' their baggies
Huarachi sandals, too
A bushy, bushy blonde hairdo
Surfin' U.S.A.
You'll catch 'em surfin' at Del Mar
Ventura County line
Santa Cruz and Tressels
Australia's Narabine
All over Manhatten
And down Doheny way
Everybody's gone surfin'
Surfin' U.S.A.
We'll all be plannin' out a route
We're gonna take real soon
We're waxin' down our surfboards
We can't wait for June
We'll all be gone for the summer
We're on safari to stay
Tell the teacher we're surfin'
Surfin' U.S.A.
At Haggarty's and Swami's
Pacific Palisades
San Onofre and Sunset
Redondo Beach, L.A.
All over La Jolla
At Waiamea Bay
Everybody's gone surfin'
Surfin' U.S.A.

—*Brian Wilson and Chuck Berry*

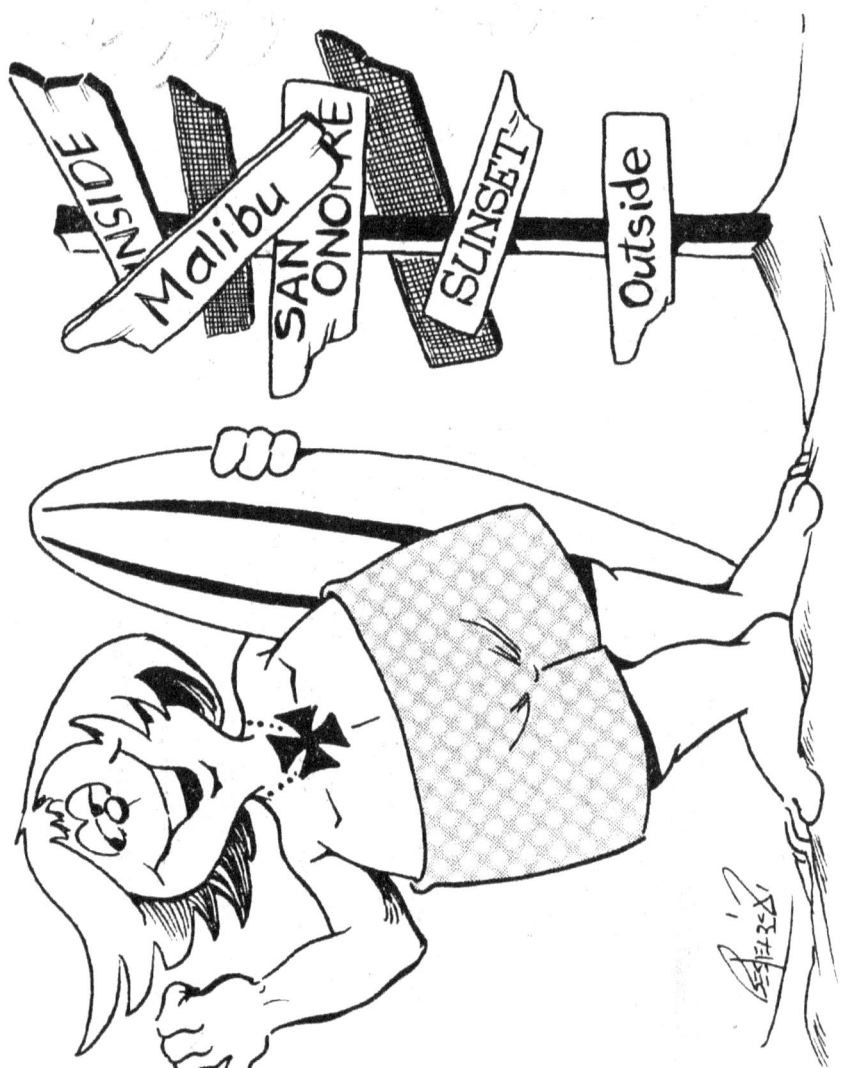

JULY CALIFORNIA CONCERT INSERT

withdrawn, the other group members had a chance to show off their their musical talents.

The Beach Boys also got involved in the Transcendental Meditation phenomenon that enveloped the Beatles and Donovan.

Commercially, the group was at an all-time low, however, and it left Capitol in a departure that neither party seemed too upset about.

It signed with Reprise and released a single, *Add Some Music to Your Day*, for it in early 1970.

Despite much promotion by the new label, the record failed to do much saleswise. A shame, for it was one of the best things the group had done, celebrating the joys of music, noting the various, sometimes subliminal ways that music is a part of our lives.

Soon thereafter, the group released *Sunflower*, which, like *Add Some Music*, was a commercial flop but a critical success, probably the best album since *Pet Sounds*.

The Beach Boys continued touring, mixing some of their new songs with several of the old surfing standards. They were enthusiastically received wherever they played. Of particular success was a gig in late 1970 at the Whisky a Go Go in Los Angeles.

During the Whisky dates, it was planned that Brian would at long last rejoin the group on stage, but after one night he decided he wasn't ready after all. Still, the other five, backed by Daryl Dragon (not yet famous as the Captain of Captain and Tennille fame) on keyboards, kept the crowds happy.

The next album, *Surf's Up*, was built around an ecological theme, but the notable track, other than Brian's gorgeous *Till I Die*, was the title song, one of the main tracks from *Smile*.

Written by Brian and Van Dyke Parks, the song was full of chord changes and word plays, and helped give the album respectable sales.

Bruce Johnston left the group in early 1972 and was replaced by Blondie Chaplin and Ricky Fataar, two musicians who had been with a group called the Flame. But sales were down again for the next album, *Carl and the Passions — So Tough*, released as a double set with a reissue of *Pet Sounds*.

So Tough was probably the group at its lowest, at

Turn to Page 6

JULY CALIFORNIA CONCERT INSERT

Good Vibrations

I love the colorful clothes she wears
And the way the sunlight plays upon her hair
I hear the sound of a gentle word
On the wind that lifts her perfume through the air

I'm picking up good vibrations
She's giving me excitations
I'm picking up good vibrations
She's giving me excitations
Close my eyes, she's somewhat closer now
Softly smile, I know she must be kind
Then I look in her eyes
She goes with me to a blossom world
I'm picking up good vibrations
She's giving me excitations
I don't know where, but she sends me there
Oh my, my, what a sensation
Gotta keep those good lovin' good vibrations
A-happening with her

—*Brian Wilson and Mike Love*

JULY CALIFORNIA CONCERT INSERT

From Page 5

least on record. As with any of their albums, though, there were standouts, this time Brian's *Marcella*, a throwback to the *Help Me, Rhonda* kind of song. But Brian's overall contributions were minimal, and it was sad that the group's greatest artistic success, *Pet Sounds*, should be coupled with its least.

Things picked up a bit on *Holland*, released in early 1973. The featured cut was *Sail On, Sailor*, which had Chaplin singing lead. It made for a great concert tune, and was on their next album, a double set of concert recordings, released later that year.

The drawback of that live album was that Brian had no involvement at all. Indeed, he was against the release.

Soon after, Chaplin and Fataar left the group.

Capitol, noting that the group was a huge concert success, released *Endless Summer*, a two-record set of their pre-*Pet Sounds* hits, in mid-1974. Amazingly enough, the album hit No. 1, providing the group with the frustrating problem of competing with itself.

While their new releases kept selling at a relatively poor pace, these old tracks were becoming popular all over again. And while they were a hot concert band, it was always the old stuff that fans reserved their biggest cheers for. They had become trapped by the dream they had first sold 12 years earlier.

Capitol repeated the success a year later with *Spirit of America*, which consisted of more pre-1966 material, so Reprise, frustrated at not receiving any new material from the group, released a greatest hits set of songs released since 1966 (Reprise had acquired all of the albums since *Pet Sounds* from Capitol).

Meanwhile, Brian had become an even more mysterious character, sometimes not leaving his house, sometimes not even leaving his bed, for weeks. Psychologist Eugene Landy began working with Brian in therapy sessions designed to bring the absent Beach Boys leader out of his shell.

And in early 1976, Brian joined the group in the studio to produce a half-and-half collection of old favorites, such as *Palisades Park* and *Just Once in My Life*, and new songs.

The album, *15 Big Ones*, (the title had two purposes — there were 15 songs and it was their 15th year as a recording group) was their best seller in years, propelled by their first top 10 single in 10 years, a remake of Chuck Berry's *Rock and Roll Music*.

Al Jardine started singing with his friends in high school.

Brian even returned to the stage act for good, although just playing piano and singing a few harmonies. Even the singing was a strain for Brian, whose once-beautiful falsetto had become scratchy and flat.

But the emotional lift for both the group and the fans was just seeing Brian out there with them and knowing that he was once again in the studio.

The Beach Boys continue to have personnel problems, such as when the group became polarized over its choice of management a few years ago.

Likewise, the sales have dipped again, as subsequent albums didn't even dent the top 100.

But they remain a viable force on the music scene, as the fans at their concerts demonstrate.

And while the group itself may be strictly devoted to surfing, each of the members continues his individuality — Mike, the boisterous on-stage leader with the nasal twang, deeply into transcendental meditation; Al, the quiet rhythm guitarist; Dennis, the fun-loving, erratic drummer; Carl, the introspective lead guitarist (who will *not* be at this particular concert because he's taking time off for a solo stint); and Brian, simply described as just, well, Brian.

The California myth may never die, and the Beach Boys will probably continue to be frustrated by having their past hamper their present plans.

But they're celebrating their 20th year in show business, so maybe they still find that it's fun, fun, fun.

JULY CALIFORNIA CONCERT INSERT

Surfer Girl

Little surfer, Little one
Make my heart come all undone
Do you love me, do you, surfer girl?
I have watched you on the shore
Standing by the ocean's roar
Do you love me, do you, surfer girl?
We could ride the surf together
While our love would grow
In my woodie I would take you
Everywhere I go
So I say from me to you
I will make your dreams come true
Do you love me, do you, surfer girl?

—*Brian Wilson*

JULY CALIFORNIA CONCERT INSERT

Time for something new from the fun-in-the-sun boys

By Mark Faris

"Next year," said Mike Love just before he and the rest of the Beach Boys strolled onto the Blossom Music Center stage in Cleveland, Friday, "we might be back here doin' somethin' with the Cleveland Orchestra. Wouldn't that be nice?

"Yeah," he continued, realizing the little play on words (*Wouldn't It Be Nice* is the title of one of their songs). And maybe it would be nice, although the thought of the Cleveland Orchestra doing *Surfin' Safari* or *Surfer Girl* seems all wet. Still, at this stage of the game, the Beach Boys are probably in the market for something a little different.

After all, after 20 years of pounding out the same fun-in-the-sun music about girls, cars and surfin' they've got to be getting a little stale.

And it's beginning to show.

Although the Beach Boys have without a doubt produced some of the greatest summer party music that's ever been written, the boys just don't seem to be into it the way they used to be.

Last Friday, for instance, they sounded flat, forced and out of tune — a lot like some middle-aged guys trying half-heartedly and at times almost pitifully to recapture the spirit and exuberance of their youth and the early and mid-'60s.

Brian Wilson, the one-time creative force behind the group, has been reduced to little more than an empty-eyed piano-bench warmer. His singing, particularly on *God Only Knows*, was embarrassing. And, in view of his enormous girth, his tune *In My Room* seems more of a tribute to his love affair with room service.

Brother Carl Wilson, the guitarist, has departed for a solo career (he'll be the opening act for the Doobie Brothers July 14 at Blossom).

Brother and drummer Dennis Wilson, guitarist Al Jardine and singer Mike Love round out what remains of the original quintet.

Singer-keyboardist Bruce Johnston, Ed Carter, Bobby Figueroa and Mike Meros pick up the slack.

And there was lots of that Friday.

Love's adolescent, adenoidal whine — a trademark of the group — was generally flat and off-key.

As front man for the group he wasn't much, either.

Mostly, he'd just sort of hobble around the stage, cautiously slapping five with folks in the front row and occasionally filling pregnant pauses by telling the audience what a nice bunch it was.

Although there were a lot of shortcomings in the performance, the 18,500 folks (it was Blossom's first sellout of the young season) who jammed the open-air showplace didn't seem to mind — in the least.

When it's summertime and the Beach Boys are on stage there's only one logical thing to do — party.

And that's what they did, from the beginning of the 90-minute set to well past its end.

The group raced through about 25 of their best-known tunes, including *California Girls*, *Sloop John B*, a rousing version of *Do It Again*, *In My Room*, *Good Vibrations*, *Surfer Girl*, *Little Deuce Coupe*, *Help Me Rhonda*, *Barbara Ann* and all the rest.

But it was the seventh tune, *Surfin' Safari*, that really got things going. It burst off the stage like a tidal wave, and from the moment it splashed down on the crowd Blossom was one big beach party without a beach.

Mark Faris, a staff writer for the Akron (Ohio) Beacon Journal, saw last week's Beach Boys concert in Cleveland.

JULY CALIFORNIA CONCERT INSERT

Survival guide for the 'biggest concert' in Long Beach

By Jill Stewart

If you are thinking about loading down a camper with cases of beer and sneaking out to the Beach Boys concert site the night before, forget it.

In fact, if you were thinking about getting up early Sunday for first crack at the line into the 6 p.m. concert, you might want to reset your alarm clock. Wrather Corp., Concerts West and the Long Beach Police Department, all planning for what police are calling "the biggest concert" ever in Long Beach, have put together what they hope is a crowd-control scheme to discourage those kinds of plans.

But the good news is that if you arrive too late to be one of the lucky 25,000 people admitted to the Queen Mary parking lot, you can still hear the concert from the Queensway Bridge or from the dirt area near the Convention Center lagoon.

And because the three-hour concert is being televised live by satellite to an estimated 53 million households nationwide, officials are promising that the 6 p.m. event will start on time.

"No bands will be late," said Bob Liljenwall, vice president of marketing for Wrather Port Properties Ltd., which is providing the concert space.

"We don't have a contract with God, but we do have the satellite network contract, and that's close enough," he said.

Here is the line-up for the bash:
6 p.m.-6:15 p.m. **Rick Springfield.**
6:20 p.m.-6:35 p.m. **Three Dog Night.**
6:40 p.m.-7:15 p.m. **Pablo Cruise.**
7:30 p.m.-8:40 p.m. **Beach Boys.**
8:45 p.m.-9 p.m. **All-band grand finale encore, including Jan and Dean.**

Promoters for the concert have hinted that another surprise "big name" musician will perform.

Here are the dos and don'ts to follow if you plan to attend the concert, which will be broadcast locally on KTLA Channel 5 and KHTZ-FM 97.
— Fans will not be allowed to cross the Queensway

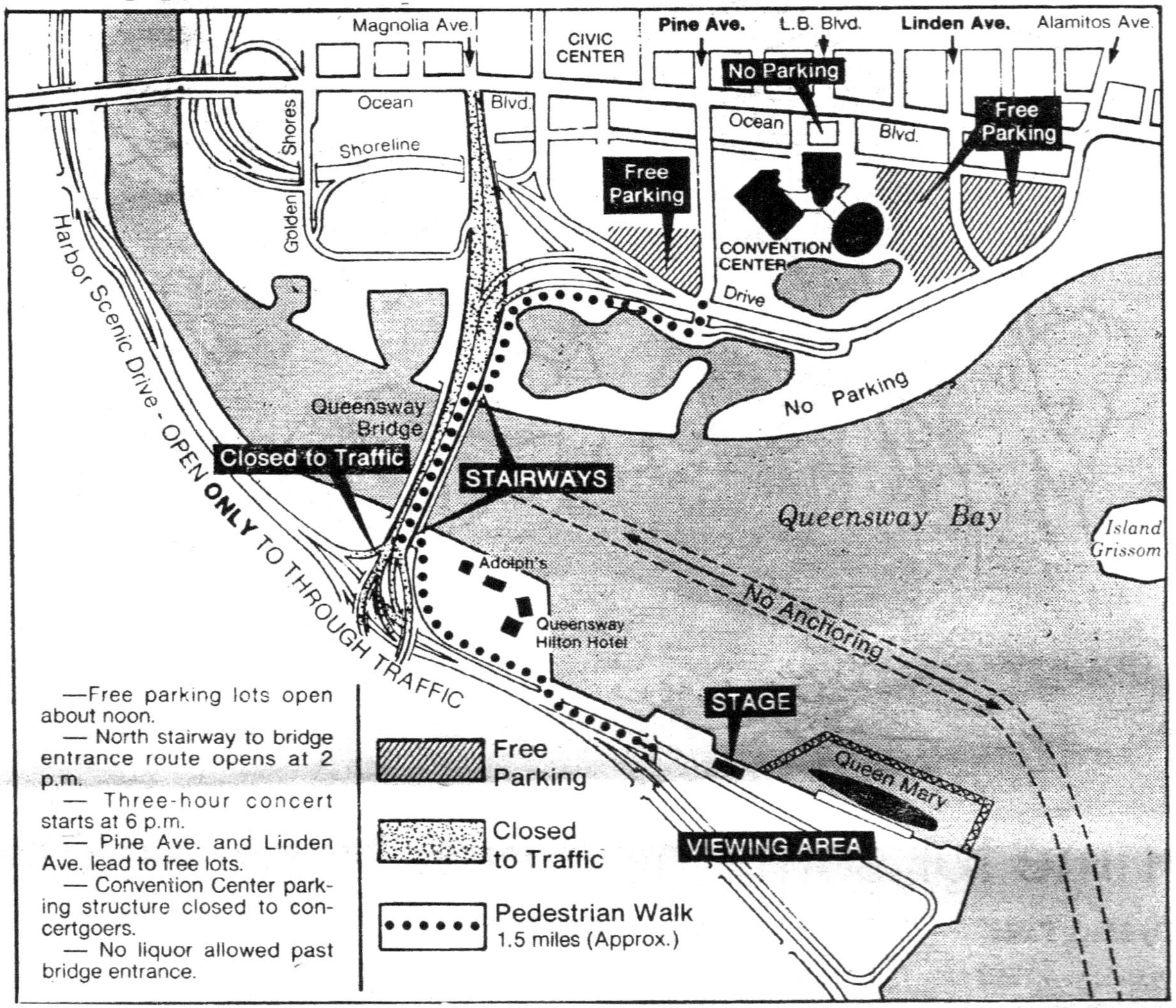

— Free parking lots open about noon.
— North stairway to bridge entrance route opens at 2 p.m.
— Three-hour concert starts at 6 p.m.
— Pine Ave. and Linden Ave. lead to free lots.
— Convention Center parking structure closed to concertgoers.
— No liquor allowed past bridge entrance.

JULY CALIFORNIA CONCERT INSERT

Bridge to the concert site until 2 p.m. Early birds can congregate near the Convention Center lagoon. The route (see map) is over a mile long and is the only way to enter the concert area, so don't plan to carry unusually heavy coolers or baby strollers. Fans must walk from the end of Pine Avenue through a rough dirt area near the lagoon, up a stairway to the bridge, across the bridge, down another set of stairs and along Queensway Drive to the Queen Mary.

— No alcohol will be allowed through admitting areas at the concert site. But food and soft drink concessions will be available to concertgoers.

— No cars will be allowed to park overnight Saturday in the Queen Mary parking lot. Police will conduct a sweep at about midnight Saturday to get rid of any vehicles in the area, except those of registered hotel guests, who will have special passes.

— No parking will be available on Pier J near the Queen Mary, but the Convention Center will provide 3,000 free parking spaces. Three free parking areas are available — a large dirt and pavement lot west of Pine Avenue and south of Ocean Boulevard and the two Convention Center parking lots on either side of Linden Avenue south of Ocean Boulevard. In addition, fans will be allowed to park for free on all surface streets south of Ocean surrounding the Convention Center. The lots open at about noon Sunday.

— Concertgoers cannot park in the undeveloped dirt area south of Shoreline Drive, which is traditionally used for recreation vehicles during Grand Prix week. That area has been fenced off during construction of the new downtown marina.

— No parking will be allowed in the Convention Center's 800-space pay parking structure, which is reserved for the play *The Best Little Whorehouse in Texas* in the Terrace Theater Sunday night.

— More than 8,000 vehicles are expected to be jockeying for spaces, so police are cautioning that parking will be hard to find. If the free lots are full, there is parking in legal spaces in the city's downtown area. In addition, several pay lots will be open as usual downtown, and nearby residents are expected to rent out their front lawns and driveways.

— The Queensway Bridge will be closed to vehicle traffic. Regular harbor district traffic will use Harbor Scenic Drive.

— No seating will be available at the concert, but fans are encouraged to bring blankets, pillows and warmer clothes for nightfall

— Fans will be refused entrance to the site once the crowd count reaches about 25,000. The turnaways will be allowed to watch from the Queensway Bridge. Once the bridge fills up, fans will be allowed to congregate near the lagoon on the opposite side of the flood control channel. Several loudspeakers will be aimed at the lagoon, but no toilet facilities or food concessions will be available.

— Boaters who look for a view of the concert will be cited by the city's Marine Department if they anchor in the center, where a wide path will be kept clear for the regularly operating vessels from Catalina Cruises. Boaters can anchor on either side of the channel, but no boats will be allowed to dock on the shore near the Queen Mary. Speed limit in the channel is 15 mph.

— Swimming will not be allowed from the rocks along the Queen Mary. The city's lifeguards have cautioned that the rocky shoreline and unknown swimming areas along that beach are hazardous.

Officials said that crowd control plans for the concert were still being arranged late this week. Dick Woods, public information officer for the Long Beach Police Department, said that in his 18 years on the force, "this is the biggest concert we've ever had. Even the Rolling Stones concert in 1972 didn't attract the group we're expecting for this one."

Although nobody is sure how many fans might turn up on Sunday, estimates range up to 30,000. By comparison, the Rolling Stones concert at the Long Beach Arena in June 1972 attracted a turnaway crowd of 14,100 and took four weeks of security planning by local officials.

Despite the last-minute change in location, officials said that everything is expected to go smoothly on Sunday, and they do not anticipate problems with angry fans who can't get onto the site.

"We have a very sensitive concert security group who are extremely experienced," said Wrather vice president Liljenwall.

"Our chief of security says it best: If we treat the fans with respect, they will treat us with respect."

Liljenwall said a heavy turnout of fans in the 25-35 year-old age group is expected, but it is not sure how many teen-agers will be attracted to the event. Because of the age group expected on Sunday, Wrather officials said it will be a "family-type concert."

"We'll get a pretty peaceful crowd that is looking for a day at the beach with the Beach Boys," said Brian Pallas, director of marketing for Wrather.

Wrather Corp., which operates the Queen Mary for the city of Long Beach, agreed to turn over its parking lot for the event after a controversial decision by the City Council to not allow the concert at its original location at Bluff Park. The City Council responded to complaints by nearby homeowners about noise and possible rowdy behavior.

But, aside from the headaches caused by the shift in location, Wrather Corp. officials said they are "very happy" to be throwing the concert.

For instance, Liljenwall said that because the concert will cause "tremendous losses" at the Queen Mary's regular tour and museum attractions, Concerts West has agreed to give Wrather Corp. 30 seconds of free air time during the satellite show.

Despite early threats from the promoters that they would not mention Long Beach during the live telecast as punishment for the unexpected location change, Liljenwall said the Queen Mary and the city of Long Beach will be "prominently featured" throughout the show.

"This is going to be a great thing for the image of Long Beach," he said.

JULY CALIFORNIA CONCERT INSERT

Betty Collignon and Paula Perrin, two of the Beach Boys' faithful.

JULY CALIFORNIA CONCERT INSERT

From concert to concert, faithful fans live for the dream

By D'Arcy Fallon

They live from concert to concert. The time in between is filled with the little footnotes of life: work, friends, family. They're the faithful, holding fast to ballads written almost 20 years ago.

Betty Collignon packed all her belongings six months ago, looking for a place she'd heard about in the lyrics of songs. When she came to Los Angeles, it was all here, just as they'd promised. She wears a delicate gold necklace with the words "Calif Girl" at her throat. Now it's official. She's a Beach Boy fan.

"The Beach Boys sang about the sun and the surf, the cars and kids and all that," says Collignon, 20, sitting in her Los Angeles apartment. She's dressed for the part: bright red cotton pants, print shirt, high heels. "That's where I wanted to be. When I came here I wasn't disappointed. A lot of people thought I would be because I built up this whole concept. There's just this *thing* about California. And what the Beach Boys said — that's what I wanted.

"They're still surfing and once in a while we'll see a Woody out there," she says stubbornly. "They're still playing the songs on the radio."

She and her roommate, Paula Perrin, also rabid about the group, have transformed their small, one-bedroom apartment into a Beach Boys Hall of Fame. Memorabilia of every kind is displayed to its best advantage, from Beach Boy frisbees in the kitchen to

---

She packed all her belongings six months ago, looking for a place she'd heard about in the lyrics of songs.

---

mobiles to hair curler bags. It's all here. Collignon offers to model her Beach Boys jacket, then thinks twice. She explains: "I'm working on my third jacket; I don't want anything to happen to this one."

The hallway doubles as an art gallery; the walls are covered with candid shots of the group, including a rare shot of two women — Brian's ex-wife, Marilyn, and her sister. Collignon pauses before the photo. "She's not that cute, but she's had a nose job since."

In the bedroom there's a small photo of Collignon and Carl Wilson, cheek to cheek, in a heart-shaped frame. His eyes are closed, with a curious half-smile on his lips. He looks like he's slow-dancing or drugged. Not Collignon; she's wide-eyed and grinning, face bared to the camera.

Their Beach Boy collection is extensive. Some of it is squirrelled away in closets, but the records are all out on display. "All this stuff is worth money," says Collignon, waving towards the stacks of records on the floor. "A lot of this stuff you can't get anymore.

It takes years to build a collection. If you go by face value for what we paid for it at the time, I've got about $4,000 worth of stuff. And that's *face* value." Perrin adds, "An album I've paid $25 for, well, I've seen it go for $300. Every year they go up. It's like an investment."

It may be an investment, but these girls will never sell. They have napkins, belt buckles, hats, posters, kites, postcards, and Beach Boy pens. It's a never-ending obsession, fed by obscure photos or a glass Dennis once used.

"The other day I almost got us killed driving down Santa Monica Boulevard," says Perrin. "I happened to see a Beach Boys poster, right there, by the Greek Theater and I was in a lane where there was no way anyone could pull around me. I just slammed on my brakes jumped out and got the poster. I backed up traffic, but I got my poster.

"Six months ago we didn't even know one another," says Perrin, 25, who works in customer service for the Press-Telegram. She and Collignon met at a Beach Boys Fan Party, and became close friends. They recall the dates and places of half a dozen parties and concerts with ease.

"I missed Christmas with my family because I wanted to come out here and see the Beach Boys and it was the only flight I could get," says Collig-

Turn to Page 10

JULY CALIFORNIA CONCERT INSERT

Faithful fans live for the dream

From Page 9

non. "That was the night they got their star." Their star? "Yes, their star. On Hollywood Boulevard. We got to go watch them lay it down. We were there yelling and screaming. I had a police escort to that star."

Keeping up with the Beach Boys is an expensive habit to maintain, especially for Collignon, who works as a "secretary-manager" at McDonald's. "It's the only thing I can find right now," she says, embarrassed. Yet now that she's here, she's found that people "don't care for the Beach Boys like they do back East." If she wants to see the Beach Boys she goes elsewhere. "I don't stay in California." Collignon and Perrin have big plans for the upcoming Beach Boys concert in Long Beach. They've made reservations in a hotel close to the Queen Mary so they can get in line early. Neither wants to miss the boat.

They know their men. They're intimate with their problems. "Brian's always been a shy person," says Collignon with a knowing shake of the head. "Brian is, well, to us, he's a genius. In my experiences with him, he's just as normal as everyone else." They agree that Dennis has always been vain, but is it any wonder? "He's *always* been told that — for 20 years now," she says. The nicks and grooves in their men are the stuff of which fan clubs are made.

"It starts off when you begin by collecting a record, and from there, somehow it goes deeper," says Perrin. "You just go further and further and further into it. Pretty soon you know who they're dating, where they live, what they drive, what they eat, what they drink."

There are bound to be favorites. Al Jardine is Perrin's. He's deep. He's sensitive. He lives in Big Sur. She blushes when asked what she'd do if she had an evening with him to herself. She regains her

President of fan club owes the group dedication in return for so much joy

By Tim Grobaty

It takes roughly eight minutes of conversation with Alice Lillie to come to the realization that, if necessary, she would hurl herself off a cliff if it meant saving the Beach Boys. She owes them that much.

They're her boys: Carl, Brian, Dennis, Mike, Al and the others who have drifted in and away from the group in the past 25 years. They've given Ms. Lillie so much joy, she figures she owes them something. Like a fan club.

In 1973, Ms. Lillie, of Los Angeles, started an unofficial club, Beach Boys Freaks United (BBFUN), a small circle of friends who exchanged notes on the band, tour schedules and other items of common interest via a single-sheet, mimeographed newsletter.

Then, "from out of the clear blue sky," she says, "the Beach Boys' manager," then Steve Love, "called and asked me if I would make the club the official Beach Boys fan club. I said I most certainly would."

She certainly did. BBFUN's newsletter — now funded by the Beach Boys — grew to a four-page tabloid newspaper brimming with facts and interviews, and Ms. Lillie, now 31, is president of the international Beach Boys fan club with nearly 2,000 members.

"We have people all over the free world," boasts Ms. Lillie, "and some behind the Iron Curtain — Yugoslavia, Poland, the Communist countries that aren't too strict."

Having the 'fan club' in its official title means that the club receives full cooperation from the Beach Boys. Rather than print a newsletter filled with hearsay and gossip, it's filled with facts and interviews and Ms. Lillie and other contributing writers are sometimes treated to pre-release audi-

—Staff Photo by BILL HODGE

Paula Perrin is one of the dedicated fans.

Fun, Fun, Fun; Help Me, Rhonda; Surfin' U.S.A.; Good Vibrations; and *Barbara Ann.*

Ms. Lillie has never seen a bad Beach Boys concert — there's no such thing. And the worst album the band has put out is good. "Their records range from good to superb," she says. "Personally, I like

JULY CALIFORNIA CONCERT INSERT

had an evening with him to herself. She regains her composure enough to venture: "His lifestyle is different from that of most rock musicians — it doesn't revolve around Southern California. It's very different than the way Rod Stewart would live."

Collignon's favorite was Dennis until he was replaced by Carl. "Carl is sweet," she says softly. "He's very gentle. Very funny. Very gentle. Always goes out of his way to say hello. He's divorced. He's got a steady girlfriend. I'd like to spend some time with him, doing different things. Just watching him rehearse, and after the show, just, uh, be with him."

What it comes down to is the Beach Boy values. Solid. Old fashioned. Perrin says their values are her values, yet she's hard pressed to explain what they are. "I don't know. It's like their music — very pure." Collignon laughs, and Perrin looks embarrassed.

"They're family," Collignon adds, in a burst of warmth. "They're our family group. They treat their fans like their family. It's just a big...family."

Perrin picks up her dog, Sassy, and adds: "I don't feel like they're up there and we're lowly fans, like in *some* rock groups."

"We're fans and friends, we're not groupies," says Collignon. "Those people (groupies) are around for one night. They get used. One night and that's it," said Collignon. "They're 'sweetheart' and 'darling.' We're Paula and Betty. And after this one's over you just think, 'Oh my god, what do I have to look forward to now?'," says Perrin. "But then you think, 'there's always the Greek Theater. Two concerts. All right.'

"I've been living like this for five years. You don't plan your life around 'well, next year I'm going to get a college degree and go out and get a real job or something.' If there's something more, I haven't found it."

writers are sometimes treated to previews and mentions of albums. Plus, the club's mailing address is printed on the back of the Beach Boys' album jackets.

What does it take to be the Beach Boys' No. 1 fan?

The Beach Boys don't pass through California without Ms. Lillie seeing them four or five times. After the group's 20th anniversary performance on the Queen Mary, she'll drive up to Lake Tahoe to watch them play for three nights at Caesars Tahoe. Similarly, Ms. Lillie caught a week's worth of Beach Boys' concerts at the Universal Amphitheater in 1979.

She saw the group for the first time in 1965 in the New York Academy of Music. "I had been a fan of the Beach Boys since 1962 and I wanted to see if they sounded as good live as they did on record. I said, 'Let's just see how good they can sound.' Well, they were great, every bit as good as their records. The first song I heard them do was, *Do You Wanna Dance*, and everybody was screaming. All that screaming: It was terrible — or wonderful — depending on how you want to look at it."

By 1975 she had seen the Beach Boys 45 times and she stopped counting. "It must be over 100 now," she says. "I used to travel as far as San Francisco when the air fares were lower. Now I'll go down to San Diego or sometimes they play in San Bernardino."

The show, she says, has changed "in a great many ways" since the '65 performance, but a lot of the songs are the same. "It's funny," says Ms. Lillie, "but the younger the crowd, the older the songs they want to hear."

The obligatory songs, the songs she says she's never heard the Beach Boys omit from the scores of concerts she's seen, are, *I Get Around; Fun, Fun,* from good to superb," she says. "Personally, I like their middle period, 1968 to 1974, better than the early or post-'74 periods. A lotta times we sit around and argue about which period is best."

But these are the best of times for Ms. Lillie and her fellow Beach Boys fans. A "wonderful celebration," the anniversary concert will expose still more young people to the sound of the band and bring more members to Beach Boys Freaks United. And, it'll be a good time, despite the fact that Carl Wilson, spending some time promoting his solo album, won't be there.

"I would have been happier if the concert was on the beach like they originally planned," says Ms. Lillie, "simply because more people could have seen them. A lot of younger people can't afford to buy a ticket to see them in a regular concert and this would have been a great opportunity for them. But I was worried about somebody drowning. The way they're setting up the concert now, I don't think anybody will get hurt, but a lot of people will be turned away and not get a chance to see the Beach Boys.

"I'm going to leave at 8 in the morning and I'll stay on the freeway until I hit the traffic jam then I'll get out and park and take the bus the rest of the way. It's the parking that bothers me the most. If they start turning people away at 10, I'll get turned away. I'll make some noise, though. I'll make a fuss, but if I can't get in I'm going to stay as close as possible and listen to a radio. (The concert is being aired live on KHTZ 97 FM).

For membership information, send a self-addressed, stamped envelope to:

Beach Boys Freaks United
P.O. Box 84282
Los Angeles, Calif.
90073

JULY CALIFORNIA CONCERT INSERT

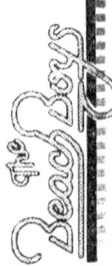

Once upon a time, they were younger

By Mark Faris

There was no long black limousine sweeping in ahead of gaggles of giddy, giggling girls.

There was no fanfare, no TV cameras, no nothing. Just a massive silver and red bus that silently rolled into the loading dock backstage at Blossom Music Center in Cleveland.

As the doors of the imposing coach flipped open, four solemn faces were immediately recognizable amidst the entourage of musicians, roadies and girlfriends that emerged.

They were the faces of Dennis and Brian Wilson, their cousin Mike Love, and Al Jardine — the Beach Boys. Only brother Carl Wilson, who left the group earlier this year to do some solo work, was missing.

The Beach Boys, for those who have never listened to a radio, are the guys who recorded all those million-selling records in the 1960s, rock 'n' roll records that told the world about surfing, sun-tanned young ladies, fast cars and growing up in Southern California sunshine — records that made kids from Ohio grind their teeth in envy.

As the four of them made their way into the backstage area of this breathtaking open-air arena in the rolling, wooded hills of suburban Akron, something seemed wrong.

These guys didn't look like beach boys. Brian, for instance, a monstrous paunch looming beneath his billowing shirt, looked more like a beach ball.

And Al, in his Lacoste tennis shorts, sneakers, socks, polo shirt and small white cap concealing thinning hair, appeared headed for the same fate. Only Dennis and Mike seemed fit. And even Mike was walking with the stiff, brittle stride of an older man.

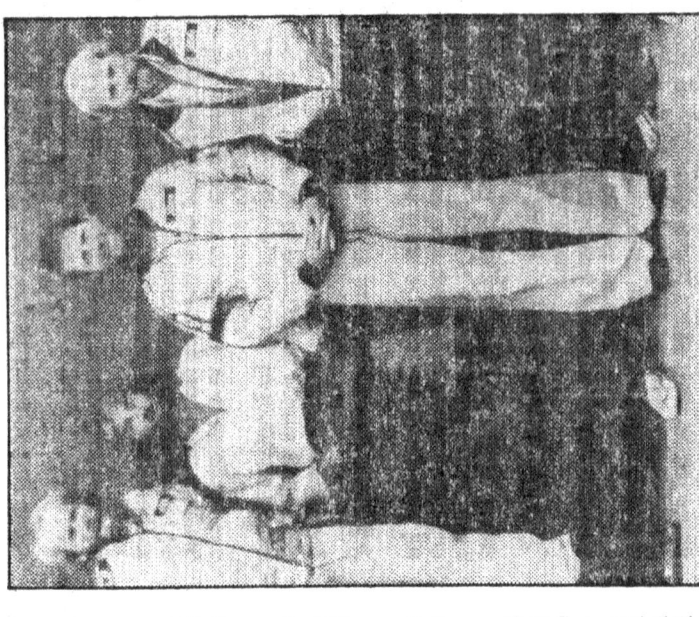

"Like most of those kinds of shows, there were about eight or 10 acts on the bill, and each of them would do about three numbers. "We did *Surfin'* and I think we did *Finger Poppin'* and *Johnny B. Goode.*

"We got $300 for the show and couldn't believe it. I mean, for us it was fun. We'd have probably done it for free just for the chance to sing in front of a crowd."

Although the Memorial Auditorium performance marked the official beginning of the Beach Boys, Mike said that he and Brian, Carl, Dennis and Al had been singing together for years.

"It was like a hobby for us," he said. "We were always getting together and singing at the Wilson house over in Hawthorne.

"Sometimes it'd just be me and Brian. Sometimes it was all five of us. Sometimes even Aunt Audree and my sister Maureen would sing with us. There was always music. Brian's father, Murry, was a frustrated songwriter. Aunt Audree was a piano teacher. And my mom, well she was really into classical music. We had a grand piano, a harp and an organ right in the living room and she made me take all kinds of music lessons that I hated.

"When she let us play rock 'n' roll on the hi-fi, she'd make us keep the volume on about six. But when she played her opera records, she'd crank it all the way up to 10 or whatever was the max."

Mike says he and Brian, Carl, Dennis and Al decided to become the Beach Boys one afternoon in the late summer of 1961.

"Aunt Audree and Uncle Murry had gone to Mexico for a vacation and me and Al and the Wilsons got together and decided to write a song about surfin'

The Beach Boys, whose first concert was on New Year's Eve 1961 in the Long Beach Memorial Auditorium.

ing meditation from the Maharishi in December of 1967. That was the best 'thing' I got from the Beach Boys experience — other than money and lots of gold records.

"But I like the future plenty good. I think about it a lot."

JULY CALIFORNIA CONCERT INSERT

> Writing the music came pretty easily because they were writing pretty much about themselves.

Together, the four of them looked more like middle-aged bowlers taking some time out for sight-seeing between frames — or something like that.

They didn't, however, look like folks who'd be whining about 409s, little deuce coupes and surfin' safaris.

But that's exactly what they did. And the fact that they did it before a capacity crowd of 18,500 people of nearly all ages attests to the enormous and continuing impact of the group and its music.

Yes, the Beach Boys have come a long way since that New Year's Eve in 1961 when they performed in the Long Beach Memorial Auditorium.

That was the very first time they performed as the Beach Boys, the very first time they were ever paid to sing as the Beach Boys. And they loved it.

"A few months earlier, I think it was in September, we had recorded our first record," recalls Mike in a soft, articulate voice. "It was called *Surfin'* and it was doing pretty well I think it was number one or two on the L.A. charts at the time.

"So we were asked to perform at this annual show and dance in Long Beach. It was called the Ritchie Valens Memorial Show and Dance (in memory of the singer who died Feb. 3, 1959, in a Clear Lake, Iowa, plane crash that also took the lives of Buddy Holly and the Big Bopper).

together and decided to write a song about surfin' cause nobody'd ever done a song about surfin'. We never really expected anything to come of it. We never really wanted anything to come of it. We just thought it'd be a fun thing to do."

Even after their Long Beach performance, Mike says the group had no thoughts of fame and fortune. He said it wasn't until several months later, when they signed with Capitol Records and recorded *Surfin' Safari*, *Surfer Girl* and *409* that they began to realize their potential.

"After those three tunes, we did our first tour. It was in the Midwest, and once we saw the crowds that started showing up to see us, we had an idea we might be able to make a career out of our music."

According to Mike, writing the music came pretty easily because, he says, they were writing pretty much about themselves.

"You know, just like our music, we were into our cars, our girlfriends, the beach, goin' to school and whatever. Actually I was workin' at the time. I was in the oil business, you know — gas, oil, check the tires, that kind of oil business. But over all, I'd say we all led a pretty average middle-class existence, just like most of the other kids we knew."

After 20 years, Mike is the first to recognize that the Beach Boys are past the "boy" stage. Still, he says he isn't one to live in the past.

"As far as I'm concerned," he explained, "the future is what I'm into. I think things get better.

"For instance, now, instead of just having one nice house, I have nice houses. I have a beautiful place in Tahoe, I have a beautiful place in Santa Barbara and I have a beautiful place in Hawaii. We've had a lot of success in the past. The best time for me was learn-

Although Mike admits that the demand for old Beach Boy tunes — as well as Brian's departure from dynamic involvement in writing and recording — has somewhat inhibited the group's creative opportunities, he says they still have plenty of latitude.

"We're not credible as a disco band," he says. "And we're not a country act or a psychedelic act in the sense of (Jimi) Hendrix-style guitar, although *Good Vibrations* was psychedelic. But we do rock 'n' roll and ballads. And we've found that some rock songs have a formula, like *Rock & Roll Music* and *Surfin' U.S.A.*, for instance. They're essentially the same.

"But what you've got to understand is that following a success story like we had in the 1960s isn't easy. I mean, that's a real hard act to follow. Our hit singles are still being played on the radio, year after year. With the exception of the Beatles, I think our records are probably played more than anybody else's.

"So creatively we may not be doing as much as we once did. But hey, it's not a bad deal getting all the adulation we receive after 20 years. Just look at that crowd out there.

"Overall, we've done real well musically and goal-wise. We've played a couple thousand shows together, made a few million dollars and had a pretty good time. And although there's a few things we'd like to go back and do better or forget about altogether, I can't complain.

"After all, nothing in this world is perfect."

Mark Faris is a staff writer for the Akron (Ohio) Beacon Journal.

JULY CALIFORNIA CONCERT INSERT

the Beach Boys

Strife and tension often mix with the sun-and-fun music

By Steve Elders

It may be the Beach Boys' 20th anniversary concert, but Carl Wilson, one of the founding members, doesn't think much of it.

Or at least that's how it may appear to some who attend the show Sunday night because Carl won't be there.

While it hasn't been announced that the youngest Wilson brother has permanently left the group, he has not performed with them on this tour. Instead, he is pursuing a solo career and is opening for the Doobie Brothers on some dates.

This will be a disappointment to longtime Beach Boys fans, because in concerts of recent years Carl usually sang the group's ballads, leaving the surfing and fun songs to nasal-voiced Mike Love.

But things have never been completely sunny for the Beach Boys.

Throughout the lives of both the group and its members there has been strife and tension; with the Wilsons' father, Murry; among each other; with their 1960s record label, Capitol; and within themselves.

Murry Wilson, father of Brian, Dennis and Carl, was a strict disciplinarian.

He could be gentle and sensitive at one moment and sadistic and cruel at another.

As Dennis Wilson once said, "Our father beat the s--- out of us. His punishments were outrageous." These punishments would range from verbal abuse to physical beatings.

Murry always somehow found fault with his sons. Brian remembers that no matter how well he did, either in class or in sports, Murry always found something wrong with him.

"I used to catch it from him all the time over that stuff," Brian said. "It bothered me because it made me feel like I was inferior (and) worthless."

And yet, there were the other times in the Wilson household, the times that Murry made sure were filled with music. When Brian was 6, Murry bought him lessons on a toy accordion for six weeks. At other times while the boys were growing up, he would just sit back and enjoy their singing.

—Staff Photo by BILL HODGE

JULY CALIFORNIA CONCERT INSERT

would just sit back and enjoy their singing.

He was the group's first manager, however, and it was his hustling that enabled the band to get its first contract.

The group fired him in this capacity in 1964 because "We decided he was better as a father than a manager," Brian said.

The next emotional incident for the group occured in December 1964.

While on tour in Texas, Brian suffered a nervous breakdown and had to go home to Hawthorne. The other four members finished the tour without him.

Brian began to devote his full time to the studio, and told the group in early 1965 that he was giving up touring with them.

Mike, Carl, Dennis and Al took the news with much sorrow, and Brian later said that Mike even questioned whether the Beach Boys should continue.

But cooler heads prevailed and the group continued on the road without their creator and inspirational leader.

So while the road group was still singing about sunshine, surf and girls, the studio group was exploring new musical dimensions.

But then the "studio group" was becoming mainly Brian Wilson, and the other members weren't so sure they liked moving away from the safe and successful surfing sounds.

Although there was some grumbling by the other members about the "new kind" of lyrics on the *Pet Sounds* album, the released record was still just about as Brian had conceived it.

But while Brian was considering various ways to do *Good Vibrations* the disagreements began to show through more.

But *Good Vibrations* became one of their biggest hits.

The *Smile* album project was the crusher, though.

A collection of the Beach Boys.

It was during this year that Brian's studio perfectionism and ultimate paranoia really overtook him.

Smile was dumped after a year, but not before several colorful stories had emerged.

Brian's ambition was to write and produce the most complex and far-reaching album in rock music to that time.

Meanwhile, tales of Brian's eccentricity were becoming known also. He had a giant sandbox built around his piano in his home so his feet would be comfortable while he was playing.

A huge tent was pitched at the Wilson house. While on a physical fitness kick, he turned his living room into a gymnasium.

While recording one part of the *Elements Suite* devoted to fire, Brian recreated in the studio the sounds of firemen putting out a blazing fire. But some time later, when a building down the street from the studio burned, he was convinced that his musical piece somehow had something to do with it, so he reportedly burned the tapes.

And finally, believing he was in competition with the Beatles, Brian thought that the British group's release of *Sgt. Pepper's Lonely Hearts Club Band* indicated that they had won the race to be out first with the "everything" album. Thus, *Smile* was dumped.

Bits and pieces of *Smile* have appeared on some of the albums the Beach Boys released in the next few years, but the project as a whole remains a sonic legend to this day.

Problems during this time also came from Capitol Records, which wanted the group to stick to the tried-and-true formula of hit-making. After all, the group's sales were down after *Pet Sounds*, and even though *Good Vibrations* was a big seller, the label

would have preferred to see Brian go back to the happy days. But he never did, and sales continued to plummet.

One stigma that landed on the group in the late '60s was Dennis' friendship with aspiring songwriter and cult leader Charles Manson.

The group actually recorded an alleged D. Wilson-Manson collaboration, *Never Learn Not to Love*, on its 20/20 album, even though Manson's name is omitted on the label.

In the 1970s, Brian's contributions to the group's records were scant, working on a song here and there. Instead of the studio, he spent most of his time at home, sometimes not even getting out of bed.

His body also grew to balloonlike proportions, and he was taking drugs heavily.

As a last resort, his wife, Marilyn, finally convinced him to see psychologist Dr. Eugene Landy, who came equipped with bodyguards, a diet and a daily schedule for the eldest Beach Boy.

The sometimes painful (for Brian) rehabilitation worked, for Brian was soon back in the studio, writing and producing for the group.

He also regained his desire to join the band on stage, and after 12 years, audiences could once again see the original Beach Boys.

In recent years there has been talk that the group would disband over members' squabbling about who should manage the group, but until the recent incident with Carl it appeared this latest hurdle has been overcome.

Nevertheless, the Beach Boys will be out there Sunday. The group will consist of the remaining four, old friend Bruce Johnston and other backup musicians.

JULY CALIFORNIA CONCERT INSERT

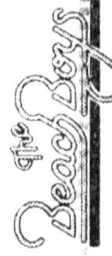

A selected collection of albums — 1962 through 1980

Most Beach Boys albums are still in print. Many, however, do not have the original title or have had songs deleted in subsequent printings. For example, *Today* can sometimes be found as *Dance, Dance, Dance*, while *Wild Honey* and *20/20* have been released as a double set.

Current versions of *Summer Days (and Summer Nights)* don't include *Amusement Parks, U.S.A.* Other mid-1960s albums before *Pet Sounds* are also missing certain tracks these days.

Capitol released the Beach Boys' records through 20/20, when the group switched to Reprise. In 1974, Reprise obtained all the albums from *Pet Sounds* to 20/20 from Capitol and released them under its own label. The group's last two albums are on Caribou.

Most of the '60s albums are now found in budget bins, along with some smaller-label records featuring their pre-Capitol songs.

Here is a list of Capitol-Reprise-Caribou Beach Boys albums and the month of release:

SURFIN' SAFARI — December 1962
Surfin' Safari; County Fair; Ten Little Indians; Chug-a-Lug; Little Miss America; 409; Surfin'; Heads You Win — Tails I Lose; Summertime Blues; Cuckoo Clock; Moon Dawg; The Shift.

SURFIN' U.S.A. — April 1963
Surfin' U.S.A.; Farmer's Daughter; Miserlou; Stoked; Lonely Sea; Shut Down; Noble Surfer; Lana; Surf Jam; Let's Go Trippin'; Finders Keepers.

SURFER GIRL — July 1963
Surfer Girl; Catch a Wave; The Surfer Moon; South Bay Surfer; The Rocking Surfer; Little Deuce Coupe; In My Room; Hawaii; Surfer's Rule; Our Car Club; Your Summer Dream; Boogie Woogie.

LITTLE DEUCE COUPE — October 1963
Little Deuce Coupe; Ballad of Ole Betsy; Be True to Your School; Car Crazy Cutie; Cherry, Cherry Coupe; 409; Shut Down; Spirit of America; Our Car Club; No-Go Showboat; A Young Man is Gone; Custom Machine.

SHUT DOWN, VOL. 2 — March 1964
Fun, Fun, Fun; Don't Worry, Baby; In the Parkin' Lot; "Cassius" Love vs. "Sonny" Wilson; The Warmth of the Sun; This Car of Mine; Why Do Fools Fall in Love; Pom-Pom Playgirl; Keep an Eye on Summer; Shut Down, Part II; Louie, Louie; Denny's Drums.

ALL SUMMER LONG — July 1964
I Get Around; All Summer Long; Hushabye; Little Honda; We'll Run Away; Carl's Big Chance; Wendy; Do You Remember; Girls on the Beach; Drive-In; Our Favorite Recording Sessions; Don't Back Down.

CHRISTMAS ALBUM — October 1964
Little Saint Nick; The Man with All the Toys; Santa's Beard; Merry Christmas, Baby; Christmas Day; Frosty the Snowman; We Three Kings of Orient Are; Blue Christmas; Santa Claus is Comin' to Town; White Christmas; I'll Be Home for Christmas; Auld Lang Syne.

CONCERT — October 1964
Fun, Fun, Fun; Little Old Lady From Pasadena; Little Deuce Coupe; Long, Tall Texan; In My Room; Monster Mash; Let's Go Trippin'; Papa-Ooo-Mow-Mow; The Wanderer; Hawaii; Graduation Day; I Get Around; Johnny B. Goode.

TODAY — March 1965
Do You Wanna Dance?; Good To My Baby; Don't Hurt My Little Sister; When I Grow Up (To Be a Man); Help Me, Rhonda (version one); Dance, Dance, Dance; Please Let Me Wonder; I'm So Young; Kiss Me, Baby;

Turn to Page 14

JULY CALIFORNIA CONCERT INSERT

97FM KHTS PRESENTS A FREE CONCERT

TWENTY YEARS OF GOOD VIBRATIONS OVER AMERICA

PABLO CRUISE
RICK SPRINGFIELD
THREE DOG NIGHT

JAN & DEAN
PLUS SURPRISE GUESTS
HOSTED BY KHTZ'S CHARLIE TUNA AND WOLFMAN JACK

LIVE FROM THE QUEEN MARY IN LONG BEACH
SUNDAY, JULY 5, 6PM
STEREO SIMULCAST ON KHTZ 97FM AND KTLA 5

JULY CALIFORNIA CONCERT INSERT

From Page 13

She Knows Me Too Well; In the Back of My Mind; Bull Session With "Big Daddy."

SUMMER DAYS (AND SUMMER NIGHTS) — July 1965
The Girl From New York City; Amusement Parks, U.S.A.; Then I Kissed Her; Salt Lake City; Girl, Don't Tell Me; Help Me, Rhonda (version two); California Girls; Let Him Run Wild; You're So Good to Me; Summer Means New Love; I'm Bugged at My Old Man; And Your Dream Comes True.

PARTY — October 1965
Hully Gully; I Should Have Known Better; Tell Me Why; Papa-Ooo-Mow-Mow; Mountain of Love; You've Got to Hide Your Love Away; Devoted to You; Alley Oop; There's No Other (Like My Baby); Medley; I Get Around, Little Deuce Coupe, The Times They Are A-Changing; Barbara Ann. (Out of print.)

PET SOUNDS — May 1966
Wouldn't It Be Nice: You Still Believe in Me; That's Not Me; Don't Talk (Put Your Head on My Shoulder); I'm Waiting for the Day; Let's Go Away for a While; Sloop John B; God Only Knows; I Know There's an Answer; Here Today; I Just Wasn't Made for These Times; Pet Sounds; Caroline, No.

BEST OF THE BEACH BOYS — July 1966
Surfin' U.S.A.; Surfer Girl; Catch a Wave; Little Deuce Coupe; In My Room; Fun, Fun, Fun; The Warmth of the Sun; Louie, Louie; Kiss Me, Baby; You're So Good to Me; Wendy.

BEST OF THE BEACH BOYS, VOL. 2 — August 1967
Surfin' Safari; I Get Around; Don't Worry, Baby; When I Grow Up (To Be a Man); Little Saint Nick; Please Let Me Wonder; Long, Tall Texan; Help Me, Rhonda (version two); Let Him Run Wild; California Girls; Barbara Ann; 409.

SMILEY SMILE — September 1967
Heroes and Villains; Vega-Tables; Fall Breaks and Back to Winter (W. Woodpecker Symphony); She's Goin' Bald; Little Pad; Good Vibrations; With Me Tonight; Wind Chimes; Gettin' Hungry; Wonderful; Whistle In.

WILD HONEY — December 1967
Wild Honey; Aren't You Glad; I Was Made to Love Her; Country Air; A Thing or Two; Darlin'; I'd Love Just Once to See You; Here Comes the Night; Let the Wind Blow; How She Boogalooed It; Mama Says.

FRIENDS — May 1968
Meant For You; Friends; Wake the World; Be Here in the Mornin'; When a Man Needs a Woman; Passing By; Anna Lee the Healer; Little Bird; Be Still; Busy Doin' Nothin'; Diamond Head; Transcendental Meditation.

20/20 — January 1969
Do It Again; I Can Hear Music; Bluebirds Over the Mountain; Be With Me; All I Want to Do; The Nearest Faraway Place; Cottonfields; I Went to Sleep; Time to Get Alone; Never Learn Not to Love; Our Prayer; Cabinessence.

SUNFLOWER — August 1970
Slip on Through; This Whole World; Add Some Music to Your Day; Got to Know the Woman; Deirdre; It's About Time; Tears in the Morning; All I Wanna Do; Forever; Our Sweet Love; At My Window; Cool, Cool Water

SURF'S UP — September 1971
Don't Go Near the Water; Long Promised Road; Take a Load Off Your Feet; Disney Girls (1957); Student Demonstration Time; Feel Flows; Lookin' at Tomorrow (A Welfare Song); A Day in the Life of a Tree; Till I Die; Surf's Up.

CARL AND THE PASSIONS: SO TOUGH — May 1972
You Need a Mess of Help to Stand Alone; Here She Comes; He Come Down; Marcella; Hold on, Dear Brother; Make It Good; All This is That; Cuddle Up. (Released with Pet Sounds as a double set.)

HOLLAND — January 1973
Sail on, Sailor; Steamboat; California Saga: Big Sur, The Beaks of Eagles, California (On My Way to Sunny Cal-if-or-n-i-a); The Trader; Leaving This Town; Only With You; Funky Pretty; Mount Vernon and Fairway (A Fairy Tale); Mt. Vernon and Fairway — Theme, I'm the Pied Piper, Better Get Back in Bed, Magic Transistor Radio, I'm the Pied Piper, Radio King Dom. (The Mt. Vernon suite was a smaller record within the jacket.)

IN CONCERT — November 1973
Sail on, Sailor; Sloop John B; The Trader; You Still Believe in Me; California Girls; Darlin'; Marcella; Caroline, No; Leaving This Town; Heroes and Villains; Funky Pretty; Let the Wind Blow; Help Me, Rhonda; Surfer Girl; Wouldn't It Be Nice; We Got Love; Don't Worry, Baby; Surfin' U.S.A.; Good Vibrations; Fun, Fun, Fun. (A double set.)

ENDLESS SUMMER — June 1974
Surfin' Safari; Surfin' U.S.A.; Shut Down; Surfer Girl; Catch a Wave; Little Deuce Coupe; In My Room; Be True to Your School; Fun, Fun, Fun; Don't Worry, Baby; The Warmth of the Sun; I Get Around; All Summer Long; Wendy; Girls on the Beach; Help Me, Rhonda (version one); Girl, Don't Tell Me; California Girls; Let Him Run Wild; You're So Good to Me. (A double set.)

JULY CALIFORNIA CONCERT INSERT

Six Beach Boys pose for this photo.

SPIRIT OF AMERICA — April 1975
Hawaii; 409; Spirit of America; A Young Man is Gone; Break Away; Custom Machine; This Car of Mine; Why Do Fools Fall in Love?; Hushabye; Little Honda; We'll Run Away; Do You Remember?; Drive-In; Don't Back Down; Graduation Day; Do You Wanna Dance?; Good to My Baby; When I Grow Up (To Be a Man); Dance, Dance, Dance; Please Let Me Wonder; Salt Lake City; Tell Me Why; Barbara Ann. (A double set.)

GOOD VIBRATIONS — BEST OF THE BEACH BOYS — April 1975
Sail On, Sailor; Darlin'; Sloop John B; Do It Again; Add Some Music to Your Day; Wouldn't It Be Nice; God Only Knows; Good Vibrations; Friends; Heroes and Villains; Caroline, No; Surf's Up.

15 BIG ONES — July 1976
Rock and Roll Music; It's OK; Had to Phone Ya; Chapel of Love; Everyone's in Love With You; Talk to Me; That Same Song; TM Song; Palisades Park; Susie Cincinnati; A Casual Look; Blueberry Hill; Back Home; In the Still of the Night; Just Once in My Life.

'69 (LIVE IN LONDON) — November 1976
Darlin'; Wouldn't It Be Nice; Sloop John B; California Girls; Do It Again; Wake the World; Aren't You Glad; Bluebirds Over the Mountain; Their Hearts Full of Spring; Good Vibrations; God Only Knows; Barbara Ann.

LOVE YOU — April 1977
Let Us Go On This Way; Roller Skating Child; Mona; Johnny Carson; Good Time; Honkin' Down the Highway; Ding Dang; Solar System; The Night Was So Young; I'll Bet He's Nice; Let's Put Our Hearts Together; I Wanna Pick You Up; Airplane; Love Is a Woman.

MIU ALBUM — September 1978
She's Got Rhythm; Come Go With Me; Hey Little Tomboy; Kona Coast; Peggy Sue; Wontcha Come Out Tonight; Sunday Kind of Love; Bells of Paris; Pitter Patter; Diane; Matchpoint of Our Love; Winds of Change.

L.A. (LIGHT ALBUM) — March 1979
Good Timin'; Lady Lynda; Full Sail; Angel Come Home; Love Surrounds Me; Sumahama; Here Comes the Night (disco version); Baby Blue; Goin' South; Shortenin' Bread.

KEEPIN' THE SUMMER ALIVE — March 1980
Endless Harmony; When Girls Get Together; School Day (Ring! Ring! Goes the Bell); Sunshine; Santa Ana Winds; Goin' On; Some of Your Love; Oh, Darlin'; Livin' With a Heartache; Keepin' the Summer Alive.

STEVE ELDERS

JULY CALIFORNIA CONCERT INSERT

Mike Love on the concert, on the group and on Love

By D'Arcy Fallon

Summer is the time of our warmest reception," says Beach Boy Mike Love. He recites the different places they've played in their 11-city tour: state fairs, amphitheaters, coliseums, an amusement park in North Carolina. It seems as if every state but their native state is willing to accommodate the Beach Boys, and Mike Love is not pleased. Welcome home.

In a phone interview from Charleston, N.C., Love voices his displeasure with the plans for the final stretch of their tour, a free concert in Long Beach. "We're going to play on the Queen Mary. Originally we were going to do it on the barge in front of the beach, which would have been superior from a visual point of view, but apparently the city council or somebody — a bunch of Long Beach old ladies — got all uptight about the fact that there might be some people at the beach. I would think they would be there anyway, on July Fourth weekend. So the city council canceled the permit to do it on the beach. We had a permit and everything.

"It was a big disappointment to us that Long Beach people would do something in that way — that capricious. To issue a permit and then revoke it."

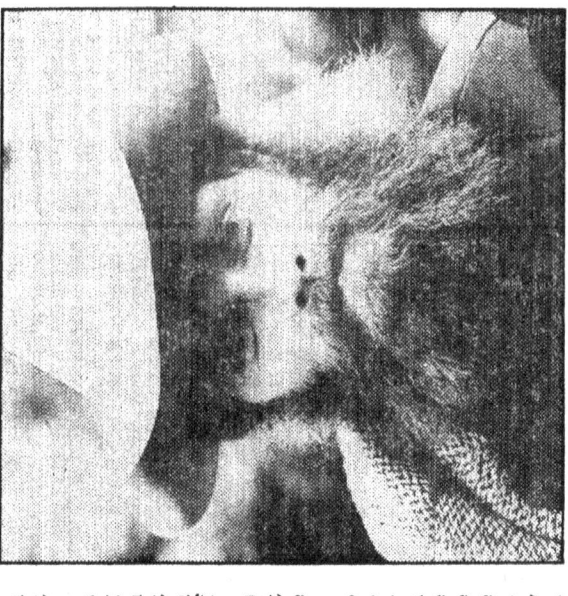

Love says they don't have a total on how much money they've lost because of the decision but that it's a sizeable sum.

"In contrast with that, the Wrather Corporation has been really, really nice to us. They're providing us with a whole lot of rooms on the Queen Mary on the nights of the fourth and the fifth. It's worked out just fine from a television standpoint, but from a beach standpoint it would have been a lot better if we could have been on the beach.

"I think they're (those who vetoed the barge idea) just being political, afraid to do anything that might get a complaint from the little old lady with the beach chair."

In the meantime, they've toured Chicago, Atlanta, Nashville, and half a dozen cities in between. They're practiced showmen; concert touring is something they have down to a science. "We've been going for about a week and a half. It takes us three days to really get to our peak," says Love. "These last few nights have been really good, the pace of the show has been really good. It takes a while for musicians and singers to click in perfectly. We really enjoy concerts and tours. We get such a great response — it's hard not to like having adulation thrown your way.

"We get a tremendous response almost everywhere we go, luckily enough. I think the California lifestyle tends to give people a certain mood when they go out, whether it's to the beach, or to a drive-in, or to a concert. We were in Indianapolis and the crowd was a lot more conservative-acting for the first three-quarters of the show. I mean, they just mainly sat there, they applauded enthusiastically, but it took them quite a while to get into it.

"Most places we play - we walk out on stage and people are ready to get into it. In California, we start off with *California Girls* or something; people start right into it."

The Beach Boys, minus Carl Wilson, who is out doing a solo album promo tour, have kept pace with a grueling tour schedule — 10 cities in 10 days so far — by leapfrogging from city to city on chartered planes. It can get old.

Mike Love likes to travel when the stress of the Beach Boys schedule gets too heavy.

of the country, and then we'll take a break. After we finish on July Fifth in Long Beach, we'll have a few days off. Then we'll be up for a week in Lake Tahoe."

When Love wants to escape the pressured world of the Beach Boys he goes to a TM retreat and meditates. Or he travels. "I have a beautiful place in Tahoe on the North Shore. I have a little hot tub and I just get out on my sun deck and relax. Just basically take it easy. See my kids. I have five kids, but I spread them over different girls just to be fair."

Future plans in the works for the Beach Boys include symphonic arrangements in the fall. "We've already got the Detroit Symphony Orchestra on the line for late November. We're also talking about the

---

July 4th Picnic Specials

LEAN PASTRAMI
$1.98 full lb.
Reg. $3.98

JULY CALIFORNIA CONCERT INSERT

Philadelphia Orchestra, probably one of the best orchestras in the world. We're planning on going to Australia and South Africa next January, so we'll be doing something in the Sydney opera house with them. We hold the all-time attendance record in Australia for outdoor concerts; we'll be doing more rock concerts there.

"We're also working on putting together a movie, *California Beach*, which is basically a comedy and musical combined. We're trying to put together the financial part of it now. We have a couple of scripts that have been written, pretty fast moving and funny, involving the group as personalities and also as entertainers."

The group is working on a new album entitled *Brothers, Cousins and Friends*, which will involve other musicians the Beach Boys have worked with through the years. They hope to do a television special using the same concept.

Love is working on a solo album now called *Looking Back with Love*, a retrospective of the '60s. "The songs deal with a reminiscence of the '60s, looking back over the ups and downs of a rather tumultuous period for a lot of people. We lived through it all."

"I meditate twice a day regularly and that has kept me from getting too stressed up," Love says. The transcendental meditation lowers your metabolism into a deeper rest for a few minutes a day. That deep rest gives you a lot of relaxation and also helps expand your creativity. That's been a big help career-wise and just life-wise.

"Brian sometimes gets real withdrawn and that's a drag because he's written about 90 percent of the music that has made so many people happy. It's kind of a drag to see him when he's depressed. But he gets out of those moods, too. He has his ups and downs — it's called manic depressive.

"The only time we get really burned out is when we tour too long. We learned a long time ago not to tour for more than a couple of weeks at a time. The only exception to that rule is if we go out

SEE WHAT YOU WANT WHEN YOU WANT IT
RENT ONE
VIDEO TAPE
and get one
FREE
with this coupon
(worth up to $10)
Offer expires July 31, 1981

OVER 2000 TAPES AVAILABLE

TELFORD VIDEO
CASSETTES & DISCS
5305 E. 2nd, L.B., 90803
Belmont Shore at Glendora
(213) 439-4547
Open 11-7 Mon-Sat 1-6 Sun.

Kitchen Cabinets
30 TO 40% OFF

Pre-finished or
Custom Made
Do It Yourself
or We'll Help

WE MANUFACTURE CUSTOM
FORMICA COUNTER TOPS

2470 BRAYTON AVE
LONG BEACH
Lic. No. 210132

Kitchens Are Our Only Business
VISIT OUR MODEL SHOWROOM

DAILY 10-6
SAT. 9-3
FREE ESTIMATES
595-6549
426-6804

Pacific Coast Kitchens
By Pacific Plastic Counter Tops Inc.

KOSHER STYLE
SALAMI $1.49 1/2 lb.
Pure Beef

BBQ RIBS
Beef or Pork **$3.98** full lb.
Reg. $4.98

the GALLEY
DELICATESSEN SANDWICHES

We have everything you need for your Picnic, Meats, Cheese, Breads, Salads, Desserts, Condiments, Paper Supplies, Beer, Wine, Soda, Ice. Call ahead... Bring your Picnic Basket, We'll fill it up.

New Summer Hours   Phone
Open 7 to 9 Daily   **597-8327**
4500 E. LOS COYOTES DIAG., LONG BEACH
At the Traffic Circle

NOW OPEN SUNDAY 10-7

JULY CALIFORNIA CONCERT INSERT

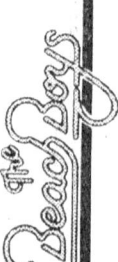

Joining the Beach Boys in Sunday's lineup are (left to right) Rick Springfield, Pablo Cruise, the reunited Three Dog Night and Jan and Dean.

Four old friends join the concert

The Beach Boys *are* the big name on Sunday's bill, and it *is* a recognition of their 20th year in show business.

But there will be other performers preceding them on stage, and some old cohorts will join them at the end of the show.

Featured as the Beach Boys' special guests are Pablo Cruise, a five-man band from the Bay Area.

Beach Boy Mike Love has called Pablo Cruise the Beach Boys' California musical cousin.

The members' new album, *Reflector*, was released this week, and a single from it, *Cool Love*, is climbing the charts.

They will perform five songs Sunday, including *Cool Love* and their two top-10 hits of recent years, *Whatcha Gonna Do?* and *Love Will Find a Way*.

Opening the show will be Rick Springfield.

In the ensuing years, Torrence became a graphic artist and designed several album covers.

But Berry's persistence paid off as, after his lengthy rehabilitation, the twosome began touring again a few years ago.

They headlined an evening at the Greek Theater last summer and have played at other local clubs and parks in the area.

HAMMOND ORGANS

OWN THE BEST AND PAY LESS — Two Convenient Locations —

COME SAVE AT: Select From Over 400 Organs & Pianos
New and Used Pianos Available

ORGAN & PIANO CENTER

SPINETS, CONSOLES, LESLIE SPEAKERS, RHYTHM UNITS

WHERE PRICES ARE LOW ON BRANDS YOU KNOW

1100 LONG BEACH BLVD., LONG BEACH 437-2271
102 LAKEWOOD CENTER MALL, LAKEWOOD 531-6751
MUSIC • LAMPS • LESSONS • CONCERTS • SERVICE • TUNING

Daily 10-9
Sat. 10-6
Sun. 12-5

EASY FINANCING CAN BE ARRANGED

In Celebration of our FIRST ANNIVERSARY
a
MEMBERSHIP SPECIAL

JULY CALIFORNIA CONCERT INSERT

MEMBERSHIP SPECIAL

from

THE BELMONT

A RACQUETBALL & ATHLETIC CLUB

A LIMITED NUMBER OF MEMBERSHIPS AVAILABLE AT SPECIAL DISCOUNTED PRICES!

$195.00 Single Membership
Regularly $350.00 SAVE 44%!
$395.00 Family Membership
Regularly $550.00 SAVE 29%!

This Beautiful Club Includes:
- Nine racquetball handball courts
- Two full sets of Nautilus Exercise Equipment
- Aerobic exercise classes - Free to Members
- Locker facilities for men & women
- Saunas, steamrooms, jacuzzi & massage
- Pro shop (open to the public)
- Murphy's Bar & Restaurant (open to the public)
- Lounge Areas & Wide Screen TV

JOIN NOW — ENJOY THE SAVINGS — WE KNOW YOU'LL LOVE THE BELMONT!

4918 E. Second Street, Belmont Shore ● 438-1176

Opening the show will be Rick Springfield. Springfield started his career in 1972 with the hit single *Speak to the Sky*, becoming a teen idol in the process.

After his 1976 single, *Take a Hand*, Springfield left music and his teen-idol image for TV acting. He appeared in episodes of *The Rockford Files* and *The Incredible Hulk*. Two months ago, Springfield was cast as Dr. Noah Drake on the soap opera *General Hospital*.

Besides his acting career, Springfield is making a comeback in the music business. His new album, *Working Class Dog*, is in the top 20 on the national charts, and the single, *Jessie's Girl*, is in the top five.

Three Dog Night, which had a string of hit singles in the 1970s, is also making a comeback, and the group will play some of its hits Sunday in an opening set.

The band broke up 5½ years ago, but each member of the original band except the bass player will be there. They have been touring since May, and plan to record a new album later this year.

One of Three Dog Night's attractive qualities was their having three lead singers — Chuck Negron, Cory Welles and Danny Hutton.

Some of their biggest hits include *One*, *Eli's Coming*, *Mama Told Me (Not to Come)*, *Joy to the World* and *Black and White*.

They will perform four songs Sunday.

Joining the Beach Boys at the end of the evening will be old surfing-music pals Jan and Dean.

Jan Berry and Dean Torrence were second only to the Boys in being the ambassadors of the California myth.

It was Brian Wilson who wrote their first No. 1 hit, *Surf City*, which may have summed up what the myth was all about even better than any Beach Boy song.

Other top 10 hits for the group in 1963-64 were *Drag City*, *The Little Old Lady from Pasadena*, *Honolulu Lulu* and *Dead Man's Curve*. The last title proved to be prophetic.

Two years after it was released, Berry was injured in a car crash that nearly killed him.

He was paralyzed for more than a year.

www.ingramcontent.com/pod-product-compliance
Lightning Source LLC
Chambersburg PA
CBHW081131170426
43197CB00017B/2824